Anarchism and Art

SUNY Series in New Political Science

Bradley J. Macdonald, editor

Anarchism and Art

Democracy in the Cracks and on the Margins

Mark Mattern

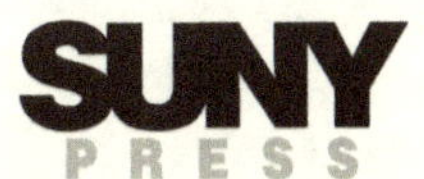

Cover image: “Madison Near Pitt—NYC 2000” by Dan Witz. © Dan Witz, 2000.

Published by State University of New York Press, Albany

Printed in the United States of America

For information, contact State University of New York Press, Albany, NY
www.sunypress.edu

Production, Eileen Nizer
Marketing, Anne M. Valentine

Library of Congress Cataloging-in-Publication Data

Mattern, Mark, 1954–
Anarchism and art : democracy in the cracks and on the margins / Mark Mattern.
pages cm — (SUNY series in new political science)
Includes bibliographical references and index.
ISBN 978-1-4384-5919-6 (hc : alk. paper)—ISBN 978-1-4384-5920-2 (pb : alk. paper)
ISBN 978-1-4384-5921-9 (e-book)
1. Politics in art. 2. Arts—Political aspects. 3. Democracy and the arts. 4. Popular culture—Political aspects. 5. Art and society. I. Title.

NX650.P6M37 2016
700.1'03—dc23 2015006075

10 9 8 7 6 5 4 3 2 1

Contents

Acknowledgments

I would like to thank Michael Rinella, SUNY Press editor, and his assistant, Rafael Chaiken, for their assistance in completing this project. I also thank Bradley Macdonald, editor of the New Political Science series at SUNY Press, for his excellent work in developing the series. I gratefully acknowledge the scholars and activists of the Caucus for a New Political Science, who make the series possible.

Nick Riley and Jeremy Feador deserve special thanks for helping me enter the world of DIY punk music. I thank Alix Olson for her generous insights about poetry slam, and apologize if I managed to get it wrong anyway.

I thank Baldwin Wallace University (BW) for its financial support during the research and writing of this book. I thank Donna McKeon, BW Political Science Department secretary and office manager, for her endless patience and capable assistance. I thank BW students Dan Clapper, Matt Kusznir, Alex Nagy, Jenna Perry, and Rich Teel for their research assistance.

Chapter 4, "Poetry Slam," is adapted from my essay, "The Message in the Medium: Poetry Slam as Democratic Practice," in Nancy S. Love and Mark Mattern, *Doing Democracy: Activist Art and Cultural Politics* (Albany, N.Y.: SUNY Press, 2013), 121–42.

1

Introduction

"We don't believe in waiting until after the revolution. . . . If you want a better world you should start acting like it now."

—Unbound Bookstore, Chicago[1]

"We need not conquer the world. It is enough to make it anew."

—Subcomandante Marcos[2]

"All human experience teaches that methods and means cannot be separated from the ultimate aim. The means employed become, through individual habit and social practice, part and parcel of the final purpose; they influence it, modify it, and presently the aims and means become identical. . . . The ethical values which the revolution is to establish in the new society must be *initiated* with the revolutionary activities of the so-called transitional period. The latter can serve as a real and dependable bridge to the better life only if built of the same material as the life to be achieved."

—Emma Goldman[3]

In this book, I argue that some forms of popular art exemplify anarchist principles and commitments that, taken together, prefigure deeper forms of democracy than those experienced by most people in today's liberal democracies. Prefiguration has two meanings, one descriptive and the other prescriptive. First, it means descriptively that current social forms contain hints of future possibilities. In this book I will explore hints found in popular art forms of specifically more democratic future possibilities.

Second, and prescriptively, prefiguration means that the ways we organize our lives in the present *should* model the characteristics of the world we want to create in the future. Our means should match the ends we seek.[4]

The forms of art that I address in this book include DIY (Do It Yourself) punk music, poetry slams, graffiti and street art, and flash mobs. Marked as they are by tensions and contradictions, none prefigure utopian worlds. Yet each directs us toward alternative possibilities and new horizons. Each embodies commitments and practices that challenge contemporary political, economic, and cultural forms of domination while offering promise of more creative, satisfying, and democratic worlds. People involved in these alternative worlds of popular art expressly or implicitly signal to the world their unwillingness to play by (all) the rules imposed on them by others and by institutions and structures of domination. They instead carve out spaces—both physical and temporal—where they live parts or all of their lives according to central anarchist principles. My task in this book is to describe their efforts and show how they prefigure a different, more democratic world.

Before turning to those art forms, I outline in this chapter the rationale for pursuing a prefigurative strategy and defend a focus on popular arts and culture. In the second chapter, I address anarchism and democracy, exploring their affinities and tensions while identifying analytical footholds for interpreting the case studies that follow. Chapters 3 through 6 are case study chapters addressing, in order, DIY punk music, poetry slams, graffiti and street art, and flash mobs. In chapter 7, I return to the themes of prefiguration and political strategy.

Strategies for Progressive Change

Sociologist Erik Olin Wright identifies three general strategies for progressive change that he calls ruptural, symbiotic, and interstitial. *Ruptural* strategies, which Wright identifies primarily with revolutionary socialism, entail a direct assault on the state and capital, and are considered successful to the degree that a wholesale and complete rupture with those institutions is achieved. The vestiges of state and capital must be decisively destroyed or abandoned for a new order to emerge. Revolutionary individuals and groups seek not to engage productively and positively with existing institutional forces; rather, they seek to destroy them via direct confrontation. Wright characterizes this bluntly as a "Smash first, build second" strategy.[5] Social classes are the main historical actors in this war of competing forces, with the working class serving as the primary agent for driving ruptural change.

Some theorists and activists continue to view this ruptural strategy as viable, despite the apparently long odds. The dissolution of the former Soviet Union took with it the most obvious threat to neoliberalism, capitalism, and liberal democracy; and, anyway, few progressives viewed the former Soviet Union as an example worth emulating. Worldwide, the primary agent of revolutionary change in Marxist theory, the working class, has largely not fulfilled expectations. According to Marx, the working class would eventually recognize the exploitation it experiences and its own class interest in overturning capitalism. Marxists anticipated that workers' widespread disenchantment with capitalism would lead to revolt to overturn capitalism in favor of socialism and, eventually, communism. Instead, most workers in industrialized countries have largely abandoned whatever revolutionary goals they may have at one time embraced in favor of higher wages, better working conditions, and social welfare spending that mitigates the harsher edges of capitalism. Many have become enthusiastic believers in ideologies that naturalize capitalism and its attendant inequalities. Overall, workers in the United States and elsewhere hardly seem poised to assume a revolutionary role.

On a smaller scale, some activists engage in ruptural strategies such as social banditry and sabotage in various forms. James Buccellato, for example, describes the social and political role of outlaws in U.S. history in terms of their direct assaults on institutions of state and capital.[6] According to Buccellato, despite—or perhaps because of—their illegality, these outlaws were widely viewed favorably by common people who saw them as representing struggles against the odds that resonated with their own struggle to attain material security. Buccellato also cites cyberjamming, factory occupations, graffiti art, rioting, and squatting as examples of outlawry in direct attack on the state or capital. At least some contemporary anarchists embrace these forms of outlawry. As noted by Pattrice Jones, "Outlaws routinely disregard the authorities and boundaries established by people while working cooperatively with one another to pursue their own purposes in the context of human exploitation and expropriation. This is anarchy in its purest form."[7] Whatever success one can ascribe to these outlaws, it is largely temporary, brief, and falls far short of achieving significant ruptural change. Those who view this ruptural strategy skeptically advocate some form of gradualist, evolutionary strategy that would produce desired changes through a process of metamorphosis. Wright's second two strategic categories reflect this shift to gradualism.

Wright's *symbiotic* strategy, which he associates with social democracy, accepts that, at least in the present, the state and capital must be reckoned with; they cannot simply be ignored or frontally assaulted. They must be engaged, while seeking to gradually transform them. This engagement requires the forging of coalitions between progressive forces and regressive forces of state and capital, and a process of collaboration with them.

A symbiotic strategy requires at least some willingness to work "within the system." Attempts to work within the current political system to democratize power and challenge domination have occasionally met with some success. For example, social democracy in Europe, and the New Deal and Great Society programs in the U.S., rounded off the rougher edges of capitalism with social welfare spending to limit the deprivation experienced by millions on the bottom of the socioeconomic scale. Also, President Obama's support for gay marriage, and the U.S. Supreme Court's 2012 decision to uphold the Affordable Care Act, also point to marginal steps forward.

Despite gains, there are nevertheless reasons to avoid relying entirely on this strategy. First, as Wright notes, gains achieved using a symbiotic strategy are always "precarious and vulnerable to counterattack."[8] Since the surge of neoliberalism during the 1980s and beyond, many of the previous decades' gains have been reversed. In the United States, social welfare spending has been attacked successfully by Republicans and centrist Democrats, resulting in the partial dismantling of public assistance welfare, the steady decline of spending on education, constant threats to Social Security and Medicare, and an increasingly regressive tax code.

Second, despite undeniable gains in progressive directions, most steps forward are marginal victories that fail to fundamentally challenge elite domination. Many progressives understandably question whether significant change can occur within the existing liberal democratic framework. Third, success within a liberal democratic political framework often comes with high costs. For example, electoral victory today requires enormous expenditure of time and money. It also increasingly requires negative campaigning, dissimulation, propaganda, lies, half-truths, and pandering. The costs to civic and public life are often steep, resulting in widespread cynicism, distrust and enmity against public leaders, and deep, often-hostile fractures separating members of the public from each other and from any hope of common ground.

The likelihood of progressive symbiotic change in the near future appears remote, and may instead decline. Electoral politics in the U.S.

appear to promise little more than slight variations on the Democrat-Republican centrism that occasionally offers progressives small victories, but overall they yield the same end result: domination by entrenched economic and political elites. Moreover, what passes for centrism has shifted dramatically to the right since the 1980s. While these variations are important at the margins, they stop short of moving in the transformative direction favored by most progressives. Without dismissing this strategy outright, it appears to many progressives that, in the foreseeable future, this symbiotic strategy offers scant hope and promises little movement forward.

In this context of declining confidence in ruptural and symbiotic strategies, some theorists and activists are turning to a third strategy, one that Wright calls *interstitial*, referring to those efforts occurring "in the spaces and cracks within some dominant social structure of power."[9] The notion of an "interstitial" space emerged earlier in the writing of anarchist Colin Ward: "Far from being a speculative vision of a future society . . . [anarchy] is a description of a mode of human organization, rooted in the experience of everyday life, which operates side by side with, and in spite of, the dominant authoritarian trends of our society. . . . [T]he anarchist alternatives are already there, in the interstices of the dominant power structure. If you want to build a free society, the parts are all at hand."[10]

Interstitial strategies begin from the recognition that dominant institutions contain contradictions and weaknesses; they are riven with fissures, discontinuities, and inconsistencies. Pursuing an interstitial strategy entails identifying existing cracks and fissures, while opening new ones where possible. Over time, these cracks and fissures can be widened, drawing new and more participants into them. In theory, these cracks and fissures may grow to the point that they threaten major institutions of domination. This strategy focuses on the present, but with an eye to the future of gradual emancipation.

Although social movements represent the paradigmatic interstitial form of collective action, Wright also offers as illustrations of existing interstitial strategies and activities "worker and consumer co-ops, battered women's shelters, workers' factory councils, intentional communities and communes, community-based social economy services, civic environmental councils, community-controlled land trusts, cross-border equal-exchange trade organizations, and many others." Each of these has in common "the idea of building alternative institutions and deliberately fostering new forms of social relations that embody emancipatory ideals and that are created primarily through direct action of one sort or another rather than through the state."[11]

Sociologist John Holloway explores themes similar to Wright's interstitial strategy in his *Crack Capitalism*. According to Holloway, there is a growing awareness that we "cannot wait for the great revolution." Instead, we must begin now altering the conditions of our lives. He emphasizes the necessity of beginning with a great refusal, of saying, "Enough! Ya Basta! We have had enough of living in, and creating, a world of exploitation, violence and starvation."[12] But "cracking capitalism" entails more than simply refusing to play by established rules. It also involves creating a different world by seizing the initiative and setting the agenda. Holloway advocates an experimental approach to develop new forms that will represent "the embryos of a new world, the interstitial movements from which a new society could grow."[13] These new forms are to be created in the interstices and cracks that can be found within capitalism. Over time, this process will "expand and multiply the cracks and promote their confluence," leading eventually to systemic change.[14]

These cracks can be either spatial or temporal, or both. Spatial cracks are new spaces within which new forms of life can be identified and created. Individuals find each other within these spatial cracks, and embark together on the creation of alternative forms of life. Temporal cracks entail going off the clock, resisting the dominant pressures and narratives of efficiency and instrumental rationality, substituting instead the possibility of doing things more for their own sake. As Max Horkheimer earlier lamented,

> Less and less is anything done for its own sake. A hike that takes a man out of the city to the banks of a river or a mountain top would be irrational and idiotic, judged by utilitarian standards; he is devoting himself to a silly or destructive pastime. In the view of formalized reason, an activity is reasonable only if it serves another purpose, e.g. health or relaxation, which helps to replenish his working power.[15]

Resisting this logic of instrumental rationality and action opens a temporal crack; it challenges the logic of efficient use of time for production and consumption. Holloway's vision anticipates that as these cracks multiply, there will be "radiating waves of rebellion" that can ultimately threaten the viability of capitalism.[16]

Like Wright, Holloway associates "crack capitalism" at least partly with anarchism. Like Wright, he links an interstitial strategy to larger transformational change, arguing that living and working within the cracks can create the conditions for large-scale progressive change. And like Wright, he demonstrates empirically that the interstitial experiments he condones are already well under way. The bulk of *Crack Capitalism* includes descriptions of existing interstitial efforts.

Neither Wright nor Holloway, however, focuses on artistic and popular cultural efforts in the interstices of state and capital. Both focus their empirical research primarily on interstitial efforts in civil society, and on alternative economic forms such as cooperatives. Examples cited by other thinkers similarly ignore the arts and popular culture. For example, James Horrox lists "autonomous social centers, popular assemblies, small-scale decentralized agriculture, LETS (Local Exchange Trading Systems), alternative currencies, mutual banking, credit unions, tenants committees, food cooperatives, allotments, directly democratic extended neighborhood communities, household and home assemblies, employees' associations, cooperative housing associations, alternative education institutions and progressive forms of home schooling, temporary and permanent autonomous zones, community gardens, guilds, co-housing, alternative and sustainable technology and numerous different kinds of low-impact living initiatives."[17] Ruth Kinna cites co-housing, health clinics, creating an alternative economy, co-ops, neighborhood services, schools, radio stations, squatting, hactivism, monkey-wrenching, unions, neighborhood collectives, and various forms of decentralized self-governing units.[18]

This book addresses artistic and popular cultural practices found in the interstices—in the cracks and on the margins—of dominant institutions of state and capital. It attempts to give the same careful attention to several popular art forms that Wright, Holloway, and others give to civil society and the economy. I argue that these popular art forms have the potential to "radiate waves of rebellion" outward, to increase political vision, and to demonstrate alternative ways of organizing our everyday lives. Taken together, they, like the practices described by Wright and Holloway, challenge or circumvent dominant institutions of state and capital. On a daily basis, each is deeply practical, in that the people involved in them are already creating alternative worlds and living within them. Each is prefigurative: each realizes and expresses alternative anarchist values in everyday cultural production, circulation, and reception, while promising a more democratic future.

Art and Popular Culture

Fine-arts purists may wish to reserve the term "art" for the works of famous canonical painters whose work hangs in museums and composers whose music is performed in grand halls and theatres. The line between so-called fine art and popular cultural art is blurred. I take as art any attempt to express ideas and emotions through a medium that includes aesthetic and affective dimensions, as well as potentially analytical and intellectual dimensions. Artists employ imagination and skill to create objects, experiences, or environments that typically include an aesthetic dimension. It is a powerful means of expressing and sharing experience, one that potentially engages the whole person.[19]

Since the translation in 1971 of his work into English, many scholars and activists interested in the political significance of arts and culture have turned to the work of the Italian Marxist of the early twentieth century, Antonio Gramsci (1891–1937).[20] Gramsci believed that revolutionary transformation would be won or lost partly on the terrain of culture. He described the convergence of ideological and material social forces in terms of hegemony, or a relatively close fit between dominant ideology and the material forces under which a society is organized and which are legitimated by that dominant ideology. In a context of hegemony, people generally accept the circumstances of their lives without question. The political economy in which they live and work appears as natural and inevitable. It appears to them as common sense. In a context of neoliberal hegemony, for example, capitalism appears as the best—and perhaps only—way to organize society's productive forces and, more generally, everyday life.

Gramsci advocated a "war of position"—a protracted, patient struggle in various social realms including cultural—as part of an overall revolutionary struggle to subvert that common sense and the hegemony it represents as a necessary precondition for changing the material bases of social organization. The leaders of this war of position, dubbed "organic intellectuals" by Gramsci, are embedded in, and drawn from, the working class. Their role is to express the revolutionary interests of the working class, to begin showing members of the working class that their common sense is distorted, to open the possibility for a new critical consciousness, and to help imagine a different world in which their exploitation would end. It was a natural step to count artists among the ranks of organic intellectuals in this war of position. Many subsequent scholars have taken Gramsci's lead and applied his theoretical and practical framework to the study of art and popular culture.[21]

Gramsci's insights have given theorists and activists new analytical tools for understanding and challenging domination. And he has provided a convincing rationale for treating arts and culture as terrains of political struggle. Yet his understanding of domination was firmly rooted in one form of domination: class. And his revolutionary strategy emphasized class struggle, with little attention to other forms of domination and struggle to overcome it. Additionally, like Marx himself, Gramsci's war of position focused on seizing control of the state, albeit temporarily, to use it as an instrument for revolutionary change. In Marxist theory, this seizure of the state would be temporary; eventually, the state would wither away, leaving a classless society. Anarchists are not alone in wishing to broaden the scope of understanding of domination. While class domination remains a defining element of a capitalist, neoliberal society, progressives have broadened the discussion to include other forms of domination based on gender, race, sexual orientation, the environment, and other social categories. Anarchists are unique, however, in rejecting the use of the state under any circumstances to advance a revolutionary agenda, fearing the centralized power it represents and the inevitable threats to autonomy and freedom.

Like Gramsci, the pragmatist and participatory democrat John Dewey (1859–1952) viewed culture as a site of domination, a source of democratic capacity, and a terrain of political action. From the 1920s until his death in 1952, he focused much of his attention on attacking "the existing system of control of power" that produced a culture of domination, and to developing democratic alternatives.[22] Dewey's *Individualism Old and New* (1929/30) can be read as an extended analysis of the culture-wide domination imposed by economic interests in the capitalist political economy of his time. In it he addressed two related problems: a culture dominated by a "pecuniary" ethos—everything is about money, making money, amassing money, and spending it—and a culture dominated by powerful economic interests that exert hegemony over all areas of life. This pecuniary ethos extended throughout culture, well beyond such obvious targets as advertising, banking, and shopping malls to include education, technology, science, and even religion.[23]

In *Freedom and Culture* (1939) Dewey reiterated earlier points, especially the dominating impact of a political economy oriented toward private gain at public expense and an educational system that emphasized fitting into the existing political economy rather than critical intelligence. He also increased his attention to popular culture and art, and their role in legitimizing domination. According to Dewey, "the theater, the movie and music hall, even the picture gallery, eloquence, popular parades, common sports and recreative agencies, have all been brought under regulation as part of the propaganda agencies by which dictatorship is kept in power without being regarded by the masses as oppressive." Although Dewey wrote this passage with the growing European fascist threat in mind, he viewed Americans as susceptible to the same misuse of art and popular culture to legitimize domination and oppression. Repeating themes from his *Art as Experience* (1934), Dewey argued that "emotions and imagination are more potent in shaping public sentiment and opinion than information and reason. Indeed, long before the present crisis came into being there was a saying that if one could control the songs of a nation, one need not care who made its laws."[24] Unfortunately, he believed, this power of art and popular culture was increasingly used for undemocratic rather than democratic purposes.

If culture represented a terrain of increasing domination, it also represented for Dewey a terrain for creating critical consciousness and deepening and extending democracy. Like Gramsci, Dewey saw a vital role for artists. Dewey's democratic vision emphasized widespread access to art and participation in art. In a democratic culture, art would not be something consigned to museums for consumption by elites; it would be spread throughout daily life, a potent form of everyday experience.

His *Art as Experience* earlier detailed his belief in the communicative power of art and its role in creating democratic communities and expanding horizons. Art powerfully captures human experience, renders it intelligible to others across differences, and breaks through barriers to understanding. Dewey called art the best form of communication that can occur in "a world full of gulfs and walls that limit community of experience." Art "strikes below the barriers that separate human beings from one another." Art helps people recognize common experiences, and potentially helps them understand and adapt to different experiences of different people.[25] Art gives us access to others' lives, and through the encounter we gain a critical foothold for examining our own lives and experiences. It helps us to see ourselves differently. This potentially forces us to rethink our assumptions and beliefs. The "function of art," according to Dewey, "has always been to break through the crust of conventionalized and routine consciousness" in order to see more clearly and critically.[26] This is the "moral function" of art: "to remove prejudice, do away with the scales that keep the eye from seeing, tear away the veils due to wont and custom, perfect the power to perceive."[27] Through the sharing of experience, we expand our horizons; our vision is deepened, sharpened, and broadened. In short, art can prefigure new, more democratic ways of life.

Gramsci and Dewey both saw clearly that culture is a terrain where identity is formed and reformed, for better and for worse; where beliefs and ideologies are contested; where political action occurs; where the capacities of democratic citizenship are both developed and undermined; where horizons are opened and closed; and where the struggle for democracy is won or lost. Both viewed the artist as a key player in this struggle for democracy, one whose imagination and creativity is summoned to forge new democratic identities, organize political action, build capacity for critical thought and action, open new vistas and horizons, and lead others in the struggle for liberation and justice. Both gave the artist an important role in shaping and contesting the character of our everyday lives. Additionally, Dewey's emphasis on the visionary capacity of art is especially relevant to this book's theme of prefiguration.

Art, Prefiguration, and Everyday Life

The prefigurative potential of art lies in the arts as a domain of creativity and imagination, where artists constantly innovate new cultural forms. Each new artistic or cultural form represents new potentialities for human thought and action. Of course, artists also often simply reflect changes that are occurring in other domains. Artists constantly strive to put their feelings and ideas onto canvas and onto stage and into words, feelings and ideas that often lie outside the margins of current ways of life. In their work we can see alternative futures.

Since the inception of the anarchist movement in the nineteenth century, "the arts have been an integral part of the [anarchist] movement."[28] An early hint of this can be seen in the mid-nineteenth-century French anarchist Pierre-Joseph Proudhon's (1809–1865) book on the social role of art. Proudhon assigned art an ambitious and lofty social role: "the physical and moral perfection of our species." In words that Dewey would later echo, Proudhon argued that art is a "representation of nature and of ourselves." It reflects back on us; it reveals ourselves *to* ourselves and to others. This opens the possibility of self- and social criticism. The task of art, he wrote, "is to warn us, to praise us, to teach us, to make us blush by confronting us with a mirror of our own conscience."[29] Nineteenth-century Russian anarchist Peter Kropotkin (1842–1921) also wrote of the social role of art in anarchism. His pamphlet "Appeal to the

Young" included artists as central players in any social revolution. In it, he addressed youth as "true poets" who "will come and take the side of the oppressed because [they] know that the beautiful, the sublime, the spirit of life itself are on the side of those who fight for light, for humanity, for justice!"[30]

In the early twentieth century, U.S. anarchist Emma Goldman (1869–1940) lectured on drama, seeing it as a powerful vehicle for revolutionary ideas. According to Goldman, "Any mode of creative work which with true perception portrays social wrongs earnestly and boldly is a greater menace . . . and a more powerful inspiration than the wildest harangue of the soapbox orator."[31] Goldman also is alleged to have said, "If I can't dance I don't want to be part of your revolution."[32] She never actually said or wrote those exact words, but did express something similar in her two-volume autobiography in which she described her love of dancing, and related an incident in which she was chastised on the grounds that "it did not behoove an agitator to dance" since it was "undignified" and "frivolous." In her considered response to her accuser, she wrote:

> I did not believe that a Cause which stood for a beautiful ideal, for anarchism, for release and freedom from convention and prejudice, should demand the denial of life and joy. I insisted that our Cause could not expect me to become a nun and that the movement would not be turned into a cloister. If it meant that, I did not want it. I want freedom, the right to self-expression, everybody's right to beautiful, radiant things. Anarchism meant that to me, and I would live it in spite of the whole world—prisons, persecution, everything.[33]

Goldman also wrote that modern art should be "the dynamite which undermines superstition, shakes the social pillars, and prepares men and women for the reconstruction" of society.[34] Many anarchists, past and present, have emphasized art's role in adding beauty and joy to any life worth living, as well as its role in challenging superstition and social conventions.

Contemporary anarchist David Graeber asks, "Why is it that artists have so often been drawn to revolutionary politics?" The answer, he argues, "must have something to do with alienation." Artists imagine things and then bring them into being; and this is the essence of unalienated production. The link to imagining and then creating revolutionary alternatives is a natural one. And this is especially true "if that alternative is the possibility of a society premised on less alienated forms of creativity."[35] Graeber highlights an important point about anarchists past and present: they do not accept the often dreary, mechanical, regimented, work- and efficiency-obsessed world defined by capitalism and the liberal democratic state. It does not have to be this way, they affirm. We can create a better world, a world less marked by the mind-numbing, alienating forms of work and leisure conceived primarily in terms of consumption.[36] We can create a world marked instead by creative, joyful, satisfying work and play. We can bridge the gap between art and everyday life.

Allan Antliff's analysis of Henri-Edmond Cross's (1856–1910) lithograph "The Wanderer," contributed in 1896 to Jean Grave's anarchist publication, *Les Temps nouveaux*, exemplifies this connection between art and anarchists' critique of alienation. The lithograph portrays an old wanderer sitting in a dark foreground. Figures working and dancing around him are rendered in bright light and color, portraying a future of radiant happiness. The dancers circle remnants of the old world as symbolized by a crown and a banner. The old man represents the dreamers who seek to break from the past to create a better future. As interpreted by Antliff, the wanderer and his companions

> . . . were outcasts, but they also were free. Their freedom resided in a day-to-day life apart from capital, as well as the revolutionary vision they propagated to those encountered along the way. . . . [They] abandoned time, possessions, labor, and slavery in a refusal to obey. . . . They existed in counter-rhythm to a society in which their ideals were deemed valueless. But they also struggled for a better world.[37]

The figures depicted in the lithograph enjoyed their freedom in the "day-to-day life" rather than in some abstract sense. They were free in that they "abandoned" many of the trappings and demands of "time, possessions, labor, and slavery." They lived outside—in the cracks and on the margins—of capitalism and its imperatives. But their great "refusal to obey" also served as a "revolutionary vision" of an alternative world of autonomy. In short, their freedom resonated beyond the immediate concerns of each individual figure. They served as a model, a prefiguration of a freer, less alienated world to work toward.

Many contemporary anarchists focus on the political importance of everyday life and culture as a source of potential "counter-rhythms" to the dominant society. Deric Shannon, for example, argues that "anarchists should fight for a post-capitalist future in the terrain of ideology and culture." Echoing Gramsci, Shannon asks why exploited workers have failed to recognize their collective class interest in overthrowing capitalism. And, like Gramsci, the answer "could be found by looking at the cultural sphere." Like both Gramsci and Dewey, Shannon argues that culture itself is shaped in the interests of capital, and the interests of capital are transmitted and taught through various cultural institutions and practices. Taking a cue from feminism, Shannon argues that "the personal is, indeed, the political," and we should make changes in our everyday personal lives by creating "egalitarian cultural forms." Collective activities such as Food Not Bombs, infoshops, social centers, and "really really free markets" can also contribute to cultural transformation. As individuals and members of collectivities, we need to "recognize the value in reinventing our daily lives and the role this plays in revolutionary politics." He acknowledges that reinventing our individual daily lives will not by itself create revolutionary change, which requires linkage with social movements. However, it does begin to change the culture, to create different, alternative forms of everyday life absent the domination, and these provide the foundation for revolutionary change.[38]

Art is a space "where our assumptions about how the 'real' world works can be temporarily put on hold."[39] This liberates the imagination, allowing us to envision new possibilities. Jill Dolan's work on "utopian performatives" examines this enlisting of art as a vehicle and vocabulary for seeing outside existing worlds to alternative ways of life. Utopian performatives are artful performances in which performers and audiences alike are transported out of their ordinary, sometimes-alienating and dissatisfying lives into alternative emotional, psychological, and physical spaces that offer both the concrete experience of, and the visionary hope for, different, more beautiful worlds. They "describe small but profound moments in which performance calls the attention of the audience in a way that lifts everyone slightly above the present, into a hopeful feeling of what the world might be like if every moment of our lives were as emotionally voluminous, generous, aesthetically striking, and intersubjectively intense" as that created momentarily by the performers. Utopian performatives "make palpable an affective vision of how the world might be better."[40] In utopian performatives, performers and audience members experience those alternative worlds directly and physically. To illustrate, Dolan draws on musicians' oft-remarked testimonies of finding a groove, of getting tight, of reaching a musical state of heightened affect and joyful expression:

> There are these rare moments when musicians together touch something sweeter than they've ever found before in rehearsals or performance, beyond the merely collaborative or technically proficient, when their expression becomes as easy and graceful as friendship or love. This is when they give us a glimpse of what we might be, of our best selves, and of an impossible world in which you give everything you have to others, but lose nothing of yourself.[41]

These experiences of heightened affect do more than give us glimpses of different worlds, according to Dolan. In offering us a vision of a better world, they goad us to seek that better world; they "move us to social action" to achieve that better world.[42]

The case studies that follow in chapters three through six provide illustrations of artistic and cultural forms that prefigure "something sweeter." They give us glimpses of "what we might be, of our best selves," and of a more just, humane, and democratic world. Before turning to those case studies, in chapter 2 I develop themes for analyzing them by more systematically addressing the theory and practice of anarchism and democracy.

2

Anarchism and Democracy

A central claim of this book is that some popular art forms exemplify central anarchist commitments, and as such prefigure more democratic ways of life. But what kind(s) of anarchism do they exemplify, and what form(s) of democracy do they prefigure? Thus far I have used the terms "anarchism" and "democracy" rather loosely. In this chapter I address them in greater detail in order to explore their similarities and dissimilarities, and to develop analytical themes needed to interpret the political significance of the case studies that follow.

The idea and practice of Western democracy is often traced to ancient Greece and, in particular, to the city-state of Athens. The term itself combines the Greek words *demos*—the common people—and *kratein*—to rule. The subsequent history of democracy is long and complex. Contemporary democratic theorists identify different variants or models of democracy.[1] In this chapter and throughout the rest of this book, I will concentrate on two variants: liberal democracy,[2] the dominant model today, and participatory democracy.[3] Anarchists are united in their rejection of the former,[4] but generally advocate some variant of the latter.[5]

The history of anarchism as a distinct philosophical and political tradition, though shorter, is at least as diverse, complex, and sometimes contradictory as the history of democracy. The word "anarchy" comes from Greek and means "without rule." The term "anarchism" appeared in use during the French Revolution, and initially referred to the chaos and disorder associated by some with the French Revolution. This pejorative understanding of anarchism persists, fed by media misrepresentations and popular misconceptions. Numerous overlapping variants, by many different thinkers, have been developed or identified, including anarcho-syndicalism, anarcha-feminism, eco-anarchism, anarcho-communism,

Christian-anarchism, social anarchism, libertarian socialism, anarcho-capitalism, anarcho-primitivism, lifestyle anarchism, individualist anarchism, libertarian anarchism, pacifist anarchism, practical anarchism, and ontological anarchism.[6] Contemporary anarchism locates its more immediate roots in the overlapping social movements of the 1960s and beyond, which addressed issues of feminism, ecologism, civil rights, antinuclear energy, antiwar, LGBT liberation, indigenous rights, and animal liberation. These culminated in the late twentieth and early twenty-first centuries in the prominence of anarchists and anarchist ideas within the alterglobalization movement. Today, anarchism is a diverse collection of decentralized networks of individuals, affinity groups, collectives, and communities united more or less by shared political and ethical commitments, modes of social organization, strategies for action, and a vision of anarchism as a way of life.[7]

In the following pages, I address those characteristics of anarchism and democracy that are most germane to my case studies, under the headings of social organization, political action, power, equality, and freedom. These analytical categories represent overlapping, complex, and contested commitments and practices. Throughout, I contrast anarchism with liberal democracy, while noting its affinities and tensions with a stronger, more radical form of participatory democracy.

Social Organization

The state and capitalism together constitute the dominant forms of social organization in modern times. Most liberal democratic states today take the form of relatively large representative republics by necessity and design. The rise of liberal democracies coincided with the development of the current nation-state system; democratic theory and practice were reconceived to accommodate the expansive scale of these nation-states. This process of accommodation can be seen clearly in the political thought of the American founders. Having inherited a bias against democracy,[8] they turned instead to republicanism. As would happen later with liberal democrats' redefinition of democracy itself, these founders essentially redefined republicanism to fit their needs, paring it down to "a government which derives all its powers directly or indirectly from the great body of the people; and is administered by persons holding their offices during pleasure, for a limited period, or during good behavior" (James

Madison), or even further to "a government in which the people have collectively, or by representation, an essential share in the sovereignty" (John Adams).[9] Each of these definitions drops older republican preoccupations with equality, civic virtue, and concentrated power; and each is easily satisfied via a scheme of representative government of the sort they had designed and were attempting to defend. The American founders opted for "a politics of radical disengagement" in which the institutional machinery of government substituted for the direct participation of average citizens.[10] In short, emblematic of liberal democracies, in place of smaller, face-to-face units of democratic self-governance, the American founders substituted institutions of government scaled to the needs of an expansive republic that reduced common citizens' role largely to passive observer.

One of the defining features of liberal democracy is its deep identification with a political economy of capitalism. The two emerged at roughly the same time, and liberal democratic thinkers and governments have, with few partial exceptions,[11] never seriously challenged capitalism. On the contrary, liberal democratic governments generally service the needs of a capitalist political economy by enforcing contracts, protecting property, providing infrastructure for production, distribution, and consumption, managing cyclical crises in supply and demand that produce recessions and depressions, providing sufficient social welfare spending to avoid rebellion, and providing various forms of corporate welfare.

A capitalist political economy organizes the social world along centralized, hierarchical lines at both the macro and micro levels. Although small, locally owned and controlled businesses continue to proliferate and play an important role in organizing everyday life at local levels, the economic landscape is dominated by global production and exchange networks controlled by large corporations and financial institutions. Large, powerful supranational institutions such as the World Trade Organization (WTO), the International Monetary Fund (IMF), and the World Bank exert authority over national and sub-national production and exchange. Multinational corporations operate relatively autonomously as quasi-independent bodies that rival or exceed many nation-states in size and power. Whatever the size of the firm, control is almost always organized vertically within it, with authority flowing downward from the owners of capital and the CEO to the workers at the bottom. With some exceptions, especially in the high-tech computer sector, work itself is rigidly organized physically and temporally to produce maximum efficiency.

Everyday life in a capitalist political economy is organized predominantly to facilitate production and exchange. The rhythms of daily life, exemplified by the workweek and holiday shopping, are largely determined according to production and exchange schedules. Labor is commodified to ensure its maximum efficient use. Ubiquitous invitations to consume permeate all aspects of culture, and many people devote their leisure time to the consumption needed to drive the economy. The result is a market society in which market values and market thinking reach into all corners of everyday life.

Anarchists envision a decentralized, nonhierarchical society based on direct action and voluntary cooperation, with local groups linked via networks and federations. Among classical anarchists, the Englishman William Godwin (1756–1836) proposed a decentralized society in which local communities form federations to address common social interests. Different districts would send delegates to a non-permanent general assembly of the federation absent a common locus of authority. The Frenchman Pierre-Joseph Proudhon advocated breaking society into a federation of autonomous regions in which the basic unit would be the commune. Russian anarchist Michael Bakunin (1814–1876) envisioned a social organization "from the bottom up, by the free associations, then going on to the communes, the regions, the nations, and, finally, culminating in a great international and universal federation."[12] At both local and federal levels, a coordinating association would coordinate production and resolve disputes while retaining autonomy at all levels. Another classical Russian anarchist, Peter Kropotkin, advocated an interwoven network of voluntary associations "composed of an infinite variety of groups and federations of all sizes and degrees, local, regional, national and international—temporary or more or less permanent—for all possible purposes."[13] Russian-born American Emma Goldman sought a society "based on voluntary co-operation of productive groups, communities, and societies loosely federated together, eventually developing into free communism, actuated by a solidarity of interests."[14] For each of these classical anarchists, and their contemporary counterparts, the principle of decentralization helps avoid abuses of power and allows direct participation by interested parties.

Social relations within and among anarchist groups are generally organized horizontally rather than hierarchically. Leaders may be selected, but generally their role is procedural: they facilitate consensus decision-making without imposing direction. This organizational model applies to the economic realm as well as other realms: workers control the organization of work at local levels, in the context of overall community and social control.[15]

The federal model favored by classical and contemporary anarchists is rhizomatic rather than arboreal. Whereas the latter resembles a tree, with one root system and growth coming from a single stem, rhizomes have no single root system. Instead, they branch out in all directions. They are flexible and mobile, devoid of a center, and irreducible to a single root system. Thus, contemporary anarchists are organized into collectives and affinity groups at local levels, and rhizomatically linked networks and federations at broader levels.[16]

Participatory democrats advocate localized, decentralized forms of social organization that are more compatible than liberal democracy with the vision offered by anarchists. Jean-Jacques Rousseau (1712–1778) famously imagined "bands of peasants regulating the affairs of state under an oak tree."[17] Thomas Jefferson's (1743–1826) ward system of local government, and John Dewey's community organizing at local levels, similarly placed citizens at the heart of deliberation and political action at local levels. Like anarchists, participatory democrats also advocate workplace democracy with workers assuming part or all of the responsibility for governing the firm as well as carrying out the mundane workday activities.[18] This suggests a level of horizontalism that at least resembles that of anarchists. On the other hand, participatory democrats are less opposed than anarchists to representative democracy at larger scales and wherever direct participation may be implausible.

For many contemporary participatory democrats, the ideal mode of social organization is captured in the theory and practice of community.[19] Individuals form communities of engaged citizens who organize to address shared interests. These are face-to-face communities at local levels, but at least one participatory democrat—John Dewey—also theorized a "great community" at the national level.[20] Analogous to anarchists' communes, local communities are interlinked with others by overlapping commonalities that are the basis for organizing to address shared interests. For many participatory democrats—as well as some anarchists[21]—community also provides a supportive social milieu that helps maximize individuals' development, freedom, and overall well-being.

As suggested by their emphasis on workplace democracy, participatory democrats reject the existing political economy of capitalism. Like anarchists, they seek to replace it with more democratic forms ranging from the democratic socialism of Dewey to Robert Dahl's system of democratically owned and managed workplaces competing in a market to the non-market libertarian socialism dubbed "parecon" by Michael Albert and Robin Hahnel.[22] Unlike anarchists, they generally retain the state as a potential instrument for exercising the sovereignty of the people.

For both anarchists and participatory democrats, the principle of decentralization helps avoid concentrations of power that allow domination, offering more capacity to control the circumstances of one's own life. Nonhierarchical, horizontal authority similarly broadens and deepens the capacity of individuals and groups to exercise autonomous choice and effective action by avoiding the dominating effects of powerful figures and institutionalized representatives in positions of control. A rhizomatic structure prevents the centralization of power and consequent threats to freedom. Direct participation ensures that each person has a voice and a direct role in decision-making, and helps block the exercise of domination by some over others.

Political Action

To accomplish their goals, anarchists have long advocated a strategy of direct action. Bakunin, for example, advocated a social revolution in the form of spontaneous uprisings devoid of institutionalized leaders or a priori goals other than liberation. To speed along this social revolution, he proposed "propaganda of the deed." Bakunin argued that "we must spread our principles, not with words but with deeds, for this is the most popular, the most potent, and the most irresistible form of propaganda."[23] Initially, propaganda of the deed carried overtones of violence against both property and people; most contemporary anarchists disavow it as violence against people, while some continue to advocate minor property vandalism.

Anarchists reject the strategy of seizing the state, even if temporarily. Instead, earlier anarchists emphasized labor organizing and general strikes favored by anarcho-syndicalists, leading to civil disobedience, guerrilla warfare, and hopefully the collapse of the state. Given the failure of these strategies to seriously challenge state and capitalist domination, more recent anarchists entertain visions of partial anarchy, or anarchy that exists within the cracks and on the margins of state and capitalism. They take their inspiration in part from Gustav Landauer (1870–1919).[24] Landauer was skeptical about the possibility of radically transforming state-capitalist societies either by revolution or by slow reform, in part because "the masses" could not be relied upon to instigate, or even support, change. He advocated creating new institutions alongside, rather than inside or atop, existing institutions. Landauer's strategy thus entails a willingness to coexist with these larger structures of domination, while striving to avoid contributing positive energy to them. It suggests creating alternative ways of living in the present rather than awaiting a time ripe for large-scale revolutionary change. As contemporary anarchist Richard Day put it, "there is no choice for those of us who desire to live differently but to begin to do so ourselves."[25]

Through direct action, contemporary anarchists seek to bring anarchism into immediate, everyday life, to put it directly into concrete action now. This does not require a complete rupture with the state through armed rebellion, nor does it require completely disavowing participation in existing capitalist relations. It instead requires finding and creating spaces within existing structures of state and capital where anarchist principles can be realized, albeit tempered by the need to coexist with dominant institutions of state and capital.[26] Hakim Bey (aka Peter Lamborn Wilson) theorized these as Temporary Autonomous Zones (TAZs) and Permanent Autonomous Zones (PAZs).[27] In response, Richard Day countered with SPAZs—or Semi-Permanent Autonomous Zones—arguing that PAZs are probably unsustainable except for "young White men with no attachments to such banalities as partners, children or broader communities."[28] Within these TAZs, PAZs, and SPAZs, "practical anarchists" solve housing needs by organizing squats, co-housing, and other forms of communal housing. They solve health needs by establishing free clinics. They organize and participate in alternative economic forms such as cooperatives. They establish alternative schools, radio stations, and print and electronic media. They build community-based power in unions, neighborhoods, collectives, and various forms of decentralized self-governing units. Some also engage in acts of sabotage such as civil disobedience, monkey-wrenching, hactivism, and various forms of minor property damage.

In the theory and practice of democracy, the term "participation" does the work of anarchists' propaganda of the deed, direct action, and prefiguration in spelling out the types and roles of individual and collective political action. For liberal democrats, political participation is measured primarily in terms of voting trends. Thus, for most people living in liberal democracies, participation occurs infrequently, approximately once every two years as citizens go to the polls to cast their votes. Then they return to their private lives, leaving the actual task of governing to elected officials. In some countries, especially the United States, many citizens do not bother with even this limited form of political participation. Other options for participation by average citizens generally are also tied to the electoral process via episodic campaign efforts. Although commentators regularly bemoan the low rates of participation in elections, it is not seen as a significant threat to the liberal democratic model.

Most anarchists reject the institution of representation, and many also reject participation in electoral politics more generally, on the grounds that both are unavoidably linked to authoritarian centralism, political inequality, and domination.[29] However, not all anarchists shun voting or participation in elections.[30] At least some anarchists argue that "a movement of any size will require a process of representation. . . . The attitude, 'Nobody talks for me, I am a free spirit,' will require restraint."[31] Similarly, most participatory democrats recognize that representation may have a place in democratic politics, especially in larger scales. As C. B. Macpherson wrote, "there will have to be some kind of representative system, not completely direct democracy."[32] For both anarchists and participatory democrats, however, elections and the mechanism of representation cannot substitute for direct participation. All citizens are expected to participate directly in making decisions and carrying them out.

Most anarchists also reject the principle of majoritarianism, since a majority can impose its will on members of the minority, compromising their autonomy. Proudhon called majority tyranny the worst form of oppression, since it is concealed behind "the name of the people."[33] Most contemporary anarchists favor a consensus rather than a majoritarian decision-making model. Whereas the latter entails domination of a minority by a majority, the former attempts to avoid domination by continuing discussion until and if a resolution can be fashioned that everyone can live with. When that resolution proves unattainable, the minority can either block a decision or stand aside. Contemporary anarchists have developed a rich menu of organizational tools to facilitate consensus decision-making, including spokescouncils, affinity groups, facilitation procedures, break-outs, fishbowls (two representatives for each side hash out an issue in front of the larger group), and vibe-watchers to monitor group process. Although a consensus decision-making model is often less efficient than a hierarchical model with a chain of command, it does help prevent the domination of a minority by a majority, and often leads to decisions that genuinely represent the interests of everyone concerned. Additionally, all voices stand a chance of being heard and acted upon.[34] Consensus decision-making occurs more readily at local levels and in small groups.

As described by Jeffrey Hilmer, "participatory democratic theory envisions the maximum participation of citizens in their self-governance, especially in sectors of society beyond those that are traditionally understood to be political (for example, the household and workplace)."[35] Herman Daly, Thomas Prugh, and Robert Costanza's description of "strong democracy"—a term that sometimes substitutes for participatory democracy—provides a similar vision:

> In a strong democracy, people—citizens—govern themselves to the greatest extent possible rather than delegate their power and responsibility to representatives acting in their names. Strong democracy does not mean politics as a way of life, as an all-consuming job, game, and avocation, as it is for so many professional politicians. But it does mean politics (citizenship) as a way of living: an expected element of one's life. It is a prominent and natural role, such as that of "parent" or "neighbor."[36]

For participatory democrats, the emphasis on widespread participation by common citizens follows logically from other principles. Political equality, for example, is unlikely without participation by common people since, absent it, an elite few may hijack policy in their own interests rather than the public interest. In participatory democratic theory, participation also serves the useful purpose of developing citizen character in the form of civic skills and dispositions essential for democracy to work. These include the ability and willingness to recognize and build on the needs and interests of others; to deliberate; to weigh individual interests against the common good; to assume responsibility for problem-solving; and the skills and character traits such as debate, initiative, and responsibility needed to address shared interests and problems. Finally, if democracy is about "we the people" governing ourselves, participatory democrats ask what it means when most people shun participation at even basic levels like voting. They note that "we the people" appears in practice to more nearly resemble "we the affluent white men" in liberal democracies. In other words, absent participation by common citizens, elites will govern by default, and they will likely do so in their own interests rather than the public interest.

For anarchists, the emphasis on extensive direct participation is tied to their commitment to a stateless society and to the principles of DIY (Do It Yourself) and direct action. Without a state to provide essential (and nonessential) services, individuals must assert themselves, with others, to provide them. This requires both individual and collective effort. The result is the same for both anarchism and participatory democracy: both are impossible without ongoing and active participation in decision-making and shared work by common people.

Anarchists' insistence upon direct participation finds expression in a system of direct democracy. Whether or not they endorse elections, most anarchists opt for direct democracy when feasible (mostly at local levels) where participatory decision-making occurs, and the use of delegates, whose authority can be revoked at any moment. Direct democracy occurs in small assemblies in which people gather to deliberate and make decisions, with recallable delegates sent to larger bodies. Delegates are "instructed representatives,"[37] or "instructed delegates"[38] who "re-present" the views of their home assemblies to others in larger deliberative arenas, and hear the views of other delegates. Their decision-making power is typically limited or curtailed entirely in favor of reporting back to the home assemblies, where decisions are made.

Most participatory democrats will recognize anarchists' vision of direct democracy as essentially their own. They endorse the same vision of common citizens taking direct control of their own lives, meeting directly with other citizens to determine or forge common interests, and acting collectively on them.

Power

According to Uri Gordon, "the discussion of power . . . is really the obvious place to start for anarchist political theory. It cuts to the core: hierarchy, domination, direct action, the liberation of desire—power is the stuff of these."[39] Gordon distinguishes between three kinds of power: power-over, power-to, and power-with/among.[40] Power-over, or domination, most nearly captures the average person's understanding of power as the coercive force that impels people to do what they might not otherwise do. It is a power of control over others' lives and can be wielded in direct, observable ways as coercion and force, but also more subtly through control of essential resources, agenda setting, and distortion of one's self-perception. The exercise of this kind of power by definition impedes someone's autonomy. Although power-over is most easily recognized when employed by one agent to control another, some power-over is not wielded by agents, but instead exists in social institutions and structures where it partly creates individuals' identities and structures their thought and action.[41]

Power-to concerns capacity for thought and action and is an essential ingredient in freedom and autonomy. Power as capacity entails possession of the abilities, means, and resources for independent, critical thinking and effective, self-determining action in pursuit of goals. It often requires social support in various forms ranging from voluntary associations to family and kinship ties to neighborhood groups to community assistance programs.

Gordon defines power-with/among as "the power of a strong individual in a group of equals, the power not to command, but to suggest and be listened to, to begin something and see it happen" and as "power-to wielded as non-coercive influence and initiative among people who view themselves as equals."[42] This variant of power represents his attempt to account for the influence wielded by forceful individuals in egalitarian anarchist groups. Some strong individuals in groups exert influence and control over less assertive individuals in very subtle ways by talking more frequently or loudly, and by pressing their views and interests more frequently, forcefully, or persuasively. Gordon is right to draw attention to this use of power within groups, but his attempt to separate it from domination is not entirely convincing. Sometimes, the subtle influence exercised in groups by assertive individuals shades into control and domination, and should be recognized as such.

Anarchists are united in their opposition to the state as a central source of domination. They reject the state because it relies on coercion, force, and violence. Anarchists also reject the state because it typically protects the privileges of the powerful, and the powerful everywhere are wont to wield power in the interests of domination. As Bakunin put it, "If there is a State, there must be domination of one class by another and, as result, slavery; the State without slavery is unthinkable—and this is why we are enemies of the State."[43] Similarly, according to Kropotkin, the state "not only includes the existence of a power situated above society, but also of a territorial concentration as well as the concentration of many functions of the life of societies in the hands of a few. . . . A whole mechanism of legislation and of policing has to be developed in order to subject some classes to the domination of others."[44]

Noting that concentrated economic power threatens freedom as effectively as concentrated political power, most anarchists view capitalism as on a par with, or as a close second to, the state as a structure of domination. Especially considering that work consumes most of people's everyday lives, freedom is circumscribed extensively by the hierarchical, elitist, dominating structures and institutions of a capitalist political economy. Today, many large corporations rival nation-states in size, and their economic resources give them political leverage that sometimes threatens the sovereignty of nation-states, as well as states, cities, and local communities. Large, powerful business interests often "imprison" policy at all levels of government through threats and reprisals for decisions perceived as hostile to business interests.[45] Internally, large corporations typically function as quasi-authoritarian regimes with vertical lines of authority. Decisions are made at the highest levels, then passed down to workers whose livelihood often depends on their ability to follow orders without complaint. With few exceptions, workers have little or no opportunity to participate in the decision-making that determines the circumstances of their work lives. Capitalist work itself often appears as the antithesis of freedom for the average wage earner; it is also degrading and dehumanizing for many workers. The "wage slave" must follow the orders of owners and their hired managers; the only alternative is unemployment and the deprivations that unemployment brings in a capitalist political economy.[46]

Liberal democrats are, in theory, suspicious of concentrated *political* power as a form of domination. Classical liberals such as John Locke (1632–1704) posed government as an obstacle to freedom, in that each government law adds a restraint of some kind to someone's choice and action. Yet Locke and his libertarian heirs for the most part do not completely reject the state. They do, however, seek to minimize its size and scope, largely limiting it to the protection of "life, liberty, and estate,"[47] and to the provision of limited public goods that private markets will not provide. In this formulation, while the state represents a threat to freedom, it also helps protect certain freedoms from the insecurities of a hypothetical state of nature prior to the institution of government. Locke's predecessor, Thomas Hobbes (1588–1679), viewed the state of nature as a "warre of everyone against everyone" in which life is "solitary, poore, nasty, brutish and short."[48] Locke himself painted a less dismal view of life in a state of nature, but nevertheless retained enough of its insecurities to warrant leaving it in favor of civil society requiring the institution of government. Anarchists reject the view of human nature on which this narrative is based, and conclude that the state is an unnecessary imposition since basically sociable, rational humans can work out their problems and differences without resorting to violence and coercion. They in effect turn Hobbes and Locke on their heads. Rather than the state keeping individuals from warring against each other, anarchists argue that it is precisely the state that keeps people at war with each other.

The U.S. Constitution is founded in part on the classical liberal suspicion of centralized political power. It institutionalizes this suspicion via its machinery of checks and balances, and separation of powers, designed to thwart the concentration and exercise of political power. In some ways, this system has worked well, for better and worse, to thwart the unchecked exercise of political power, including its exercise by democratic majorities. In practice, this often translates as gridlock. On the other hand, as measured by the steady growth in the size and reach of government in most liberal democracies, and by the centralization of power under the U.S. presidency, concentrated, often unchecked or weakly checked political power is a mainstay of liberal democracies.

Despite some attempts to regulate it, liberal democrats regard concentrated *economic* power largely with equanimity, embracing it as an expression of cherished economic freedom. Locke's seminal defense of unlimited property acquisition occurred in the state of nature prior to the establishment of government, suggesting that concentrated economic power is both natural and private, outside the purview of the government he advocated to protect property. In liberal democracies today, private property confers power on its owners that they can wield against non-owners. They can set the terms of common life—through access to policymakers and through control over the productive and distributive forces of society—to an extent that is so ubiquitous that it appears utterly normal, a matter of simple common sense. Anarchists challenge this normalization of private property and the power associated with it. Emma Goldman rejected private property as a form of "dominion."[49] Proudhon famously declared that "property is theft," but he also wrote that "property is freedom." The former applied to landowners and capitalists who got their property directly or indirectly through conquest and exploitation, sustained by the state; and the latter applied to peasants and artisans with a natural right to a home, land to cultivate, and tools of trade, but not to control the same rights of others. In other words, he justified property ownership so long as it did not become an instrument of domination.[50] Bakunin and Kropotkin both favored socializing property.

Like anarchists, participatory democrats are keen to reduce or eliminate domination by the state and capital. Unlike anarchists, they do not advocate the complete abolition of the state. Generally, participatory democrats accept the necessity of the state as a means of rendering economic power accountable; to provide some public goods; to organize some forms of collective action; to provide for defense; and to ensure adequate protection of rights across localities. However, like anarchists they recommend decentralization and dispersal of both political and economic power in order to make it amenable to local control and social accountability. Participatory democrats offer at least three options regarding property. First, make it politically irrelevant by eliminating class barriers to participation in politics and taking steps to ensure that inequality in property ownership does not translate into political inequality. Second, disperse property ownership widely, to ensure that everyone has sufficient property to support independence, autonomy, and self-determination. Third, socialize property in the major means of production in order to take the control afforded by property out of private hands and place it in public hands that are accountable to the popular will. Most anarchists and participatory democrats additionally advocate some form of workplace democracy.

While anarchists' opposition to the state and capital as sources of domination has not waned, the focus has considerably broadened in the last several decades to include myriad other forms of domination throughout society. Anarchists now recognize and oppose domination as expressed in social forms such as patriarchy,[51] white supremacy, speciesism, and heterosexism. The alterglobalization movement includes newer anarchist groups representing animal rights and environmental groups as well as groups opposing the state and capital. In all cases, anarchists recognize and oppose the limits to freedom imposed by the many forms of domination.

So far, this discussion has focused on power as domination. As noted earlier, power as a positive capacity is essential for freedom and autonomy. Individual capacity is a function of access to skills, resources, and aptitudes that enable critical choice and effective action. Individual capacity is gathered through community organizing, participation in social movements, and other forms of collective action. The case studies in this book explore popular art forms as means of challenging domination and building capacity for critical thinking and effective action.

Equality

Despite the partial achievements of liberal democrats in pursuing equal rights and a minimal level of substantive equality, most liberal democracies are characterized by economic and political inequality ranging from substantial to radical. *Economic* inequality is a hallmark of liberal democracy, whether measured in terms of income or wealth disparities. Liberal democrats reduce *political* equality to the principle of one-person-one-vote, equal formal rights, and equal protection under the law. While these are important, they hardly ensure political equality. In practice, liberal democracies are noted for their wide discrepancies in effective political power depending primarily on access to financial resources and institutionalized seats of power.

Anarchists and participatory democrats go well beyond liberal democratic commitments to equality. To understand why, one might simply ask: what are the consequences of inequality for freedom and autonomy? As recognized by countless thinkers, economic inequality quickly translates into dependence and subjection. Rousseau, for example, argued that the poor are "obliged to receive or to steal their subsistence from the hand of the rich," and either to accept their "domination and servitude" or engage in "violence and pillage."[52] To highlight their state of dependency and dehumanization, Rousseau compared impoverished people to slaves who, unable to make self-determining decisions, are robbed of a moral personality. Wage slavery, he argued, deprives humans of independence and initiative while in the employ of others. They must yield to the whims of their bosses and to their own desperate need for subsistence. This robs them of moral agency and undermines their freedom.

Godwin too invoked the image of slavery in his discussion of the effects of poverty. A person born into poverty, he argued, is destined to be "strangely pent and fettered in his exertions" and the "bond slave of a thousand vices." Like Rousseau, Godwin also tied inequality to the perversion of character, arguing that concentrated property creates a "servile and truckling spirit" in those who are dependent on property owners.[53] Similarly, Thomas Jefferson argued that extreme disparities of wealth and income produced corrupt luxury on the one hand, and subservience and dependence on the other. Jefferson frequently extolled the virtues of small, independent farmers of rural America, seeing in them the basis for a healthy, sustainable democracy. He proposed a progressive income tax, inheritance laws, and the confiscation and redistribution of uncultivated land as foundations for widespread equality and independence.[54] Plato, though hardly a democrat, also saw inequality as a threat to workers' independence. He argued that poverty prevents work by keeping the worker from "providing himself with tools and the other necessities of his trade."[55] This leaves the worker dependent and vulnerable to the whims of the wealthy. As these thinkers recognized, economic inequality erodes freedom and autonomy by cultivating dependence of some on others.

Political inequality also erodes freedom by forcing those with little or no political power to live by rules and laws set by the politically powerful, often in their own interest. Many anarchists believe that we are free to the degree that we obey only rules and laws that we specifically agreed to. Participatory democrats generally adhere to a less strict rule by arguing that we preserve our freedom by adhering to laws that we helped make and that represent our common interests. For both, in a context of political inequality, some people wield more political power than others. This gives them the ability to control decision-making that determines the rules and circumstances of our lives. Anarchists and participatory democrats are both deeply suspicious of this possibility. As we saw earlier, many anarchists generally further reject the principle of representation on the grounds that it puts unacceptable levels of political power into the hands of a select few, by definition a departure from political equality.

At least some anarchists and participatory democrats are committed to equality as a matter of principle. Proudhon practically equated justice with equality, writing that "man seeks justice in equality." Hierarchy, he argued, causes "special perquisites, privileges, exemptions, favours, exceptions," and these are "all the violations of justice."[56] Bakunin, too, nearly equated the two: each person, he argued, is born with an innate sense of justice, which is "simple equality."[57] According to contemporary anarchist David Graeber, democracy is "not even really a mode of government. In its essence it is just the belief that humans are fundamentally equal and ought to be allowed to manage their collective affairs in an egalitarian fashion."[58] John Dewey's commitment to equality can be found throughout his writings on topics ranging from political economy to education to art. Jefferson was offended by the extreme inequality he observed in Europe. In a letter to James Madison, he denounced the unequal distribution of property that resulted in "so much misery to the bulk of mankind."[59]

Although I have concentrated in this section on economic and political (in)equality, other forms of inequality similarly undermine freedom and autonomy. A patriarchal family, for example, by definition includes male control over female choice and behavior, undermining her self-determination and independence. Racial inequality, an enduring feature in many liberal democracies, practically ensures that marginalized people of color enjoy less freedom and autonomy than privileged white people. While earlier anarchists and participatory democrats had a mixed record on these issues, their contemporaries are solidly committed to a wide-ranging equality that encompasses class, gender, sexual orientation, race/ethnicity, species (for some anarchists), and more. The same can be said for participatory democrats.

Freedom

For both anarchists and democrats, freedom lies at the heart of their political and ethical commitments. Freedom concerns the degree to which a person is able to successfully exercise choice, volition, and action relatively unhampered or unduly influenced by external forces. The dominant Western conception of freedom—so-called negative freedom—poses freedom in terms of a self-interested individual's "freedom from" interference by others and by the government. In this liberal formulation, individuals are free to the extent that they are left alone to do whatever they want, subject to as few restraints as possible. Simply being left alone, however, may not guarantee that individuals are able to do what they want. Removing interference is a necessary condition for freedom, but insufficient. Enabling conditions may need to be added in the form of positive support and resources that will ensure individuals' "freedom to" choose and act successfully in the pursuit of their goals. This "positive freedom" requires attention to their capacity; in other words, to their power to choose and act successfully.[60]

William Connolly integrates these two kinds of freedom in his discussion of the "internal relationship" of freedom to autonomy.[61] Autonomous individuals are self-determining agents, capable of choosing their own ends and acting on them without undue interference. Self-determination means exercising control over one's life. An autonomous individual is independent of others' control, which can be exercised directly but also indirectly through control over jobs and income, for example. An autonomous person is uncoerced, either directly using observable force or more subtly and indirectly through threats, dependence, insecurity, and vicarious influence. Autonomy is the opposite of subservience, subjection, submission, and dependence, which entail a loss of control over one's decisions and actions. The principle of autonomy is applied primarily to individuals, but also to groups and sometimes to geographical areas. For example, an affinity group, a community-based cooperative, or a region is autonomous to the degree that it is self-determining, independent, uncoerced, and free of subjection to outside control.

So for Connolly, freeing individuals from restraints is important, but not enough by itself if the goal is a self-determining, independent agent who chooses freely and acts successfully in the pursuit of goals. Freedom requires additionally that an agent possesses various capacities that support autonomy. These capacities include independent critical reflection and self-understanding, so that others do not distort an individual's choices and actions. Individuals must be able to reflect on their options and understand them realistically and critically, without undue influence from outside forces such as the media, advertising, or dominant individuals. Additionally, according to Connolly, freedom requires the presence of viable alternatives. Individuals must be able to actually act on a choice with the reasonable expectation that it is within reach. And to make an alternative viable, to make it a real option and not just a hypothetical or abstract option, the addition of positive social support may be required. Freedom is necessarily a factor of embeddedness in social relationships that structure and partly determine our choices and behaviors. Disconnection from a social context is both impossible and undesirable in that social forces often precisely serve as the foundation for individual capacity. The challenge is to create social relations that support rather than undermine freedom. A social context defined by authoritarian, hierarchical, coercive social relations undermines freedom. A social context of nonhierarchical, decentralized power and equality supports free, autonomous individuality.

With few exceptions,[62] anarchists embrace a conception of freedom that closely approximates Connolly's freedom in its emphasis on autonomy, self-determination, capacity, and sociability. Bakunin, for example, wrote that

> I am a fanatic lover of liberty, considering it as the unique condition under which intelligence, dignity, and human happiness can develop and grow; not the purely formal liberty [negative freedom] . . . of bourgeois liberalism. . . . No, I mean the only kind of liberty that is worthy of the name, liberty that consists in the full development of all the material, intellectual, and moral powers that are latent in each person.

According to Bakunin, "Man can fulfill his free individuality only by complementing it through all the individuals around him, and only through work and the collective force of society." Absolute independence, he argued, is a "wild absurdity" and the "brainchild of idealists and metaphysicians" that condemns the individual to "non-existence." Society, according to Bakunin, is "the root, the tree of freedom, and liberty is its fruit."[63] Similarly, according to anarchist historian Rudolf Rocker (1873–1958), "For the anarchist, freedom is not an abstract philosophical concept, but the vital concrete possibility for every human being to bring to full development all the powers, capacities, and talents with which nature has endowed him."[64] This "full development" of "powers, capacities, and talents" occurs within a social context that supports individual development. As Wilhelm von Humboldt (1767–1835) argued, "The isolated man is no more able to develop than the one who is fettered."[65]

Additionally, self-determination and the full development of individuality should not come at the expense of others. Most anarchists embrace solidarity as a necessary complement to individual freedom. Rudolf Rocker argued that an individual with developed capacities should "turn them to social account."[66] According to Bakunin, "I am free only when all human beings surrounding me—men and women—are equally free."[67] According to Max Nettlau (1865–1944), "from isolation we take refuge in solidarity," and "all those who revolt against authority [should] work on lines of general solidarity instead of being divided into little chapels." Nettlau called for "a large sphere of solidarity" to balance the anarchist commitment to individual freedom and autonomy.[68] Errico Malatesta (1853–1932) referred to "the great law of solidarity" that he believed should predominate in society. Solidarity, according to Malatesta, "tempered" the "aspiration towards unlimited freedom," and helped ensure that "all should enjoy equal freedom."[69] Solidarity asks individuals to reject a narrow form of rational egoism, and to consider the needs and interests of others.

In recent times, Murray Bookchin accused some contemporary anarchists of abandoning this long-standing commitment to solidarity in favor of a more individualistic and self-centered "lifestyle anarchism." Bookchin distinguished between two kinds of freedom: freedom from constraint (the negative freedom of classical liberalism) and "freedom for" that entails freedom for humanity as a whole as well as the individual. He disparaged the former, associating it with contemporary anarchists pursuing prefigurative social change strategies. He associated the latter with social anarchism, and endorsed it as consistent with the collectivist, solidaristic form of anarchism of which he approved. His critics responded that he had created in "lifestyle anarchism" a straw anarchist representing everything he disliked about contemporary anarchism, and that his criticisms of prefigurative social change strategies were overdrawn.[70]

In the theory and practice of democracy, understandings of freedom both overlap and diverge from anarchist formulations of freedom. Democracy requires that citizens are free to assemble, to speak freely, to be free from unwarranted incursions in their private lives, and in general to enjoy the freedoms necessary for them to identify common interests and act on them. Liberal democrats typically interpret these requirements primarily in the terms of negative freedom from obstacles that prevent such activities as assembling, speaking, and acting on interests. In the history of liberal democracy, this kind of negative freedom is tied to rights, understood as protections for the individual against encroachments by others and the government. Since John Locke, the right of property has been central. Subsequent liberal democratic theory and practice have emphasized the central importance of property rights as expressions of individual freedom.

In liberal democratic theory, every citizen is a rights-bearer to an equal degree as everyone else, and everyone's rights are equally protected by an essentially neutral government. This leads to a political practice of protecting rights (combined with limited provision of public goods); and if a person's rights are successfully protected, the demands of freedom are satisfied. Although negative rights are useful means of protecting individual autonomy, by themselves they are insufficient. Millions of rights-bearers in the United States, and billions worldwide, suffer deprivation, insecurity, dependence, and subjection because they lack sufficient means and resources for autonomy.

Participatory democrats recognize this link between freedom and access to material resources. John Dewey, for example, argued that "effective freedom"—the freedom to actually act successfully in pursuit of goals—varies along with the possession of material resources.[71] Participatory democrats also understand freedom at least partly in terms of the freedom to help determine the rules under which we choose to live. We preserve our freedom by consenting only to those rules that we had a hand in creating. This more closely approaches anarchists' understanding of freedom, with the caveat that some anarchists consider themselves free only to the degree that they live according to rules to which they have specifically consented. In the absence of consensus, most participatory democrats are willing to apply the principle of majoritarianism, in which a minority will have to accede to the laws approved by a majority.

Much of the domination experienced in everyday life occurs in people's work lives, where they are subject to vertical, authoritarian structures of control. They obey the rules set by others, with no pretense of consent. According to participatory democrats, there is no reason in principle to limit democracy to a narrow realm dubbed "political." This limitation marks an enduring characteristic of liberal democracy, one that artificially diminishes democracy while protecting property and concentrated economic power from popular pressures. Participatory democrats and anarchists alike reject this artificial segmentation of life, insisting that individuals should enjoy freedom and autonomy in all realms, from the workplace and household to the classroom and neighborhood associations as well as more recognizably political realms, and this means participating in the decision-making within those realms.

The conceptual and practical counterpart to solidarity in democratic theory and practice is civic virtue, meaning attention to the common good as well as to one's individual self-interest. Liberal democrats for the most part have rejected or abandoned the idea of civic virtue. It has become an article of faith in dominant forms of liberal democracy that self-interest is all there is in the realm of politics. Politics is about the social organization of that self-interest into competitive factions, with elections advancing some interests against others. Like solidarity, civic virtue balances individual self-interest against the needs and interests of others. It adds an ethical commitment to the well-being of others, not just the self. Anarchists' solidarity and participatory democrats' civic virtue bind individual aspirations to social concern and obligation. They link individual struggles to the struggles of others, and recognize that one's own well-being is muted and tarnished by the deprivation and suffering of others.

No conception of freedom can wholly escape the tension between individual freedom and the communal and social dimensions of human existence. Even if the individual does not think *only* in terms of self-interest, individual freedom may raise difficult challenges for securing cooperation and collective action. With their strict emphasis on negative freedom and individual self-interest, and lacking a corresponding conception of a common good, liberal democrats must turn to a coercive state to secure mutual protection and public goods unsupplied by the market. Anarchists' commitment to solidarity, and participatory democrats' commitment to civic virtue, at least opens the possibility of extensive, uncoerced cooperation and collective action.

In the case studies that follow, popular art forms will be analyzed for what they reveal about anarchist and democratic themes of social organization, political action, power, equality, and freedom. I will argue that each art form is organized and practiced in varying ways and degrees according to central anarchist principles, whether explicitly or not. As such, each in turn prefigures more deeply democratic forms of life. The case studies do not speak equally forcefully or clearly on each of these themes, but each has something to say about them. In each case study, I ask: What form(s) of social organization and political action does this popular art form model? How does it challenge domination while increasing capacity? What does it say about equality and freedom? And in each case, how does it prefigure a more democratic future?

3

DIY (Do It Yourself) Punk Music

Writing in 2008, Uri Gordon argued that "the punk movement has been the most significant hotbed for anarchists throughout the last two decades."[1] This is particularly true of one subgenre of punk music: DIY punk music, the subject of this chapter. Tom Buechele defines the DIY punk music subculture as a

> . . . hands-on approach to playing and recording music, putting out records, making art and generally creating things on your own or in a community. What makes it a distinct scene from that of the larger punk culture, and a counterculture to the mainstream is its adherence to the DIY ethic and, more broadly, central defining commitments of contemporary anarchism. The DIY ethic can be defined as the creating and sharing of music and art through a network of DIY communities, operating as an alternative to mainstream institutions of production.[2]

DIY punk music is one part of a larger DIY music scene. I make no attempt to comprehensively address all aspects of this broader DIY music scene. This chapter does not, for example, address the DIY music of prominent mainstream musicians such as Madonna, Prince, Simply Red, and others who in recent years have adopted a limited DIY approach in producing and mass-marketing their music. While these musicians and groups are indeed taking greater control over their own cultural product, their primary motivation remains commercial rather than the generally anti-capitalist, and (sometimes) anti-state leanings of the DIY punk music scene. Moreover, I concentrate on the United Kingdom and the United States, omitting potentially illuminating considerations of DIY punk music in other countries. The musicians, bands, and fans addressed in this chapter, while unable to completely escape the influence of state and capital, nevertheless create worlds apart—in the cracks and on the margins—where they fashion a life based on alternative ideals and beliefs tied implicitly or explicitly to anarchist theory and practice.

The roots and antecedents of the DIY punk music scene are variously traced to early anarchist thought and practice;[3] the Situationist International that formed in 1957 as a revolt against dominant culture, capitalism and consumerism;[4] the London-based Albion Free State, whose manifesto of 1974 proclaimed a "network . . . of independent collectives and communities, federated together";[5] the feminists and lesbians who during the late-1960s and 1970s created their own separatist music communities doing "womyn's" music via all-women record labels, distribution networks, and music festivals in response to the male-dominated music industry;[6] and the deep alienation felt by many youth in the 1960s and 1970s, driving many of them to seek alternatives to the consumerist, capitalist culture in which they were living.[7] The DIY ethic of do-it-yourself and explicit anarchist themes—themes such as questioning conformity and authority, commitments to autonomy, direct action, and challenging the state and capital—surfaced in early punk music during the mid-1970s. The phrase "Do it yourself" is attributed to Caroline Coon, the English artist, journalist, and activist, who supposedly uttered it in 1976.[8] The DIY ethic was rapidly spelled out further by various musicians, record producers, and fanzine writers. Mark P. (aka Mark Perry), founder and publisher of the punk fanzine *Sniffin' Glue* (*SG*), for example, exhorted punk fans to "take their destinies into their own hands." "All you kids out there who read '*SG*,'" he wrote, "don't be satisfied with what we write. Go out and start your own fanzines."[9] The U.K. anarcho-punk band Desperate Bicycles stated the DIY case bluntly on the sleeve notes for their second single, "The Medium Was Tedium?"/"Don't Back the Front" (Refill Records, 1977): the band would "really like to know why you haven't made your single yet. . . . So if you can understand, go and join a band. Now it's your turn." The group adopted as their slogan, "It was easy, it was cheap, go and do it."[10]

Thousands of bands scattered throughout the U.K. and U.S. now "go and do it." They create, develop, and sustain DIY communities and networks through music and related cultural activities. The DIY punk music scene is both large and diverse,[11] making generalizations difficult. Some musicians and bands continue to identify explicitly with anarchism, while many others do DIY absent overt political commitments. The politics of the latter are found in the prefigurative practice of DIY punk music as an alternative way of life.

Social Organization

The highly decentralized and extensively networked world of DIY punk music closely resembles the rhizomatic model of social organization characteristic of contemporary anarchism. The basic units of the DIY music scene are the bands, houses, and other performance venues; DIY recording labels; and DIY-friendly bookstores, cultural centers, and community centers. Although some DIY musicians perform solo, most are members of bands. Some of these musicians live in DIY houses in residential neighborhoods where living rooms, basements, and attics are converted to performing spaces for DIY concerts. Sometimes, DIY musicians convert old warehouses, commercial storefronts, or other buildings into performing spaces that often also include residential space (whether or not the local zoning permits it). Other performing venues include bars, coffee shops, and restaurants. Decision-making within bands and houses generally occurs informally, without resorting to formal or hierarchical lines of authority. It is more difficult to generalize about bars, coffee shops, and restaurants. While some are worker-owned and worker-managed in nonhierarchical ways as anarcho-punk collectives, others are privately owned and managed along hierarchical lines of authority.

Many of the early DIY punk bands created their own recording labels. This was partly driven by necessity: given some of the lyrical and visual content of the bands, the big labels were reluctant to record them. However, it was also inherent in the DIY philosophy of autonomy, of controlling your own message, and of circumventing dominant capitalist institutions. These labels took on a recording industry that emphasized centralization of media technologies; a gatekeeping role that denied access to most musicians; hierarchical management structures; centralized power in the hands of recording executives; exploitive contracts that typically allotted a small percentage of around 7 percent in royalties and required long-term commitments that favored the recording company; a tendency toward homogenized sound; and an uncertain commitment to promotion. These independent labels offered instead greater autonomy; participation and access; decentralization of media technologies and organizations; a leveling of power; a more collaborative and cooperative management model; more equal patterns of rewards and status; a more diverse and innovative aesthetic; and more dependability in distribution commitments.[12]

The most important of the early labels was arguably Rough Trade, formed in 1978 in London by Geoff Travis, owner of a record store of the same name. Although not formed by a DIY band, Rough Trade embodied many of the aesthetic and political commitments of DIY. It recorded bands with explicit anarchist political commitments that the big labels shunned, and also offered members of those bands unprecedented access to decision-making processes within the company, as well as jobs within the company. It led a decentralizing process in the recording industry that by 1982 would result in the release of at least sixteen thousand different punk records worldwide by approximately three thousand independent labels.[13] Rough Trade self-consciously leveled power both within the organization and between the label and its musicians by broadening stock ownership among employees, equalizing pay grades, forming decision-making boards composed of representatives elected by employees, and encouraging debate and discussion over both policy and strategy. It negotiated alternative deals with musicians in which royalties were split 50-50, and copyrights reverted to musicians after six months. And it recorded music that sometimes fell well outside established patterns of acceptability with musical elements such as off-key vocals, unbalanced mixing, yelling, screaming, indecipherable lyrics, noise, feedback, fuzziness, static, distortion, fast tempos, three-chord song structures, and deliberate amateurism.[14]

Many of Rough Trade's commitments and practices were replicated by other DIY labels that institutionally embodied punk musicians' commitment to access, control, and autonomy and their "intrinsically anarchistic . . . approach to authority and control."[15] The labels, and the musicians that recorded with them, clearly intended to transform the relations of production, especially the relations between musicians and record companies, but including relations between musicians, record companies, distributors, retailers, promoters, and fans. Today, thousands of DIY recording labels continue to play an important role in sustaining the DIY scene. Although it is impossible to say accurately how many labels are currently operating, the number must be considerable, given the accessibility and relatively low cost of recording technology. In 1999, Craig O'Hara estimated the number simply as "thousands" of DIY labels in the U.S.[16] Since then, recording technology has increased in sophistication while decreasing in cost, so today the number of active labels is likely considerably higher. With a relatively small investment of a few thousand dollars, any modestly ambitious band can now record itself as well as any other interested bands with which they have connections. Many of the indie labels are run from private homes, by one or two people.

DIY-friendly bookstores, cultural centers, and community centers also provide organizational resources for DIY punk music. Among the best known are Profane Existence in Minneapolis; New York's Lower East Side ABC No Rio, a punk collective, social center, and art gallery; and 924 Gilman Street in Berkeley, California, notorious for its success on a largely volunteer basis.

These various organizational units of the DIY punk music scene are connected via "an international DIY network of labels, musicians, fanzines and distributors."[17] Communication occurs primarily through online resources and through bands' seemingly constant touring. Online social networking sites have dramatically opened new rhizomatic connections in the DIY scene at local, regional, national, and international levels. These online networks are less centralized, less dependent on already-existing social relations, more user-friendly, more accessible, and more diverse than older networking technologies. They enable expanded artistic control and autonomy, increased access and participation, new collaborative possibilities, and openness to widespread participation. The importance of the web can be partly seen in the rapid expansion of its use. Approximately 240,000 artists used MySpace in 2005; that number had grown to more than 5 million in 2008. Embeddable tracks allow "friends" to link a band's tunes to their pages. Artists can choose to monetize and sell tracks, albums, and other merchandise; or they can let the users decide its value, and pay accordingly. In recent years, more and more bands are self-releasing their recordings directly onto the web, bypassing hard copies. Bands can also add photos, videos, merchandising pitches, or whatever additional copy they deem useful for circulating their music. Most artists bring an existing social network to cyberspaces such as MySpace and Facebook, and then attempt to build it further online. Online sites enable musicians to find each other for collaborative projects, find new fans, connect with existing ones, and manage the actual performing and touring logistics such as promoting upcoming shows. None of this guarantees a successful band or a successful gig. With so much traffic now on the web, one band's efforts are easily swamped by the traffic.[18]

The tour is a central means of linking local efforts to a larger DIY network. Many bands tour at least once a year, for at least four to six weeks, and some tour more often over longer periods. Musicians that want to tour contact promoters, who typically are DIY house residents, collective members, or owners of performance venues. This contact is made via MySpace, Facebook, cell phone, Twitter, or email. Typically at least several bands are booked for a single night, including one or more touring bands plus some locals. Rather than a formal admission charge, small donations are requested with the proceeds typically distributed to the touring bands. Band members are typically fed and offered a place to spend the night. Musicians hope for enough pay to buy sufficient gas to get them to the next stop on the tour, and when that goal is not met, at least some bands resort to siphoning gas to make up the difference. Bands attempt to earn some additional income through the sale of tee shirts, CDs, and other paraphernalia. Few participants make a living through DIY music; almost everyone works a day job, and many go without health insurance unless it is provided through their day job or by parents, spouses, or partners.

Political Action

As the DIY label suggests, DIY punk music is defined by its commitment to direct action by participants in the production and circulation of music and other cultural creation. It is also characterized by related anarchist commitments to widespread participation and volunteerism, and to political action directed against various forms of domination.

Punk music has always been identified with rebellion, but the character of that rebellion has varied from relatively symbolic forms emphasizing style to more overtly politicized forms such as protest and civil disobedience. Especially after they quickly signed with major labels, early prominent punk bands such as the Sex Pistols and Clash combined the two. Despite the title, the Sex Pistol's first single, "Anarchy in the U.K.," did not accurately represent the emerging DIY and anarchist messages emphasizing positive political engagement. Comparing anarchists to Antichrists, and exhorting listeners to "Get pissed, destroy," the song reinforced the long-standing misperception of anarchists as nihilists advocating violence. In signing with major labels, the Sex Pistols and Clash reflected what would become a ongoing dilemma for punk bands: either "sell out" to become commercially successful, or maintain autonomy while paying the price of economic marginality.

The British punk band Crass[19] played a defining role in the early development of the DIY music scene. Crass, composed of nine male and female musicians, artists, filmmakers, and activists, did "more to spread anarchist ideas than Kropotkin."[20] From 1977 until it disbanded in 1983, Crass confronted the music industry, the church, the army, the government, and, sometimes, other punk bands they felt had sold out. They also addressed feminist and ecological themes. In a move that would become a defining element of the DIY scene, Crass circumvented the power of the music industry by creating its own recording label. Members of the group also helped others establish their own labels, produced and distributed their own music, designed their own sleeve covers and liner notes, and organized an alternative network of fans, promoters, and other musicians for performing and touring. They frequently played benefits for various leftist political causes, and donated money earned from shows to marginal political campaigns and free festivals. They took steps to obliterate the gap between performers and fans by, for example, hosting tea parties before and after performances.

Crass's 1978 song "Punk Is Dead" notoriously critiqued the punk bands they viewed as sell-outs. The lyrics openly expressed their disdain for the Clash for opting for cash over political commitment and denying that they had anything to do with revolution.[21] In an even more pointed—and humorous—critique, the cover of their 1980 single "Persons Unknown"/"Bloody Revolutions," issued with Poison Girls (their frequent performing partners) as a benefit record for the Anarchy Centre in London and a protest against the trial of four anarchists indicted on conspiracy and bomb charges, made visual fun of the Sex Pistols by superimposing the heads of despised authority figures over the bodies of members of the Sex Pistols. The head of Margaret Thatcher replaced that of Johnny Rotten, who is pictured as drinking a glass of wine rather than the more working-class can of beer; the head of Queen Elizabeth II replaced that of Sid Vicious; and Pope John Paul II's head replaced that of Steve Jones, whose arm now bore a "Mum" tattoo.[22]

Their 1979 album, "Stations of the Crass," included a booklet detailing crimes of organized religion, and its cover art referenced the graffiti campaign it was currently waging in London's underground railway system. Crass's "Big A, little a"[23] was a call to direct action and social change. The song exhorted listeners to challenge dominant powers, and to stop playing by rules created by those powers. Crass frequently commented through their art on contemporary events. They bluntly and publicly opposed the war in the Falklands in their single "How Does It Feel To Be the Mother of a Thousand Dead." Directed at Margaret Thatcher, the song asks her how it feels to be the cause of so many deaths, and accuses Thatcher of arrogance, deceit, lies, "filthy pride," vanity, inhumanity, lust for war, having a "stone heart," using the war to advance her domestic political agenda, and a lot more. It makes the larger antiwar claim that throughout history, leaders like Thatcher have sacrificed young lives to their twisted imperial ambitions. The song concludes with the familiar anthem: "1 - 2 - 3 - 4 - We don't want your fucking war!"[24]

Crass bass player and vocalist Pete Wright bluntly stated the group's commitment to direct action:

> ATTENTION. Stand up and fight. Choose life or destruction, love or hate. You cannot have both and survive. Go forward. Get out in the streets. Down the sewers. Snap the rules. Creep through the net. Fuck their diseased system. The words are no longer enough. The information has been given. The lies have been exposed. Choose your path. It's time to fucking act. No time to be nice. It's time to fucking act.[25]

Many other DIY punk bands from this period took the same path as Crass. Poison Girls' contribution to the DIY ethic has been immortalized in the group's hand-drawn chord chart with the blunt DIY exhortation: "here's one chord, here's another, now start a band."[26] Other prominent U.K. DIY punk bands from this early period included Flux of Pink, Subhumans, Buzzcocks, and Desperate Bicycles.

On the other side of the Atlantic, similar efforts were under way, especially in California. The Dead Kennedys formed in San Francisco in 1978. By 1979 they were recording on their indie label, Alternative Tentacles, which, like the band itself, would become a key player in the DIY movement. The Dead Kennedys highlighted their critique of the mainstream recording industry in 1980 while performing at the Bay Area Music Awards, attended by music industry insiders. The band wore white shirts with a large *S* painted on the front. Fifteen seconds into their first song, they stopped, pulled black ties from around their necks so that each tie and *S* together formed a large dollar sign, and then launched into a new song entitled "Pull My Strings." The song satirized the mainstream music industry with lyrics that tied mainstream success to small brains and selling one's soul. During the 1980s, the Dead Kennedys used their music to critique Reagan-era politics. Its 1981 "In God We Trust" EP featured a gold Christ figure nailed to a cross of dollar bills, and contained songs lambasting the moral majority ("Moral Majority"), skinhead punks ("Nazi Punks Fuck Off!"), and U.S. president Ronald Reagan ("We've Got a Bigger Problem Now"), in which they call Reagan an emperor, a fascist, and a shah who tramples on human rights.

Black Flag, formed in 1976 in Hermosa Beach, California, set a course similar to the Dead Kennedys. They established their own label, SST, toured seemingly constantly, and tirelessly promoted the DIY values of autonomy and independence. Partly of necessity given the lack of venues at the time for punk bands to perform, members of the band arranged and promoted their own gigs in parks, basements, churches, and wherever else they could book a performance. They created their own artwork for flyers and album covers. Their self-promotional efforts included spray-painting the band's logo—four vertical black bars on a flag, representing anarchy—all over Los Angeles. They released numerous albums, continued touring nationally and sometimes internationally, and finally disbanded in 1986.

The commitment to direct action and widespread participation remains a constant and prominent element in the contemporary DIY punk music scene. Profane Existence, an anarcho-punk collective formed in Minneapolis in 1989 and still sporadically active today, quickly became an important clearinghouse for DIY punk music as well as other anarchist cultural and political material. According to its mission statement, Profane Existence is about "contributing to building a stronger and more politically active punk rock movement. . . . Our politics are anti-state and anti-oppression . . . and our community is from within the DIY punk rock movement."[27] Collective members organize tours and concerts, publish a zine, produce and distribute LPs on their own record label of the same name, and publish anarchist, punk, and DIY material. Especially through its zine of the same name, Profane Existence promotes direct action against the state, capitalism, nationalism, militarism, religion, racism, and patriarchy. In addition to political organizing, collective members seek to develop and control the means of production and dissemination of culture. As expressed by one member,

> The driving ethic behind most sincere Punk efforts is DIY—Do It Yourself. We don't need to rely on rich business men to organize our fun for their profit—we can do it ourselves for no profit. We Punks can organize gigs, organize and attend demos, put out records, publish books and fanzines, set up

> mail-order distributions for our products, run record stores, distribute literature, encourage boycotts, and participate in political activities. We do all of these things and we do them well.[28]

Berea Fest V, a DIY music festival held in Berea, Ohio, on July 16–17, 2010, exemplifies DIY punk music as a rhizomatic network for organizing direct action and participation. Its organizers described it as "a celebration of national and local DIY music and the community it creates. With support from all who are involved, we can create something that is relevant on our own terms. We all have the ability to inspire and impact each other and the world around us." The event was organized through online venues and via an extensive network of personal relationships cultivated through years of performing, touring, and recording. The organizers refused corporate sponsorship and booked no bands through agents. The nominal entrance fee of five dollars went toward paying for gas for touring bands, with some left over to donate to the nearby Berea Children's Home (in 2009, the event raised $2,525 for the home). The website for Berea Fest urged attendees to claim ownership of the event and to volunteer: "THIS EVENT IS YOURS, so if there is something going on that you like, support it. If there is something negative going on, help address the issue." The informal organization of the event was exemplified by the pitch for volunteers: "You can just help with this, you don't need to ask, just stick around." Organizers also requested that everyone pitch in to help feed the musicians, and to provide housing for anyone who needs it. Housing support was recruited and supported via an online "Sleep Over Board" in which people offering space could list their names and contact information, and people needing space could find it. Bands were asked to cooperate by sharing equipment. Although no explicit political messages were included by the Fest organizers, clues hint at political commitments. For example, the presence of Cleveland Food Not Bombs helping with food arrangements suggests a commitment to anarchist peace organizing. The website concluded with a familiar DIY exhortation: "There is always room for more fests/shows in Berea. Do it! We know you can. DIY!"[29]

As Berea Fest V illustrates, the DIY punk scene relies on widespread direct participation by fans, musicians, zine writers, house residents, and others. Since relatively little money circulates through the scene, cash cannot serve as the primary basis for participation. This means that other motivations propel individuals into the scene and keep them there. It also means that there are no significant class barriers to entry. One of the hallmarks of liberal democracy is precisely these financial barriers to participation in market, state, and cultural institutions. In the DIY punk music scene, these barriers are systematically eliminated. Anyone with a guitar or drum set can form or join a band, and recording songs now requires very little financial investment. Promoting recordings and live performances costs almost nothing, since most of it now occurs electronically. Fans must pay nominal amounts for the recordings, and small "donations" to attend live performances, but nothing rivaling the costs associated with consuming the cultural product of mainstream artists. The cafés and bookstores that dot the DIY scene tend to price their goods at below-market rates, or offer inexpensive alternative fare such as rice and beans as a routine entrée. These various aspects of the DIY punk scene have clear democratic implications of broadening and deepening participation.

Participation in the DIY scene is also democratized by "removing the audience/performer separation."[30] As noted above, early anarcho-punk bands attempted to narrow the gap between performers and fans by, for example, serving tea to fans after performances. In the contemporary scene, the performing spaces themselves tend to be easily accessible for most people. Gigs occur most often in basements, garages, community centers, private homes, and at free or inexpensive festivals. Stages are often eliminated as an intentional way of putting musicians literally on the same level as listeners. Bands often enter the performing area—whether a stage or not—from and through the audience, and often play in basements surrounded by fans. Creating music and performing it still requires relatively accessible musical skills compared, for example, to those required of classical musicians. Concert billings typically are shared by several or more bands, and sometimes with other performing artists such as poets. Hierarchies between headline and supporting acts are deliberately undermined. Most of necessity haul their own gear, do their own sound checks, develop and distribute their own promotional materials, and generally do the physical as well as creative work associated with music production and circulation. As already noted, established musicians and bands exhort others to form their own bands, write and record their own music, start their own recording labels, and in general seize control of cultural production.[31]

The various social networks also democratize participation by opening practically unlimited and inexpensive avenues for it. Thanks to MySpace, Facebook, YouTube, Twitter, the Internet, and cell phones, individuals can easily find each other, make connections, and identify openings for participation in the DIY music scene.

Much of the political content of the DIY punk music scene is embedded in the organization and everyday practices of its participants; in the "doing it." The politics are enacted daily in the autonomous production, circulation, and reception of the music, and related activities. The do-it-yourself ethic of the scene itself rehearses the central political commitments of participants. Many DIY participants' political action is limited to their work in the DIY punk scene. Others organize, or enlist in, various forms of collective action both inside and outside the DIY scene. The DIY punk music network is frequently used as a resource for mobilizing for various causes such as the alterglobalization, antiwar, and ecological movements. Many houses and other performing venues sponsor benefits for various causes. But there is a limit imposed on the frequency of benefits by the need of touring bands to earn enough to continue touring. Many DIY punk music participants now advocate for ecological protections, and there are likely more vegans and animal rights activists per capita in the DIY punk scene than in the general population. Many profess a commitment to anti-consumerism, but this may be borne more of necessity than political commitment, given the meager economic resources of most participants. Yet, it can be said with certainty that many DIY punk music participants consciously choose an alternative path, at least temporarily, to the careerist, materialist, consumer-oriented path taken by most other residents of affluent countries. Many formulate this explicitly in terms of anticapitalism.

Power

Within the DIY punk music scene, formal concentrations of power are limited. Some level of concentrated power can be found residing informally in strong personalities, in individuals who control the booking of touring bands, and in rhizomatic hubs such a bookstores, houses, storefronts, and other performing venues. But these are generally limited in scope and depth. Given the dispersed, decentralized rhizomatic nature of the DIY punk music scene, concentrations of power that mimic the centralized power of the state and capital in liberal democracies are generally difficult or impossible to produce and sustain. No individuals or institutions can fully control the availability and circulation of information, music production and reception, or other aspects of the DIY punk music scene. This dispersal is aided by social media and independent labels that serve as countervailing forces against concentrated power. The various social media create avenues of information sharing and dissemination that broaden access and limit centralized control. Small, independent DIY labels are "an institutional challenge to the majors' dominant discourses . . . , part of an attempt to spread power out, to re-distribute cultural capital and encourage self-expression."[32]

At least some of the contemporary opposition within the DIY punk music scene to domination likely originates in rebellious teenagers and twentysomethings who either in principle or viscerally oppose the domination imposed by various authority figures and institutions, but largely lacking the focus on ending domination by the state and capital. That said, many contemporary participants intentionally engage in practices that subvert state and capitalist domination. According to the website of Cleveland's DIY punk music performing venue Tower 2012, the goal of the collective is to "promote and maintain this space in order to ensure that we have an alternative to the capitalist-model venues. We do not profit monetarily from this. We gain something more: fun, friendship, killer bands and awesomeness." The collective members of the Marburg Hotel, a community recording studio and performance space in Cincinnati, write that they "strive to be a meaningful resource for the city's creative community, empowering those who would not traditionally have access to arts production, promotion, and distribution." They offer their creative and technical services at "low-cost, no-cost, and trade-based community negotiations." Some performing venues will not book bands that are signed to major labels. According to the organizers of the Berea Fest V (2010) DIY music festival, "we will not book any band through a booking group/agent, period . . . ever." They "take pride in the fact that there are no sponsors for this event." As noted above, whatever money is left after paying gas for touring bands and covering other costs is donated to the Berea Children's Home, so no one profits. These examples can be multiplied many times over.[33]

Additionally, participants avoid the Internal Revenue Service by paying each other in cash and by asking for "donations" in lieu of required fees to enter performance spaces. Some dumpster-dive for food, and some siphon gas from others' cars. The latter is, of course, illegal and as such a direct—if relatively trivial—challenge to the authority of the state. Many share living quarters to reduce housing costs, and some squat in abandoned buildings. They live partly off the grid, flying under the radar, in the cracks and on the margins of both state and capital.

Yet, whatever their relative success in avoiding or subverting the concentrated power of the state and capital, inevitably most DIY punk music participants must contend with them sooner or later. Most work day jobs because their DIY punk work pays too little or not at all; and they pay taxes based on their day-job wages. Those who drive must buy licenses for their vehicles. All are more or less subject to the same laws that structure everyday life for all residents. Small, independent DIY music recording labels must compete against the major labels for listeners' attention and dollars. As noted by Robert Strachan, the small labels, and small-scale cultural producers more generally, "cannot be seen as autonomous from either the dominance of large-scale institutions or the larger field of power"[34] given the impossibility—or desirability—of complete retreat to the cracks and margins.

Despite the explicit feminist commitments of some bands, the DIY punk music scene has always been dominated by men, at least as measured in terms of number of participants. Nevertheless, women have made their mark in various ways. In the early 1990s, the Riot Grrrl movement appeared on the scene. This decentralized, underground feminist punk movement addressed many of the same DIY themes as its male counterparts, while also tackling issues left under- or unexplored by previous punks. These included, for example, rape, female empowerment, sexual abuse, and female sexuality. The "Riot Grrrl Manifesto," published in 1991, summarized many of the new movement's commitments. The manifesto expressed the need for records, books, and fanzines that address the specific needs and interests of girls and women. It also noted that the punk rock anthem of "you can do anything" applies equally to girls and women. The manifesto included a long list of "isms" that its adherents need to "figure out" and address. And it insisted that "girls constitute a revolutionary soul force that can, and will, change the world for real."[35]

A separate, more informal "Punk Rock Feminism" manifesto also appeared around the same time. This second manifesto repeated some of the same themes of the "Riot Grrrl Manifesto," while making even more explicit the anarchist theme of autonomy: "It's about AUTONOMY: gaining more and more control over my life. Creating the stuff, music, porn, writing, I want to hear and read instead of waiting and consuming and being bored and unsatisfied. Girl autonomy means we need our own fanzines/magazines/music/films/books/venues . . . the things boys can take for granted."

The manifesto also emphasized the themes of community and networking. It concluded with the familiar DIY exhortation to "get on and do stuff."[36] The Riot Grrrl movement, like DIY punk music more generally, was a decentralized network of musicians, bands, artists, and fanzine writers, and was led by anyone willing to step forward and form a band, label, or fanzine. Some of the best-known bands included Bikini Kill, Lucid Nation, CWA (Cunts With Attitude), Emily's Sassy Lime, and Voodoo Queens. These bands at least partly countered male domination in the DIY punk music scene.

Prefiguring its anarchist rejection of domination, DIY punk music participants create alternative spaces—TAZs, SPAZs, and (perhaps for some) PAZs—where domination is challenged and, at least sometimes, reduced or eliminated; where power is leveled, and central authority figures or structures are reduced or eliminated. Participants create and sustain communities and networks of support, building capacity for autonomous living. Some DIY punk music participants, anyway, create sufficient power within the scene to make a living on their own terms. Many more draw everyday sustenance and experience autonomy and agency within the scene that can carry over into other aspects of their lives. The participants in the scene must coexist with larger structures and institutions of domination. Moreover, most participants live much of their lives outside the cracks and margins within which DIY punk music culture resides, working capitalist jobs, consuming mainstream media, and generally participating in various forms of everyday life ensnared in dominant and dominating mainstream institutions and structures.

Equality

The anarchist commitment to equality permeates the DIY punk music scene. Equality is integral to the principle of DIY itself. The presumption underlying "do it yourself" is that anyone is capable of "doing it"—of initiating, organizing, and assuming responsibility for taking direct action. Participants are exhorted to take direct action to start a band or zine, learn to play an instrument, write a song, address and solve a problem, organize a house concert or festival, or create a recording label. Volunteers at various DIY punk music events are expected to figure out what needs to be done, and to take the initiative to get it done. These various exhortations and expectations suggest a deep faith in the capacity of ordinary people to take direct action and accomplish their goals.

The DIY punk music scene lacks any overarching hierarchy of decision-making or control. Each DIY house, recording label, fanzine, community, and affinity group is independent. Authority and power are horizontal and dispersed. Each DIY participant and group is more or less autonomous and self-determining within constraints imposed by resource limitations that different individuals and groups face in variable ways.

The commitment to equality is sustained materially in several ways. For example, a strong commitment to affordability pervades the scene, and this helps eliminate class obstacles to participation. This commitment to affordability extends to the sale of records, tee shirts, beverages, food, and other artifacts in addition to the low cost of donation requested to attend a concert. The commitment to equality is also sustained materially via the technology of recording. As noted above, almost all DIY punk music recording is now done by individuals and bands that have assembled some recording equipment, or by micro-labels operating on a shoestring budget where simple survival marks you as a successful label. The widespread availability of inexpensive musical technology supports a relatively egalitarian access to DIY punk music production and distribution.

Nevertheless, class challenges and contradictions can be seen in the political economy of the houses, bars, and other performing venues. In order for these performing venues to stay open and continue participating in the production and circulation of DIY punk music, they have to be funded in some way. While no admission is charged for attending (in part to thwart IRS attempts to levy taxes on the venues), a minimal voluntary donation is requested and expected. This money typically goes to the touring bands, and generally does not fund the performing venue itself. House members typically must work day jobs to pay their rent and other house expenses; and given that many house members also do their own touring, the jobs they hold tend toward the temporary and part-time variety, without benefits. In the case of bars, coffee shops, and restaurants, sufficient income is needed to stay open, and this income is often generated from the sale of corporate products such as nationally branded beer and other beverages, in addition to locally crafted brews. In most cases, these aspects of the DIY punk music scene add up to a marginally sustainable lifestyle for the participants. As O'Hara notes, "almost no Punk bands are able to live off of their earnings"; it is "near impossible" to sustain a successful DIY business, and record stores and music clubs are constantly on the edge.[37] One result is that most view their deep participation in the DIY punk music scene as necessarily temporary, likely to change when interests such as raising a family become more pressing. This marks an enduring challenge and raises grounds for skepticism regarding the durability and sustainability of the DIY punk music scene as currently constituted. On the other hand, given the large number of venues that remain open, it also serves as a testament to the commitment of those creating and maintaining the DIY spaces. It also ensures that sustaining the DIY punk music scene remains a collective, communal, egalitarian effort. Volunteerism sustains the scene, even in bars, coffee shops, and restaurants where participants are sometimes asked to repair electrical and plumbing systems, design promotional materials, collect donations at the door, and other tasks.

The commitment to equality also manifests itself in blunt denunciations of inequalities based on gender, race, sexual orientation, and class. For example, the Brown Town house in Athens, Ohio, proclaims that "racists/sexists/homophobes/jerks need not apply" to play there. The Leathershop of Lima, Ohio, puts it even more bluntly: "racist/sexist/homophobe/haters can fuck off."[38] Some of these houses and collectives require bands to submit lyric sheets prior to booking them in order to weed out the racists, sexists, homophobes, jerks, and haters.

These commitments to equality are not fully realized. As noted above, despite the explicit commitment to anti-sexism, the DIY punk music scene is dominated by boys and men, with relatively few girls and women involved in the production and distribution of music. Most of the DIY houses and other performing spaces are occupied by young men, with relatively few women in residence. Similarly, the contemporary DIY punk music scene remains dominated by white participants. With few exceptions, African Americans appear infrequently at performances and in web video and photographic renditions of the scene. There are relatively more Hispanics involved than African Americans, especially in the Chicago area, but the trend overall is the same. One noteworthy attempt to integrate more African Americans is Brooklyn, New York's annual Afro-Punk Festival. Although it increases the presence of African Americans in the punk scene, its DIY credentials are suspect, given its reliance on corporate sponsorship.[39]

Freedom

In chapter 2, I noted that anarchist Murray Bookchin disparaged "lifestyle anarchism," the term he used to refer to some contemporary anarchists who pursue prefigurative social change strategies of living their ideals in the present. Bookchin accused these "lifestyle anarchists" of focusing too heavily on an individualistic approach to freedom divorced from collective concerns and commitments, in essence abandoning the historical anarchist commitment to solidarity. Bookchin's critics responded that his criticisms were oversimplified and exaggerated. The contemporary DIY punk music scene helps us to understand why this is so.

First, although pursuing a prefigurative strategy may entail determined willingness by individuals to live for themselves as free of domination as they can, it also reverberates socially. We saw this in Allan Antliff's interpretation of Henri-Edmond Cross's lithograph "The Wanderer," which captured important elements of anarchists' understanding of freedom. On the one hand, at least some DIY punk music participants, like the characters in Cross's lithograph, engage in a great refusal: they refuse to spend their lives working in senseless and mind-numbing occupations so that they can participate fully as consumers in a capitalist political economy. Like Emma Goldman, DIY punkers refuse to stop dancing.

In this refusal lies a valuable lesson for a world addicted to seemingly endless and oftentimes mindless work where play is reserved for relatively short intervals between work, sleep, and trips to the shopping mall. DIY punk music participants sketch out an alternative world of greater freedom that entails creative, fulfilling, satisfying work, where work and play overlap. They model choices generally left off the table in a capitalist political economy, and these new choices expand the range of possible thought and action. In short, they increase freedom as autonomy for all who care to heed the message. While seeking greater individual freedom, they serve a valuable social function of modeling for others an alternative, more autonomous world.

Second, Bookchin's criticisms of "lifestyle anarchists" overlook an important social dimension of freedom within anarchist circles. Consider that the phrase "do it yourself" is actually misleading. None of the DIY punk musicians, zine writers, promoters, house residents, and fans does it alone. Each does it in a highly social context defined by an extensive web of social relationships. DIY punkers do their work and play as part of a dispersed, decentralized network of autonomous but interlinked communities. They depend on each other to sustain this network of communities. This means that, as suggested by Evan Landon Wendel, DIY could actually be more appropriately labeled as DIT, or Do It Together. As Wendel notes, "DIY modes of music making required broader social networks (labels, fanzines, radio, fans) and a cooperative togetherness to be effective or sustainable."[40] For the most part, Wendel focused narrowly on the music production and distribution industry, but his suggestive argument can be generalized to encompass the DIY punk music scene as a whole. This DIY scene presents a more nuanced, sociable understanding of freedom than Bookchin's criticisms of "lifestyle anarchism" suggest. DIY punk music participants gain individual freedom by refusing to turn their lives over to mindless work and endless consumption. But in dropping out, they drop into an intensely social, communal network where work and play is reimagined in terms of voluntary participation in groups and collectivities oriented toward the creation of art and an alternative, more satisfying and humane culture.

The individual freedom understood in terms of rejecting mainstream ways of life is inseparable in the DIY punk music scene from the solidaristic freedom suggested by DIT. As Emilie Hardman writes:

> DIY stresses an active engagement in creating the cultural material and the venues for the expression of culture and ideology in opposition to consuming the ready made products of the culture industry. From the anarcho-punk perspective, this is seen to be not just important on the individual level of resistance, but is central to the production of community as well, because all who participate in the community are involved constantly in the process of asserting what that community is and what it stands for through the creation and dissemination of their own cultural material.[41]

As this discussion suggests, the freedom embodied in DIY punk music does not exclude the possibility of deep social and political commitment. In fact, the freedom found in DIY punk music would be much more difficult, perhaps impossible, without that deep social and political commitment. Participating individuals secure and maintain their freedom by helping create the cultural conditions of an autonomous life. The social connections and the interconnected communities that constitute the DIY punk music scene would be impossible without the commitment of countless volunteers who contribute to the scene and make it possible. DIY freedom is understood as rooted in social networks of solidarity, mutual responsibility, and aid.

Prefiguring Democracy

DIY punk music prefigures a rhizomatic social organization of dispersed, decentralized, networked individuals and communities. Individual musicians, fans, and groups take direct action to create the social bases for cultural production and consumption, in the process circumventing the concentrated power of the music industry. Power is dispersed and horizontal, residing in multiple rhizomatic nodes, but collected as needed to create and maintain the capacity for autonomous cultural production and consumption. DIY punkers' commitment to equality is expressed in its faith in everyone's capacity to "just do it," in its dispersal and leveling of power, in its elimination of most class barriers to participation, and sometimes explicitly in its lyrics. Individual freedom and autonomy are set within a highly sociable network of DIY musicians and fans whose ability to "do it together" is made possible by solidarity and mutual commitment. Taken together, these central components of anarchist theory and practice prefigure an alternative, more democratic future.

Robert Strachan argues that DIY cultural production provides "a symbolic resistance to the totalizing discourses of capitalism" and a "critique from the margins" that counters concentrated media power.[42] While these claims are undoubtedly true, it must be emphasized that DIY punk music goes well beyond symbolic resistance and critique. DIY punk music participants create alternative spaces in the cracks and on the margins of mainstream society, and they live parts of their lives within those spaces. They develop and sustain the infrastructure of an alternative culture and community, one that deliberately avoids reproducing at least some of the domination and oppression constitutive of liberal democracy.

George McKay says of punk music that "small wonders have grand repercussions."[43] In a time when liberal democratic domination may appear impervious to challenge, small wonders offer glimmers of hope and the material bases for pursuing those grand repercussions. DIY punk music offers glimpses of a more democratic world marked by greater freedom, autonomy, equality, decentralized and horizontal power relations, solidarity, and participatory community. It opens new democratic possibilities, and keeps them open.

The core principle of DIY—of taking direct action to solve a problem, address an issue, create art, build an alternative world—is also central to participatory democratic understandings of citizenship. Participatory democrats ask common people to do the work of self-governance, and to stop turning that responsibility over to elected officials and powerful elites. This requires retaking power where it has been relinquished, and it requires turning attention from working, shopping, and leisure to devote parts of our lives to civic concerns. In a participatory democracy, common citizens would "do it themselves" and they would "do it together."

The alternative world created by DIY punk participants is tiny in contrast to the larger world defined by the dominant structures of the state and capitalism, its cultural production and circulation swamped by the cultural messages and symbols routinely circulating through the mass media. DIY punk music remains financially unsustainable for most participants. Yet a scene in which hundreds of thousands, perhaps millions, participate on an everyday basis can hardly be discounted as irrelevant or utopian. For these participants, the DIY punk music scene offers daily sustenance, not just a utopian vision. It is a transformative experience for many participants, even if the impact is limited to relatively small spaces, and even if many or most participants eventually move on and into mainstream life. The DIY punk music scene offers a hopeful vision of an alternative world where participants routinely engage in a great refusal to play by the rules imposed by dominant outside forces, and where their refusal opens new possibilities for anarchistic sociability, community, and democracy. Do more art, DIY participants tell us, and less mindless work and consumption. For them, this is more than a hollow exhortation or utopian vision. It is a way of life.

4

Poetry Slam

Stripped to its bare essentials, slam poetry is poetry that is performed in a competitive environment before a live audience. Judges, usually five, are chosen randomly from the audience with no attempt to first ascertain their ability to judge good from bad poetry. They rate the poets on a scale of zero to ten, with high and low scores tossed and the remaining three averaged. Generally, poems must be three minutes or less with points deducted for going over the time limit, though this can vary significantly across local slams. Poets are judged on the poem itself and its performance. A slam master emcees the show, and also does much of the organizing and preparation.

The roots of slam are traced back several millennia to ancient oral traditions found in the Homeric epic, African griots, Zuni priests, Japanese Kojiki poets, and Greek bards who related communal stories via song, poetry, and narrative. According to one source, slam as a competition goes back at least to the first century B.C. when the Greek lyric poet Pindar was bested five times by a lesser-known poet, Korinna, and Pindar went on to ridicule her as a sow. Others note that the ancient Olympics included poetry competitions, with winners receiving laurel crowns. Other competitive roots include Japanese haiku contests and African word battles called "signifying."

Twentieth-century roots and influences include Dadaism, emphasizing childlike spontaneity, intellectual nihilism, and moving art outside the museum and concert hall. The 1950s and 1960s beat poets, who sought to transform poetry from a sedate, genteel diversion enjoyed by elites into something more immediate and accessible, are also cited as influences on slam poetry. Beat poets read in coffeehouses, bars, lofts, and cellars. They broke other rules of academic poetry by inviting audience participation, adding music, and injecting elements that sometimes made the readings appear like drunken chaos. Beat poets also began hosting open mic readings. Many of the same dynamics occurred in the Black Arts movement of the mid-1960s and early 1970s. Affiliated with Black Nationalism, this movement primarily sought to address black audiences, celebrate black culture, and increase black cultural autonomy. Black Arts poets anticipated slam in treating the poem as a performance script rather than simply a written text. They drew from various African and African American cultural elements including street vocabulary and cadence, West African vocabulary, percussion and other musical elements, call-and-response, African spirituality, and the speech cadences of black preachers. Their use of live performance, nontraditional performance venues, an attitude of political resistance, democratic ideals, and a conscious stance of marginality from dominant and official verse cultures would eventually be found in slam poetry as well. Performance art and hip-hop culture of the 1970s and 1980s also laid the foundations for slam. The genesis of slam can also be found in a reaction against the mid-twentieth-century literary world's "New Criticism," with its focus on structure and content of literary texts in isolation from both audience response and social context. Finally, slam poets would react against the perceived poverty of the traditional poetry scene of the 1970s and 80s; and against the elitism of traditional poetry and literary worlds.[1]

By the early 1980s, these various influences were congealing into new forms of performance poetry. In 1980, Stone Wind poet Al Simmons began hosting poetry bouts. He formed the World Poetry Association (WPA) modeled after pro wrestling and boxing. These poetic boxing matches introduced entertainment and show into the world of poetry.

Marc Smith, a construction worker and poet in Chicago, is widely cited as the person who created the poetry slam in its modern form.[2] In the late 1970s and early 1980s, various Chicago venues hosted poetry readings either routinely or occasionally. One early venue was the Get Me High Lounge, on Chicago's north side in a blue-collar neighborhood. Smith secured Monday nights for poets, and this became the Monday Night Poetry Readings and open mic, starting in 1984. In 1986, he started a poetry cabaret on Sundays at the Green Mill Cocktail Lounge, known mostly as a jazz club, on Chicago's north side. The first slam was held there on July 20, 1986, although no official competition occurred. Instead, Smith came up with the competition idea out of creative desperation: he ran out of material to finish an ensemble show. He turned it over to the audience to judge via boos and applause. Smith was also creatively responding to some of the perceived problems associated with poetry readings, especially poets who read too long in open mics, and the lack of surprise and variety in many readings.

The new format quickly took off, and the idea began spreading to other cities. The first National Poetry Slam occurred in 1991 in San Francisco. Since then, the National Poetry Slam has been held annually in a different city each year, often with upwards of one hundred cities competing. Slam continued its rise to attention and prominence in 1994 with its inclusion in that year's Lollapalooza tour through more than thirty cities. At each stop, a poetry slam was hosted in a "Revival Tent." To help promote the event, local slams were also held in host cities in advance of the arrival of the tour. This tour led to the proliferation of local slams in places like Austin, Dallas, and Pittsburgh. Slammers formed Poetry Slam, Inc. (PSI) in 1997. PSI began hosting three major annual events: National Poetry Slam (NPS), Individual World Poetry Slam (iWPS), and Women of the World Poetry Slam (WOWps). It also began hosting a Cross Training Poetry Camp with three days of workshops, discussions, open mics, feature performances, and slam competitions.

A host of regional slams deepened and broadened the poetry slam landscape. Examples include Southern Fried Poetry Slam, Rust Belt Slam, Western Regional Slam at Big Sur, Midwest Poetry Slam League, Berkeley's The New Word Series, Battle of the Bay (Bay Area), Taos Poetry Circus, and the Canadian Spoken Word Olympics. One of the defining features of slam poetry in recent years has been its reach into youth communities. Various groups formed to introduce slam to younger populations.[3] Youth began participating in their own national and regional slam competitions through such organizations as the College Unions Poetry Slam Invitational (CUPSI) and the Brave New Voices National Youth Poetry Slam Festival.

Slam has also gone international, with competitions now occurring routinely in many other countries. At various levels of organization and among many different populations, slam poetry is now an established feature of culture production and consumption. Marc Smith's claim that slam poetry is "the largest and most influential literary arts movement of our age" may be exaggerated, but there is no denying that its rapid growth marks it as an important component of contemporary cultural production and consumption.[4]

This chapter will emphasize the political significance of the poetry slam form itself, the way it is organized and practiced. Wholly apart from the content of the poems themselves (which often enough do carry overt political significance), slam poetry is organized and performed along lines resembling central anarchist principles that prefigure a more democratic world.

Social Organization

With the partial exception of PSI and the national competitions it sponsors, slam poetry resembles the rhizomatic model familiar to anarchists: it is both decentralized and highly networked. Local and regional slams are autonomous; and local and regional organizers generally favor informal, largely volunteer-driven forms of social organization rather than a formal institutionalized structure. Overall, slam poetry at local levels is a form of horizontal, grassroots cultural production and circulation, networked at regional and national levels through a combination of informal and formal practices and institutions.

The basic organizational unit of slam poetry is the local slam. Some local slams are organized on an ad hoc basis by slam poets and enthusiasts, while others acquire a level of continuity through repetition that generates a local community of slammers who expect the show to go on. Each of these local slams is autonomous, free to create and follow its own rules and rituals. Consequently, many slam variations occur. These include, for example, cover slams where the poets perform work of famous poets, erotica slams featuring sexual themes, haiku slams of seventeen-syllable poems, hip-hop slams in which performers mimic the cadences of rap musicians, prop slams where performers are invited and sometimes required to use props, speak-out slams where political advocacy is required, heckler slams where audience members are encouraged to heckle, bad poem slams where the worst wins, music slams where poems are performed to musical accompaniment, improv slams featuring improvised poems, group poem slams in which all performance is in groups, specific theme slams, and many more. Anything goes at the local level, where variations are limited only by the slam masters' and other participants' imaginations. Across all these variations, the central defining elements of slam remain: it is performed in a competitive environment before a live audience.[5]

PSI is a nonprofit organization charged with "overseeing the international coalition of poetry slams."[6] It was formed to head off others' attempts to seize control of the brand and the increasing attempt to profit from slams; to oversee competition and ensure a level competitive field; to create and enforce rules; and to attempt to ensure that the open, democratic spirit of slam remains intact. The immediate precipitating factor was the attempt by a board game manufacturer to create a trademarked board game called Poetry Slam. In response, slammers decided to trademark the name themselves. But they had to form an actual organization to do that. In effect, slammers formed a nonprofit organization to thwart for-profit commercial forces. PSI is a membership-based organization in which members can participate in policy-making decisions and cast votes. PSI's bylaws were adopted after public deliberation among participants at the time, and can be amended as needed by current members. Since voting generally occurs at meetings held either prior to, or at, national slam competitions, practically speaking, participation in these decisions is limited to local members, members of teams who are competing at that particular slam competition, and members who can travel to attend the preliminary meetings.

Slam masters at all levels play a leadership role in organizing and facilitating slam events. They are roughly equivalent to DIY punk music concert promoters in the informal but essential role they play in making slams happen. And like punk music concert promoters, their work introduces an element of informal—and perhaps unavoidable—hierarchy. The slam master's authority derives more from the informal requirements of organizing and hosting a slam than from a formal institutional structure.

A PSI SlamMasters organizing committee, representing registered venues around the country, organizes each year's national competitions, determines host sites, handles specific proposals and projects, manages rules and committee work, and elects members of the executive council. The seven-member executive council oversees the routine management of PSI. This executive council meets at least twice each year to determine host sites, conduct elections to the council, propose and approve new projects, and organize and conduct work through subcommittees. The seven members of this elective body serve two-year terms.[7] PSI thus represents a form of hierarchical organization, albeit one that is dependent on members' active participation in decision-making. Its authority encompasses all matters related to participation in NPS and other PSI programs. In all other matters, local and regional slams remain autonomous.

While local slams can, and often do, depart from scripts and rules, NPS is highly structured as a four-day tournament, with preliminary, semifinal, and final competition nights. As in all other slams, however, five judges are selected from the audience. The NPS adheres to rigid rules. The three-minute time limit is strictly enforced, with a half-point deducted for every ten seconds over the three minutes. No props or costumes are allowed, though debate often occurs over what constitutes a costume, and who pushes the boundaries too far. For example, is a naked chest a costume? Additionally, while many local slams allow cover poems, at NPS all poems must be original. Most of these rules were instituted to ensure a level playing field. For example, someone who brought along several musicians to a slam performance would have a better chance of impressing members of the audience. The three-minute rule was instituted initially as well to fend off "stage hogs" and increase the number of participants. All of these rules are subject to challenge through the governing structure of PSI. Only certified slam teams can compete at NPS. To become certified, you must provide evidence of ties to a local community, and each local slam must conduct an open competition to form a team.[8]

PSI and the various national and regional slams provide a means of networking for those local slam teams and individuals that want to participate. The slam community is also networked via an infrastructure of local slams geared in part toward touring slammers. Touring allows for "cross-pollination" across different slam scenes and venues, and makes the notion of a "national community" of slammers at least somewhat more concrete.[9] Many informal connections are developed and sustained through touring and through networking at national and regional slams. These can be translated into support during touring in forms such as shared accommodations.

Slam poetry is also networked through a variety of electronic and print resources. The NPS listserv "puts hundreds of slammers from across the country in easy contact with each other" and "has had an incalculable impact on touring and the exchange of helpful information regarding how to promote and manage a slam."[10] PSI's website features a map of active local slam venues, an online store, membership information, and a forum for posting requests for places to stay while touring.

Most slammers are of necessity relatively independent from dominant cultural institutions and commercial forces. Given the relative lack of interest in slammers' poetry by established publishers (due in part to the difficulty of translating onto paper the performance aspect of slam poetry), most slammers who want to publish their poetry must do so independently. This often occurs in the form of chapbooks, or short booklets of poetry printed on regular 8½-by-11-inch paper, folded and stapled in the middle. These are the literary equivalent of DIY punk musicians' independently recorded and produced CDs. They are inexpensively produced, often by the poets themselves, and marketed informally through web contacts, touring, and PSI's online store. Printed reading series and zines also occasionally make an appearance.

These elements add up to a mix of horizontal, decentralized, autonomous social organization at local levels with partly hierarchical, centralized social organization at the national level. PSI and NPS integrate a representative system of governing and a formal, hierarchical governing structure designed to allow democratic input from below while facilitating the business of organizing and hosting national slams and other programs. They thus represent at least a partial departure from anarchist principles of social organization. Many local slams operate independently, with no affiliation to PSI or NPS.

Political Action

Poetry slam prefigures a world in which common people embrace the anarchist principle of direct action. The DIY ethos pervades the poetry slam scene. Slammers presume that "anyone can do this," and interested individuals should "just do it." Anyone can organize a slam. Anyone can write and perform a poem before an audience. Comparable to the DIY punk music creed "here's one chord, here's another, now start a band," this DIY ethos propels common people into participation as creators of culture. Participants are in effect urged to take cultural direct action to write and perform poetry, to organize and host a slam, and to assist in the organizing of local, regional, and national slam events.

Audience members are also encouraged and expected to participate actively as critical judges of poets' performances. This is true most obviously of those audience members who are selected to serve as judges for the slam. But it also holds true for all audience members. There is "no such thing as passive listening at a slam."[11] Audience members react to the poet's performance with boos, cheers, jeers, finger-snapping (indicating the poem is boring), hissing (generally at sexist poems), stomping, groaning, and guessing-the-rhyme (shouting out the word in predictable poetry). Some venues offer a more structured role for audience members including discussion after a reading, or having an entire audience involved in scoring. Slammers hone the same poem during its shelf life, and deliver it in repeated slams. Audiences come to expect certain poems, and recite or shout certain lines along with the poet. Rather than being frowned upon, as it would be at a more formal poetry reading, this signifies positively that the poet is connecting with the audience (unless it is done sarcastically, as sometimes happens). In short, the passive silence typically expected of audience members in traditional poetry scenes is suspended in favor of a healthy (and sometimes noisy) questioning of poetic authority more consistent with anarchists' antihierarchical stance.

Like the DIY punk music scene, slam poetry relies on widespread direct participation by those who are involved in it: slam poets, slam masters, organizers, audience members, and volunteers. With little money to motivate participation in the typical slam, other incentives must drive participation. Although some slam poets are able to earn a modest living through their performance poetry, primarily through touring, most slam poets do it for the love of the art. Prize money, even at larger regional and national slams, sometimes covers costs of attendance plus a little extra for winners. For most who attend, costs have to be borne by individuals and teams themselves, either by reaching into their own pockets or fundraising at home. Local slams have even less money to distribute as prize money.

Fortunately, few if any financial resources are needed to organize, host, and participate in a slam. Organizers must identify a venue, set up a sound system with at least one microphone, and get the word out. Since many slams are hosted at bars, restaurants, and cafés whose proprietors are keen on drawing patrons in to purchase food and drink, generally no cost is required for the venue. Minimal costs may sometimes be required for promotion, but these can be entirely avoided by taking advantage of online and print resources that publicize cultural events at no charge. In short, the poetry slam scene, especially at local levels, is driven primarily by the efforts of volunteers who bring energy and effort but few financial resources to the task.

The general absence of financial resources and motivations in the slam scene largely eliminates class barriers to participation in local slams. A small fee may be required to participate in a slam competition; this money is used for prize money and to offset the minimal costs of hosting a slam. On the other hand, participation in regional and national slams requires funds for travel and, sometimes, lodging and food. These costs are often at least partly offset by the sponsoring team's slam community and by the host city's fundraising efforts dedicated to partially covering attendants' costs. Organizing a national slam competition requires many hours of work to prepare the host city for NPS.[12] Volunteers are needed to make contacts, arrange funding, work with the media and other promotional outlets, secure and prepare venues for the competition, and staff the actual slam and associated events. Volunteers are needed during the slam itself as emcees, ticket-takers, lighting and sound technicians, doorkeepers, scorekeepers, timers, judges, and retailers of chapbooks, tee shirts, and other related items.

If DIY punk music reduces barriers between audience and performer, slam obliterates them. Slam poets embrace an ethos of accessibility and widespread participation. As already noted, the dominant sensibility in slam is that anybody can write and perform poetry, and everyone is encouraged to do so. Most slams begin with an open mic in which participants sign up on a first-come-first-served basis and perform in that order. Although some slams feature invited poets who are guaranteed a slot later in the evening, most poets must earn their later performance slot by surviving early rounds and advancing to the later rounds. The competitive framework of slam ensures that every poet gets a chance to perform in the opening round and, if good enough, later rounds. Of course, this competitive framework also ensures that some poets—those who garner the favor of audiences and judges—will be more likely to advance to later rounds and thus get more performance time.

Slam venues accentuate the accessibility of slam. These typically are places where common people congregate anyway: bars, restaurants, coffee shops, community centers, and sometimes performance halls. Chicago's Get Me High Lounge hosted its slams directly in front of the bathroom, making it necessary for bar patrons to walk across stage during performances to use the bathroom. Slammers also had to compete there with local Cubs fans watching games on television. During the 1980s in Cleveland, slams were notoriously held at Pearl Road Auto Wrecking, on the back of a flatbed semi truck. Slam poets still sometimes compete not only with each other but also with the television and rowdy patrons watching a ball game on television; and audience members are not expected to stay glued to their seats through a slam performance.

Few live performers will deny that they read their audience and respond to it. But for slammers, this is arguably more important than for other live performers. Their success or failure as a performer is judged more immediately, directly, and explicitly by the scoring judges. And the scoring judges, drawn directly from the audience, often follow the audience's lead in scoring a performance. So assuming they want to advance in the competition, slam poets must heed the signals they get from the audience and respond to them. In sharp contrast to elitist, academic, and high-art poetry (hereafter referred to as Brahmin poetry), slam poetry entails a certain amount of "folly"[13] unavoidable in attempting to succeed in a competition scored by randomly selected judges who often bring little or no poetic expertise to their task. Add to this the sometimes raucous and boisterous audience participation and you can end up with "organized chaos."[14] Both help to demystify poetry and take the edge off its seriousness, making it more approachable for common people, and this increases the likelihood of their direct participation both as slam poets and audience members.

An oft-noted feature of slam poetry is the high degree of participation by minority, marginalized, and multicultural populations. The poetry slam community includes participants drawn from "the communities and populations normally not considered poetic, such as the homeless, gang members, midwives, prisoners, [and] carpenters."[15] Poetry slam audiences "constitute a diversity of age, gender, race, and sexual orientation that is resoundingly absent in the audiences found at opera, hip-hop concerts, repertory theatre, traditional poetry readings, and other performing arts events. Inclusiveness and aggressive community involvement have been the cornerstones of the success of Poetry Slam."[16] Observers note an "astonishing mosaic of diversity" at nationals.[17] Susan Somers-Willett notes an emphasis on "poets of color, working-class poets, women, and other culturally marginalized groups," and the ubiquity of poems that make a proud avowal of marginalized identity.[18] Not surprisingly, given the presence of so many poets representing marginalized groups, the poems themselves often inveigh against social injustices. At NPS, outside of the actual competition, featured poets most often are Asian American, African American, Native American, queer, female, Latino, and other poets representing marginalized identities.

As we saw in chapter 2, anarchists' rejection of the state and capitalism opens the need to rely on the direct action of individuals and groups to engage in collective action. Without state support and absent commercial backing, individuals must "do it themselves." Similarly, slammers must take the initiative to locate or open accessible spaces where, during slam performance, they become TAZs for prefigurative cultural creation. Slam poetry is made possible by the direct action of individuals who join forces to collectively create an alternative social world. They open accessible spaces where different, anarchist-inflected norms and values apply. These include an antihierarchical stance toward authority, widespread access and participation, diversity, and DIY.

Power

As noted earlier, for the most part slam poetry is organized along the horizontal, decentralized model characteristic of anarchist social organization. Power is leveled and decision-making dispersed. With partial exceptions, there is no individual or entity with the authority to impose rules and guidelines. The many local slams are autonomous, organized by local promoters, poets, and enthusiasts. Rules and guidelines are frequently adapted, rather than adopted uncritically. The partial exceptions to this general rule (PSI, NPS, and iWPS), created to thwart efforts by some to co-opt the brand and seize competitive advantages, are governed according to principles of both representative and direct democracy. We have also already seen that organizing a national slam competition requires many hours of work, almost entirely by volunteers, to prepare the host city and run the event. This grassroots approach to preparing and hosting a slam helps ensure the sharing and dispersion of control. It also helps broaden ownership of the event and slam poetry more generally.

Some power concentrates in the hands of slam masters at local and national levels. The national SlamMasters Council, comprised of rotating members, meets prior to NPS to organize and prepare for the event. At local levels, slam masters who do the work of organizing a slam inevitably wield influence and control in determining time and place, the type of slam, whether or not to feature one or more poets, and variations on local rules. At least some power also concentrates in outsize personalities, and in slam poets who have risen to the top of the competitive heap. Overall, though, the rule holds: power is widely dispersed throughout the slam community.

Slam poetry arose partly in reaction against the perceived elitism and dominance of Brahmin poetry, and it continues to play a role of challenging elitism in poetry. It challenges the "cultural privilege and institutional power" that is awarded in mainstream society to Brahmin poetry in particular and so-called high art in general.[19] It encourages participants to shed their reverence for Brahmin poetry and high art, and to see themselves as fully capable of creating, appreciating, and judging poetry and other forms of art.

Little, if any, opposition to the state per se can be found in slam poetry. Many slam organizers and venues take selective advantage of state support, especially in the form of funding. For example, slam poets' work in schools is sometimes supported by tax dollars, and organizers of national competitions sometimes avail themselves of funding from local municipalities. Sometimes, too, slammers accept invitations to perform at state-sponsored events.[20] Slam poetry is, however, replete with criticisms of specific policies and actions of the state, almost entirely from a "liberal" perspective. Slam poets also take frequent aim at capitalism, as well as class, gender, and racial domination.

Slam poets open TAZs where anarchist rules and assumptions apply: all are capable of creative expression, hierarchies of power are generally leveled, elitist attitudes about art are rejected, common people are assumed to be capable of direct, meaningful participation, and privileges of birth do not count. By putting audience members "in the seat of critical power,"[21] slam builds capacity for critical consciousness and judgment.

Poetry slam also builds capacity through its affective power. All poets marshal the affective power of words and language. In reading their work, Brahmin poets generally rely primarily or entirely on speech and voice. They convey emotion through the words themselves, through vocal inflection, and sometimes through hand gestures. They employ "words charged with their utmost meaning."[22] Poetry entails special attention to each word, to how words are put together into sentences, to how thoughts and emotions are shaped in and by language. Poets understand the power of language, and model its role in a democratic society of gathering and using power for democratic deliberation.

Slam poets draw upon a wider array of performance tools than do Brahmin poets, and so are often able to generate more affective power in their performance. These tools include, especially, bodily movement that sometimes approximates dance, and a wider range of vocalizations than the typical Brahmin poet employs. In some (primarily local) slams, poets are also allowed to add various props and costumes to their arsenal of tools for building and harnessing affective power. These range from music to puppets to an infinite variety of simple artifacts that add audio and visual texture to the performance. According to Cristin O'Keefe Aptowicz:

> To truly understand the power and attraction of the poetry slam, you can't simply read some words on a page. You have to attend a poetry slam yourself, see the faces of the poets, experience the raw and thrilling performances firsthand in a room thick with noise and people. The electricity and the emotion of these events can barely be captured by film, let alone trapped mutely in a book.[23]

The affective power created and harnessed by slam poets increases the likelihood of achieving an intense engagement, an engrossing experience shared by all participants. As John Dewey argued, this sharing of experience contributes to the possibility of community, the basis for practical problem-solving and democratic life in general.[24] Additionally, these shared moments are at least sometimes examples of utopian performatives that transport participants out of their mundane, everyday lives and offer glimpses of exalted states of consciousness and being. They expand the capacity of participants to envision different, potentially better worlds.

Equality

Slam's commitment to equality is evident from the previous discussion: in its insistence that anyone can write and perform poetry; that common people are capable of appreciating and judging poetry; that barriers to participation should be eliminated; and that control of the slam scene should be leveled and decentralized, dispersed among participating individuals and local slams. Slam poetry's commitment to equality can also be understood in terms of its open rebellion against Brahmin poetry. Brahmin poets and critics for the most part have simply ignored or casually dismissed slam poetry. Tellingly, in the midst of a renaissance of poetry as represented by both slam and rap, Brahmin voices were proclaiming the demise of poetry. Joseph Epstein, in a 1988 article entitled "Who Killed Poetry?," argued that poetry's decline was the result of the increasing migration of poets into academic writing programs.[25] Three years later in an *Atlantic* article entitled "Can Poetry Matter?," poet and critic Dana Gioia affirmed Epstein's argument, while ruing the loss of a nonacademic audience that "cut across lines of race, class, age, and occupation" and was "poetry's bridge to the general culture." Individual poets, he wrote, "are almost invisible."[26] Similarly, John Barr, while president of the Poetry Foundation, observed in 2006 that "poetry is missing and unmissed," and that "a general, interested public is poetry's foremost need."[27] These Brahmin poets and critics were either unaware of slam poetry or, more likely, dismissed it as unworthy of serious consideration as poetry.

Sometimes, Brahmin poets and their defenders have openly expressed their disdain for slam. Harold Bloom's screed against slam is illustrative:

> Of course, now it's all gone to hell. I can't bear these accounts I read in the *Times* and elsewhere of these poetry slams, in which various young men and women in various late-spots are declaiming rant and nonsense at each other. The whole thing is judged by an applause meter which is actually not there, but might as well be. This isn't even silly; it is the death of art.[28]

For the most part, slammers respond in kind: they either ignore their Brahmin critics or lob the insults back at them. Brahmin critics and poets, especially those found in academia, are charged with elitism, snobbery, and disconnection from the real world. Slammers' response reveals a deep anti-authoritarianism, and a desire to flatten hierarchies, both of which contribute to the egalitarian ethos that pervades slam poetry.

From the outset, a central goal of slam poets has been an attempt to reconnect poetry to a vital audience, and part of this mission has involved encouraging art from the masses and taking it straight to the masses. As Marc Kelly Smith and Joe Kraynak argue, slam poets are "not scholarly snobs, not preachers or saints more perfect than the masses they stood before. Slammers were, and are, just part of the crowd."[29] This embrace of common people, their everyday experiences, and their capacity for art helps explain the venues often chosen for slams: bars, nightclubs, and community centers where common people congregate. Slammers have been on a mission to rekindle popular poetry among a large and diverse audience, something that Brahmin poets have largely failed to do in several generations at least (and as admitted by Brahmin poets and critics themselves). They have sought to shatter the notion that art occurs in a rarefied atmosphere in which participation requires credentials and the stamp of approval from elite critics. They have emphasized instead that average people can create, perform, and appreciate poetry. This breaks from the Brahmin approach in which poets with credentials are featured, and where a sharp distinction is made between poet and audience. Brahmin poetry emphasizes the degree to which the credentialed poet has the necessary skills and artistic sensibility to write and judge poetry, while audience members are generally relegated to the role of passive listeners or readers.

One of the features of slam poetry that offends many of its critics is its deliberate attempt to entertain, because it requires a certain level of accessibility to audiences. Slammers ask, "Why couldn't poetry entertain as well as enlighten? Why couldn't poetry be accessible as well as intelligent?"[30] Slam poets remind us too that Shakespeare wrote to entertain common people, and his plays were widely accessible in his time.

Does the competitive element of slam undermine this commitment to equality? After all, any competitive system produces winners and losers, where winners gradually acquire status and power over others. As a general answer, it should be acknowledged that a tension exists between the competitive aspect of slam and its commitment to equality, given that some slam poets inevitably garner more attention, acquire more prestige, and claim more stage time accordingly. Some specific evidence can also be cited of competition undermining the egalitarian ethos of slam. For example, to gain a competitive advantage, in 1997 slam master Bob Holman offended many by securing corporate sponsorship for his NPS team from Mouth Almighty Records/Mercury. Similarly, the NYC-Urbana team, based in the Bowery Poetry Club, was sponsored by the manufacturer of the board game Scrabble. Many saw these as opening the floodgates of corporate sponsorship (a deplorable development in its own right to many slammers) that would tilt the competitive field toward the best-funded teams. That same offending Mouth Almighty team of 1997 was handpicked by Holman to better ensure competitive success. Prior to that, all national teams were composed of poets who had earned their way onto the team via an open competition at a local venue. Naturally, Holman's handpicking a team offended many as contradicting the open, populist spirit of slams. The following year, in response, NPS banned handpicking.

Slammers' defenders respond that the competition is not driven by money or by corporate sponsorship, but by a commitment to the art form. The competition, they insist, is "tongue-in-cheek . . . a method of enticing people to gather on a Monday night and watch poetry instead of 'Ally McBeal.' "[31] Competition is "window dressing . . . a theatrical device intended to stoke the competitive fires of the performing poets, encourage audience participation and pump some fuel into an entertaining evening of poetry, friendship, and camaraderie." It is "a way to get the audience involved." It "fires up the audience and encourages them to interact with the poets and emcees. And it provides a structure for the poetry slam that holds the whole crazy show together, energizing all those involved, including the audience."[32] Poets who care too much about winning are referred to as "score creeps"[33] whose pandering is "disgusting."[34] Defenders of slam competitions also note that, if the competition were meant to reliably separate good from bad poetry according to Brahmin standards, judges would not be selected randomly from the audience; they would be chosen based on their experience and expected ability to recognize quality when they see and hear it. The competitive dimension of slam helps maintain its nonhierarchical, grassroots element by forcing slam poets to heed their public; to listen to the "voices of the people" who judge their work; and by heading off Brahmin impositions of taste and elitism.

Despite this overt commitment to equality, informal inequalities can nevertheless develop. Aptowicz identifies an "unspoken hierarchy" in the New York City slam community that results in unequal opportunity in competing to make the national team, and this likely applies as well to at least some other slam communities that field national teams. This "unspoken hierarchy" consists of big name slammers at the top, "repeat offenders" who are big enough to be guaranteed slots on the team, those who have been on at least one team, but are still developing their craft, and the rest who have never made it onto a team. The result, she argues, is a "tacit caste system."[35] To help avoid this problem, some cities limit the number of times an individual can participate on a national team.

In removing most class barriers to participation, drawing deeply from marginalized communities, and frequently emphasizing opposition to class domination, slam poetry models a kind of economic equality. The dispersed, decentralized, autonomous nature of local slams and overall dispersal of authority and control, combined with the partly hierarchical structure of PSI and NPS, present a somewhat more mixed picture of political equality that partly diverges from anarchists' commitment to equality.

Freedom

The autonomy emphasized by anarchists requires a capacity for critical awareness, reflection, and judgment. Participation in the slam experience encourages the development and exercise of this capacity. Subjecting people to cultural forms in which they play passive, uncritical roles teaches them to be passive and uncritical. It instills character traits that are not conducive to the critical thinking and engaged activism needed for autonomy. Exposing people to slam poetry offers an alternative experience in which passivity is institutionally and structurally rejected in favor of active, critical participation. This contributes to habits of critical thinking and engaged citizenship.

What is the basis for audience members' judgment and critique? Partly in response to the perception of rigid codes and standards of quality imposed in Brahmin poetry circles, codes and standards that inevitably exclude common people, slammers have intentionally attempted to subvert Brahmin codes and standards. This does not mean that there are no codes and standards. It just means that those codes and standards, which are derived in part from the audience and what its members want and expect, emphasize different things, especially connection and resonance between poet and audience. For slam poetry, a good poem communicates deeply with audience members. It engages them as whole persons, both cognitively and affectively, in a fully engrossing experience. This requires both a good poem and a good performance—or at least a poem and performance perceived as good by the audience. A slam poem is good if it touches the lives of ordinary people in meaningful ways; if it captures recognizable experiences and shared meanings, and uses these to broaden experience and shared understandings while establishing connections between poet and audience member.[36]

All this is sometimes also true of Brahmin poetry. However, Brahmin poetry in general emphasizes the text and structure of a poem, divorced from social circumstances, more so than slam poetry. For many Brahmin poets, the questions change from "what does it mean to be human now?" and "how can we cope with our current reality and solve current problems?" to "what is a well-crafted poem?"[37] The point is not that slam poets and audiences do not admire a "well-crafted poem"; the point is that that goal is complemented and sometimes superseded by other considerations, especially meaningful connections to common people and their everyday lives.

If the slam poet must win the sympathy of audience members in order to succeed competitively, does this encourage pandering, and the expression of cheap, sentimental, and distorted ideas and sentiments? In other words, does slam imitate the distortions and manipulations of public opinion in liberal democracies? Does slam give audience members basically what they want rather than what an autonomous citizen needs to engage in critical debate? Do slammers educate and challenge members of their audience? In short, are slam poets demagogues or modern-day Socrates? A definitive answer to any of these questions is impossible. Much depends on the venue, the poet, and the makeup of the audience. Undoubtedly, some slammers pander to the audience by using clichés and cheap sentimentality in order to succeed competitively. Undoubtedly, some slams emulate the cheap, commercialized forms of entertainment that dominate much popular media in the twenty-first century. But slam is also replete with poets whose performance challenges the audience in myriad ways to examine and rethink the basic assumptions, beliefs, and practices that characterize their everyday lives and the world beyond them. Slam offers no magic pill that can fully overcome the cumulative and collective weight of a political economy and culture oriented toward misinformation, misperception, and mass propaganda. At a minimum, however, slam cuts against the grain of these dominant forces by demanding that poet and audience alike constantly read each other, exercise judgment, and think critically.

According to singer-songwriter Tori Amos, "When you write, you can be anybody or anything. Nobody controls what your relationship is in a song or who you are. And nobody owns it."[38] This expression of autonomy in creative expression applies as well to slam poetry. Yet there is an important difference, in that the freedom of self-expression and creation is inseparable from community. Slam poets, and those who write about slam poetry, emphasize its "communal nature."[39] This is most pronounced and apparent in group poems, which are created and performed collaboratively by two or more poets who weave multiple voices and sounds imitating a particular social environment. In a group poem, "four poets become one voice."[40] A good group poem exceeds the sum of its parts as individual poets' separate voices amplify each other, and the separate poets feed off each other's creativity and energy. In a sense, all slam poems are group poems since they *never* come to life in isolation. Slam poems attain their fullness in performance, which presumes an audience whose members are expected and urged to participate actively as judges and sounding boards. The affective dimension of slam poetry augments and reinforces its communal nature as poet and audience are at least sometimes drawn together in a "deep connection."[41]

Slam's deep roots in community could be viewed as an impediment to human freedom. The dominant liberal ideology that poses freedom in terms of the absence of restrictions on human choice and action—so-called negative freedom—appears in a popular conception of artists as solitary figures standing outside society and perhaps even independent of its influences. There are at least two problems with this portrayal of an artist, and the conception of freedom it models. First, while this picture of the solitary artist no doubt accurately portrays some artists and their lives, in important ways it is a romanticized caricature. No artist lives completely apart from human society and influence. Every human is at least partly a creation of human society through the myriad social influences that mold human personality and character. Second, underlying this portrayal of artists is the presumption that good art *can*, and perhaps *should*, be created in separation from social influence. It portrays a person divorced precisely from the human intercourse that generates art that can speak meaningfully to diverse audiences.

Whatever the merits of this version of art and its creation, slam poetry presents a sharp contrast. Although most slam poets actually write their poems alone, they cannot afford to do so in isolation from their audiences. They must write with their audience in mind, if they want to be competitive. They have to write poetry that they think will connect in performance with their audience. This means that slam poets must write for others, not in spite of, or while ignoring, others. In the liberal sense of negative freedom, this of course limits their choices and thus their freedom. However, it also makes necessary a more sociable conception of art than the one noted above. It also models a more sociable conception of freedom, one that is more consistent with anarchist formulations, in which the individual's freedom relies on community involvement and support, and where sociability is viewed not as an impediment to human autonomy but as a requirement for it. Slam poets experience their freedom *because of* social connections and the community ties in which they are embedded, not despite them.

Prefiguring Democracy

In its commitments to anarchist principles of freedom and equality, accessibility and participation by common and diverse people, creative expression, critical consciousness, and decentralized, horizontal power, slam prefigures a more democratic future. Slam poetry gives participants a direct experience of democracy that is deeper and more tangible than the thin version most take for granted in a liberal democracy. On the other hand, slam is not immune from undemocratic influences and pressures. The generally progressive and liberal leanings of slam poets and audiences do not ensure the absence of occasional racist, sexist, heterosexist, homophobic, and other undemocratic messages in the content of slam poetry. The slam form itself may sometimes prefigure demagoguery and degraded discourse as some audiences respond enthusiastically to manipulation and cheap sentimentality.

Despite the frequent criticisms of capitalism and an overall anti-commercial bias in slam poetry, some slam poets have attempted to take advantage of market opportunities presented by capitalism. According to Somers-Willett, despite the "anti-commercial, anti-capitalistic strain within the slam community . . . slam poets realize that's really the way they're going to make it, by 'selling out.' "[42] The dilemma is real: how to generate sufficient income from slam poetry without threatening the democratic strains that are deeply embedded in slam poetry. In addition to the selective embrace of market opportunities by individual slam poets, national slam organizing committees typically make strategic use of commercial and media opportunities to fund and promote the NPS. This is an ongoing debate within the slam community, and an easy resolution is unlikely. The dilemma is hardly unique to slam poetry. Reconciling artistic autonomy and integrity with commercial considerations is a challenge that pervades the worlds of artistic and cultural production within a political economy largely defined and structured according to capitalist principles. How can artists support themselves comfortably without falling prey to, or contributing to, the dominating influence of capitalism? Can the democratic elements of slam survive against the pressures of a profoundly undemocratic political economy whose bottom line emphasizes profit rather than genuine freedom and autonomy? These are difficult questions with no easy answers. It should be emphasized that the vast majority of slam poets perform their poetry with no expectation of financial remuneration or commercial success. They do their art off the commercial grid.

Slam poetry gives poets and audience members an immediate visceral and practical experience of free, creative expression. It offers a moment, however fleeting, of heightened joy and beauty in a world where both seem routinely beaten down, especially for marginalized people. As a utopian performative, slam poetry "make[s] palpable an affective vision of how the world might be better."[43] And whatever its flaws and imperfections, slam offers concrete visions of more democratic worlds. Like DIY punk music, slam poetry does not simply project more democratic possibilities in the future. It also opens spaces where participants can live parts of their lives according to those more democratic principles. In other words, like DIY punk music, it is prefigurative in both senses of the term. It models a different, more democratic world, and it offers the means of practicing a deeper form of democracy in the cracks and on the margins of liberal democracy.

5

Graffiti and Street Art

Graffiti and street art have been called the "the greatest art of the late twentieth century,"[1] the "most influential art movement since pop,"[2] an "important grassroots urban mural,"[3] an "act of liberation,"[4] an effective antidote to gangs,[5] and a grassroots movement that contributes vitally to a "publicly expressive culture."[6] They have also been called "a dangerous and even subversive threat to local authority,"[7] an "eyesore,"[8] a form of terrorism,[9] a crime comparable to rape,[10] "an invitation to criminals,"[11] and "a direct threat to the quality of life."[12] As these testimonies suggest, debate is polarized. Opponents of graffiti and street art see them as symptoms of social breakdown; of inner cities in disarray and decay; of raging, delinquent, criminal youth without proper character, values, and commitments; and of a narcissistic culture in which everyone is entitled to whatever they want. Proponents defend them as popular expressions of the people; as an attempt by disadvantaged and marginalized people to reclaim public space and make their presence known; as straightforward forms of art that beautify urban environments; and as a means of fighting oppression. Property owners and public authorities are likely to fall into the former category of opponents. Those who question the basic terms of the liberal democratic social contract, which awards considerable power to property owners and the state that defends them, are more likely to fall into the latter category of proponents.

Although graffiti has become a catchall term for all urban guerrilla art, it refers to a specific form: signature writing. Graffiti is sometimes adorned with other images or messages, but the central component is the signature. The most basic form of signature writing is the tag, a simplified, calligraphic signature usually done quickly with a spray can on public and private surfaces. Throwups, so-named because they are quickly "thrown up" on a surface, are slightly more complex signatures adding color and diversity of size, and typically comprised of simple letter outlines that are filled in with color. Most throwups are written in bubble style, the rounded letters resembling doughy pillow forms, and occasionally include a background "glow" to make the name pop out more effectively. Pieces—short for masterpieces—usually integrate two or more colors and more stylistic development. They tend to be large, multicolored, and stylistically complex, so they require greater skill than tags or throwups. Some resemble murals that tell a story or convey a message of some kind through the use of letters, words, and characters. However, the artist's signature remains central. Different styles include the relatively legible block letter, bubble, and 3D; the increasingly distorted, intertwined, and illegible wildstyle; and basically any combination of these or whatever the artist chooses to integrate. More stylistically complex pieces integrate arrows to simulate motion and dynamism, as well as stars and quotation marks. For most complex graffiti, the artists carefully plan ahead, sketch the design, and scope out the site prior to actually painting it. A fourth category of graffiti sometimes included in discussions is the production. A production is typically created by crews—groups of graffiti artists working together—as a series of pieces or a collaborative piece, melded together via a background.[13]

Graffiti artists, known as writers, earn respect through repetition and frequency—by covering many surfaces with their signatures—and by painting their signature in risky locations that increase the respect for the artist as the risk increases. Since more complex pieces generally require more risk, they also garner more respect. As graffiti style becomes more visually complex, the public is increasingly locked out, since most outsiders cannot read the signatures. Generally, graffiti writers are less interested in communicating with the public than with each other. An unwritten rule in the graffiti community exhorts writers not to disrespect others' work by writing over it, unless starting a battle. Tools of the trade include spray paint in cans; spray caps that offer fat, skinny, outline, and fill-in options; and wide and fat-tipped markers. The style and aesthetics of graffiti evolved in part due to its illegality, which required artists to learn to paint rapidly, and to use styles that can be done quickly. The same can be said for the tools of the trade: spray cans are easily concealed and carried, and can cover a large area relatively quickly but with sufficient control.

Street art—sometimes called post-graffiti, neo-graffiti, or urban painting—is more diverse and less tied to writing signatures. Street artists use more formal art techniques such as stencils, printmaking, and painting, and create more figurative works that range from realistic to cartoonish. Like graffiti artists, street artists use spray cans and markers, but also oil and acrylic paints, oil-based chalk, charcoal, stickers, textiles, posters, stencils, yarn, mosaic tiles, and electronic media. The choice of material is sometimes determined by practical considerations. One advantage of stencils, for example, is that they are faster, and therefore safer: the artist is less likely to get caught.[14] Another advantage of the stencil is its reproducibility: the artist can paint the same image on many different surfaces. Street artists are also more likely than graffiti artists to work with an overt political agenda. Their work is often done in accessible locations, with the intention of communicating with a public, unlike graffiti artists whose work is typically aimed at other graffiti artists.

The term "graffiti" is derived from the Italian *graffiare*, meaning "to scratch." The roots of graffiti and street art are traced to early attempts to communicate symbolically on cave walls. The Chauvet caves in France containing murals dated at approximately thirty-two thousand years old are sometimes cited as the oldest examples of graffiti. Early stencils were created when artists put paint made from charcoal, natural pigments, and earth into their mouths or hollow bones and blew it around their hands or other objects. Stencils were often used to decorate pyramids. Excavations of Pompeii unearthed more than eleven thousand wall inscriptions that included election slogans and obscenities as well as drawings. Unsanctioned inscriptions appeared on churches in the Middle Ages. The Spanish conquistadors inscribed their names on Inscription Rock near Gallup, New Mexico; and French names were scrawled on the walls of Angkor Wat in Cambodia.

Twentieth-century roots and influences cited by observers include public toilet art, children's sidewalk chalk art, and hobo graffiti on freight trains documented as early as 1914. Nazis used graffiti and street art to stir up hatred against the Jews, and dissident Germans resisted Hitler using graffiti and street art. The muralist David Alfaro Siqueiros used stencils to protest Argentinean dictatorship in 1933–34. Stencils were used in resistance movements across the world in countries such as Nicaragua, South Africa, the Basque region of Spain, and Chile during the 1970s and 1980s.[15]

Some observers root contemporary graffiti and street art in deteriorating urban environments caused by urban renewal schemes and highway projects that "laid waste to once viable communities," and in the "unfulfilled promise of '60s idealism clashing with the disappointing reality of America in the mid-'70s," leading to rebellious and antiauthoritarian art forms such as graffiti and punk rock.[16] Some urban youth reacted against the Vietnam War, and to public spaces dominated by celebrities and corporate advertising, by tagging. Pioneer graffiti writers, many of them teenagers, took some of their inspiration from comic books, typography, and mainstream popular culture rather than art school or other formal art sources. Although graffiti is sometimes conflated with gang culture and gang writing, they are separate, and graffiti and street art are sometimes described as an alternative to gangs, and even as a means of separation from gangs.[17]

The contemporary graffiti and street art movements are sometimes said to have begun with James J. Kilroy's "Kilroy was here" inscription. A World War II shipyard inspector, Kilroy wrote his inscription on ship parts and equipment upon completion of the inspection. Soldiers abroad saw it on those parts and equipment and began adopting it as their own, sometimes embellishing it with a figure of a man peeking over a wall. This iconic image is now engraved on the World War II Memorial in Washington, D.C.

In 1965 in Philadelphia, Darryl Alexander McCray began writing "Cornbread" on the walls of his reform school. After his release, he continued writing it on walls in his North Philadelphia neighborhood and once, notoriously, on the side of an elephant at the zoo. Others soon began imitating him. In 1969, the name TAKI 183 began appearing around New York City. By 1971 it was ubiquitous, prompting a *New York Times* story[18] that naturally spawned imitation by other writers. Soon a subculture of writers had developed in Philadelphia, New York, and other cities. In New York City, especially, this subculture's work was most prominently displayed on subway cars and station walls. Tags grew progressively bigger until throwups and pieces began appearing on the trains. Trains offered a useful surface for writing since more people could see the work as they traveled through the various boroughs, a "rolling art gallery" of sorts.[19]

Women have been involved in graffiti and street art from the beginning, but in fewer numbers than men. One reason for their relative absence is the additional obstacles they face compared to men. These include safety considerations associated with late hours, desolate locations, and the fear of rape that accompanies most women into those circumstances. They also include what is sometimes described as a harsh social atmosphere of a male-dominated field, where women sometimes face rumors about sleeping their way into the scene and onto a crew, or about a boyfriend doing her work for her. Those women who participate do so "in a sometimes misogynistic 'boys club' culture"[20] in which male writers "work to prove they are 'men,' but female writers must work to prove they are not 'women' [by demonstrating] that they have the same 'balls,' stamina and resilience as their male peers."[21] The graffiti and street art scenes remain a primarily "male-orientated activity," a "predominantly male bastion."[22]

That said, women have long contributed to and influenced the development of graffiti and street art. Lady Pink (Sandra Fabara) is regarded as the first woman to make a significant impact, though many women preceded her. Her best-known early work featured illustrations of sexualized young women and girls in various provocative poses. Miss Van (Vanessa Alice Bensimon) is also often cited for her influence on the scene. Her work, even more vividly than that of Lady Pink, portrays illustrations of young women and girls in assertively pouty and sexy poses.

One of the newest entrants into the street art scene, yarn bombing, is dominated by women. Yarn bombers install knitted or crocheted work in public places on bicycle racks, door handles, tree limbs, monuments, telephone poles, barbed wire, car antennas, and more. The first recorded yarn bombing occurred in 2005 when Magda Sayeg and a friend, whose public names would become PolyCotN and Akrylik, knitted a rectangular shape out of blue and pink acrylic yarn, then sewed it to the handle of a door in Houston, Texas. The two subsequently formed Knitta, or Knitta Please, the first yarn graffiti crew. Yarn bombing spread quickly throughout the world, to the Great Wall of China, throughout Europe, Canada, and the United States. Yarn bombing is now an "international guerilla knitting movement"[23] that merges installation art, needlework, and street art. The needlework ranges in complexity from a basic rectangle with simple stitches anyone can do to complex sweaters, shoes, and multi-formed shapes. Yarn bombing is even more ephemeral than painted graffiti and street art. Items sometimes disappear within minutes of their installation, lifted either by admirers who want to take the art home or by irritated authorities and citizens who destroy it. Some yarn bombers, like other graffiti and street artists, prolong the installation by placing their work in inaccessible locations.

Contemporary graffiti and street art forms quickly spread throughout the Western world, sometimes arriving alongside, or with, punk and hip-hop, as occurred in many parts of Europe. Stencil artists were at work in Paris before tags and styles emerged there. Canadian train-hoppers created "monikers," or figures and pictures on freight trains in oil-based chalk, to communicate with each other. In South America, graffiti and street art reflected the "strong opposition towards the rich upper classes from people living in the ghettos."[24] Today, urban residents almost everywhere encounter an astonishing variety of graffiti and street art. Some of it is crude and hurried, some of it complex, beautiful, and whimsical, some of it bluntly political.

Social Organization

Graffiti writers typically organize themselves into crews of several or more writers who share common social roots and aesthetic sensibilities. The crews organize the work, and play a role in fostering camaraderie, support, and solidarity. Although crews typically operate with no formal leadership or hierarchy, different individuals (dubbed kings or queens) are recognized for exceptional accomplishment, and may play informal leadership roles. Some writers are members of more than one crew. Crew members hang out together hatching ideas, developing sketches, and planning installations. In preparing for a piece, one crew member will get the paint, others check out the site, and some may serve as spotters for the police. All this congeals at the wall, where someone outlines the letters while others handle the fill-in, the final outline, the clouds and bubbles, and the surrounding area and background that ties it all together. Collaboration sometimes occurs between rival and friendly crews, or with guest writers from other areas, cities, and countries.

There are comparable street art communities around the world, but generally not as common or tight as graffiti crews. The exception, yarn bombers, often work in crews partly for social reasons and partly because of the time-intensive nature of their art: it takes a lot of knitting and crocheting, often more than one person can handle, to create enough material for a medium or large installation. Socially, yarn bombers draw on a long tradition of yarn circles—sometimes fondly dubbed "stitch 'n bitch" circles—found in many cities, towns, and suburbs. The sociality is part of yarn culture, from young mothers gathering at the playground to elderly women meeting in a kitchen to knit and gossip. These characteristics of yarn bombing, perhaps more than other kinds of graffiti and street art, prefigure anarchists' commitment to eliminating artificial boundaries between art and everyday life.

These various graffiti and street art groups are of necessity highly decentralized given the state's ongoing hostility toward them. Although the artists sometimes convene for festivals or exhibitions, for the most part the crews work independently of each other. No formal hierarchy or coordinating authority exists, but collective effort nevertheless emerges in coordinated efforts to create large-scale projects that would be impossible for a single artist. This is especially true for yarn bombing.

In the early years of graffiti, subway systems provided an essential form of communication among writers and crews. It was a common space for writing and sharing ideas, and a kind of mass-media system and communication network for circulating ideas through the city. A crew could throw up a work on a train, and "send" it off to different locations where it would be viewed by other individuals and groups. As the authorities made subway writing increasingly difficult, its importance as a communications network waned. Some writers began writing on freight trains, creating a more dispersed communications network with far-flung writers in distant cities. In the mid- and late 1980s, new writers' print and video media came into play as modes of circulating ideas and communicating with other writers. These took over some of the functions earlier played by subways and trains. Zines such as *International Graffiti Times* began appearing in the mid-1980s.

Responding in part to the transient, ephemeral nature of graffiti and street art—it may disappear literally within seconds, depending on the efficiency of abatement efforts—and the desire to document the work, the Internet has since the 1990s become a vital component of the graffiti and street art scene. It offers peer education, gathering sites for graffiti culture, a vehicle for networking and communication, and a means of documenting work and history.[25] Given the short life of most graffiti and street art in the street itself, artists began photographing their work immediately after completing it, and then uploading it to the Internet. This effectively prolongs the shelf life indefinitely, giving it an online durability impossible in the street. The Internet has become an alternative public sphere for graffiti and street artists to share their work with others, to communicate among various local, regional, national, and global audiences, and to disseminate the messages to a wider audience. Massive archives for graffiti and street art of all kinds have been developed, in addition to the many thousands of websites established by individual artists and crews to feature their own work. Art Crimes is perhaps the best known; it has become the "definitive worldwide site for highlighting the talent of many writers for a wider audience."[26] Art Crimes was launched in 1994 by a group of high school students, college students, and computer users who had been in cyber-touch via the newsgroup alt.graffiti. They began posting photos to share. *Newsweek* magazine ran a story a month after Art Crimes started, helping propel it into prominence. Most of these websites are labors of love rather than profit. Potential sponsors such as spray-paint companies are understandably leery or hostile. The two most prominent manufacturers of spray paint, Rustoleum and Krylon, feature only anti-graffiti material on their websites. Today, thousands of sites feature images of daily activity, and magazines devoted to graffiti and street art circulate throughout the world.

Not all graffiti and street artists view the role of the Internet in wholly favorable terms. They note that experiencing a work of art online is a far cry from experiencing it directly, in the street, in the urban environment in which it is sited and from whence it derives much of its potency. The Internet distances viewers from the work, mediating and diluting it. Moreover, they argue, it has led to some homogenization of graffiti and street art, and a corresponding loss of regional and local distinctiveness, given the sharing of styles and influences across borders. Anna Wacławek concludes, nevertheless, that photos provide an essential foundation on which the graffiti and street art movements rely. Without photo-based publications and websites, "the movement would quite literally have been lost."[27]

In sum, the social organization of graffiti and street art closely resembles that envisioned by anarchists. While most graffiti and street artists work in decentralized, uncoordinated units and crews, most also link to the efforts of others either directly through collaborative collective action—both spontaneous and planned—or through the Internet. Most of their work is accomplished without commercial or state support; on the contrary, most of it is accomplished in the face of overt hostility by commercial and state forces. The result is a horizontal, dispersed, highly decentralized, nonhierarchical, rhizomatic network with individual artists and crews at the nodes, connected primarily via the Internet and sometimes through coordinated, collective work.

Political Action

While many DIY punk musicians and poetry slammers express their anarchist principles indirectly by simply circumventing or ignoring the state and going off the capitalist grid, graffiti and street artists unavoidably engage in direct action against both the state and capital. At least for the duration of the artwork, graffiti and street artists stake out autonomous urban spaces—TAZs—where they visually proclaim their independence from authorities and claim the right to mark the city. The enthusiastic abatement efforts by public officials and property owners generally ensure that the TAZs created by graffiti and street artists tend to be temporary, indeed, except in inaccessible, infrequently policed locations. Given their status as direct challenges to the rules of property and the state that enforces them, all works of graffiti and street art can be considered implicitly political, whether or not they express overtly political themes. While most graffiti art is devoid of explicit political messaging, much street art carries explicit political intent and content. A few examples will illustrate.

Paul Harfleet began his "The Pansy Project—Fuck Off and Die Faggots" in Manchester, England, in 2005 in response to homophobic verbal and physical assaults he and others had suffered. He and others planted pansies at sites where the assaults had occurred, and included captions detailing the abuse and the victim's name. The project inspired others to follow suit, with pansies eventually appearing in New York, Austria, London, Berlin, and Turkey.[28] In the street art collective Monochrom's "Nazi Petting Zoo," first staged in 2008 in Vienna, Austria, a man dressed in Nazi uniform parades within a picket fence, offering a Nazi salute. Visitors are encouraged to pet him. The intent was to force Austrians to come to terms with their fascist past, while disarming the political and historical potency of Nazi symbols.[29] In 2005, the renowned street artist Banksy stenciled nine works on the security barrier wall surrounding Bethlehem in Israel's West Bank, all of them on the Palestinian side of the wall. Although whimsical and gently humorous, each functioned as a critique of Israeli West Bank policies. In one, children are shown playing with beach toys beneath a tropical paradise. Another shows children holding onto a bundle of balloons, floating upward toward the top of the barrier. Others show children kneeling at the foot of a rope ladder reaching to the top of the barrier; a huge living room setting with armchairs, coffee table, and window overlooking an inviting landscape; and a section of the wall marked out like a sewing pattern, with scissors cutting around the edges to suggest opening the barrier. His "Untitled," done in Israel in 2007, showed a young girl frisking a soldier.[30]

Street artist Dan Witz responded to gentrification in his Brooklyn neighborhood with his "Ugly New Buildings" project of 2008. He installed and painted various types of grates on the sides of buildings, one to two feet off the ground. Behind each grate he portrayed humans trying to see out or get out; behind others lay prone human forms as though dead bodies lay behind the grates. These works of street art portrayed the human spirit as trapped inside soulless buildings, the result of gentrification.[31] Blek le Rat, known as the "godfather" of the street stencil, did a series of stencil artworks portraying homeless individuals, drawing attention to the problems of homelessness. He began his career as a street artist stenciling rats on Paris streets in 1981, then moved on to full-size figures.[32] These few illustrations of overtly political street art, along with the implicit political work of graffiti artists, exemplify the politicization of public space by graffiti and street artists.[33]

Participation in graffiti and street art as an artist is limited to those who are willing to break the law. This naturally limits the number of willing participants. For those who do choose to participate as artists, access is relatively straightforward. Buy or steal your paint and other materials. Avoid the police. Overcome safety and accessibility challenges. Do it yourself or do it together with a crew.

While simple tags require little technical skill, more complicated graffiti writing styles require practice and skill. Knitting at high levels requires considerable ability, but most people can successfully knit for yarn bombing using very basic techniques, roughly comparable to punk music's two- and three-chord songs. Moreover, the tools and materials needed are very inexpensive and accessible. Similarly, while some stencil artists create and deploy technically and visually complex cutouts, newcomers can opt for something much more simple and straightforward, requiring very little skill to fashion. Once the stencil is cut out, the only skill required is the ability to hold or tape the stencil against a surface, and spray-paint over it. Some street artists, on the other hand, who work freehand without stencils, bring highly developed artistic skills to the task that are unattainable by beginners.

Participation in graffiti and street art as a viewer is open to almost all pedestrians, drivers, subway riders, and other residents. It is imposed on urban residents who prefer their urban visual space unadorned with graffiti and street art. Either way, the price of admission to this urban art gallery is free. Anyone can view it.

Graffiti and street artists embrace a simple DIY principle: "If you want to put art in the street, do it."[34] Some graffiti and street artists also emulate another DIY practice found in the DIY punk scene of encouraging active participation. The Graffiti Research Lab, started by Evan Roth and James Powderly, makes templates for inexpensive and easy devices to assist graffiti and street artists. They also fashion open-source tools such as an LED throwie, a type of LED screen that writers and artists can use to portray their work on city walls. Similarly, M-City invites participation in a virtual creation. Visitors can use its "city constructor" tool to create and employ stencils. In New York City in 2007, Ji Lee founded the "Bubble Project" in which speech bubbles were placed on ads and pedestrians were invited to write comments and thoughts in the bubble. The

DIY principles of openness and encouraging innovation are also evident. For example, the "manifesto" of Masquerade, a yarn bombing crew, states: "Patterns are for inspiration, not for following. . . . There are no mistakes, only techniques not yet invented. . . . Super glue is not cheating! . . . All colors match. . . . Nemoattexet sobrius (Nobody knits sober)."[35] Mandy Moore and Leanne Prain's book on yarn bombing is full of DIY tips and instructions for would-be yarn bombers. For graffiti and street artists, "Images and ideas are there to be co-opted, manipulated, and then transferred freely around the world."[36]

Graffiti and street artists proffer an anarchistic participatory vision, a form of participatory artistic performance. They tell us to take direct action against capitalist and state power without permission. Reclaim public visual space. Do it yourself.

Power

The anarchist character of graffiti and street art as challenges to dominant forms of power is visible and obvious. Both represent direct, explicit attacks on capital and the state and their control over urban public space. Commercial interests flood public urban space with advertisements. These invitations to consume are made possible by corporate financial control over the physical spaces and structures of urban environments, and the private property rights making that control possible. The state ensures the security of those property rights. State authorities additionally fill our vision with instructions, directives, and threats on what to do and when: where and when to turn, stop, yield, and go; how fast or slow we may go; and where and when we may cross the street. This control is backed by its monopoly on force and coercion, enforced at street level by police forces and, increasingly, surveillance technologies.

Commercial and state forces often work together. When not (re) creating and controlling urban space itself, the state regulates, controls, and sanctions how market forces work to create urban environments. Zoning laws, for example, allow or disallow certain kinds and patterns of commercial development. Government authorities often work closely with architects, developers, businesses, and other commercial entities to create, change, and maintain urban spaces. This arrangement depends on the ability of the state to create a legal, political, and economic environment conducive to commercial interests. Given pressures at all levels to maintain a favorable business climate, and despite occasional challenges by common citizens, the arrangement typically works to the advantage of commercial and state interests.

Graffiti and street art challenge this formula. Resistance to the domination of state and capital are inherent in the definition of graffiti and street art. Except under exceptional circumstances, both are illegal, and so challenge the authority of the state and its laws, including and especially its laws regulating and protecting private and public property. Each tag, each stencil, each piece, each lovingly knitted tree warmer is an affront to property, and to liberal democratic notions of ownership, in two ways. First, graffiti and street artists temporarily claim access to others' property in order to make use of it as a canvas. They trespass, impiously denying the quasi-sacred status of private property in liberal democracies. In claiming a wall, a billboard, or a sign as temporarily their own, graffiti and street artists subvert the normal rules of property and ownership. They insist on the right of community members to sign, mark, and adorn public spaces without permission from state or capital.

Second, no one owns and controls graffiti and street art. Once the artist completes the work, it is displayed for all to see; no ownership is—or can be—claimed, and control is relinquished. And as Ethel Seno argues, "In a consumer-based economy, the idea of giving anything away for nothing and making fun of the machinations of seductions that compel us to over-identify with commodities may well be the truly offensive crime committed here."[37] Doing such artistic work is an affront to a materialist culture of acquisition, since it is an act of denial of possession. The vast majority of graffiti and street artists do their work with no expectation of monetary or other material reward. Shannon Holopainen concludes from this that "tagging is a gift, given without return."[38] Critics of graffiti and street art will of course respond that, if this is a gift, it is a gift best left undelivered and unopened.

In liberal democratic thought, government originates in a social contract formed to protect citizens' lives, liberty, and possessions. Its legitimacy depends on its ability to fulfill its end of the contractual arrangement: that is, to protect citizens' life, liberty, and possessions. This requires exerting sufficient control over people's actions. Should government fail to fulfill its obligations, its authority and legitimacy are undermined. This may provoke a crisis of government in which the people withdraw their consent through elections or, in extreme cases, open rebellion.

Graffiti and street art represent vivid, creative, and sustained challenges to state authority and legitimacy, and stark illustrations of the state's failure to fulfill its obligations. Each graffiti or street artist who hits a wall, an underpass, a street sign, or a billboard challenges the authority of the state as an institution of enforcement and coercion. Each installation marks a refusal and a disruption of state authority. Graffiti and street art thus challenge the basic terms of the social contract from which government derives its authority and legitimacy in a liberal democracy.

No wonder, then, that government officials tend to react aggressively and punitively to graffiti and street art, as though their jobs depend on it. With rare exceptions, government officials have declared graffiti and street art illegal. This illegality is central to the definition of graffiti and street art, and key to its political potency. Having deemed it illegal, the state must attack it. Political authorities have made extraordinary efforts, committing massive amounts of resources, to enforcing the laws against graffiti and street art. From the beginning of the graffiti and street art movements in Philadelphia and New York City, authorities have attempted to stifle them. By 1973, New York City mayor John Lindsay was spending $10 million annually on anti-graffiti efforts.[39] The efforts proved unsuccessful since they focused primarily on repainting subway cars, which simply stimulated writing by providing more blank canvases. It also brought together writers who had been sentenced to paint over the trains, thus facilitating their networking and planning for future crews and writing. The second "war on graffiti," by New York City mayor Edward Koch in 1980–83, succeeded partly in reducing graffiti on subway trains, especially after city authorities fenced off their idle trains. New York City spent $150 million during the 1980s to clean the subway system.[40] The Metropolitan Transit Authority (MTA) declared victory in 1989 in its war against subway graffiti. In the process, however, they drove writers to do their work on city walls outside the subway system, creating more enforcement problems.

In the 1990s, Mayor Rudy Giuliani again attempted to crack down on graffiti. Arrests increased over 200 percent after he revived the Anti-Graffiti Task Force in 1995. The city budget under Giuliani allocated over $40 million annually for graffiti abatement. Whole police units were devoted to it. By 2002, a quarter of a million graffiti hits were cleaned each year off subway cars, and 3 million square feet of graffiti were buffed from highways and bridges.[41] Like previous crackdowns, this one simply increased the resolve of writers to bomb the city. Overall, according to two separate estimates, graffiti costs the United States $4 to $5 billion annually in abatement efforts.[42]

Most civic leaders and authority figures embrace the so-called "broken window theory," which holds that acts of vandalism, including graffiti, increase the likelihood of more serious forms of crime such as rape and murder. Vandalism is a slippery slope, in other words, and graffiti as a form of vandalism contributes to the tipping downward of the slope toward mayhem. Mayors and other civic authorities accordingly characterize graffiti writers as criminals who undermine civic order and contribute to urban fiscal and social crisis. The city of San Francisco offered this official advice: "Paint over graffiti within 48 hours whenever possible and advise your neighbors to do the same. Vandals will move along to a different neighborhood if their vandalism is abated quickly."[43] San Francisco Public Works Code article 23 1303(a)(1994) stipulates:

> Graffiti is detrimental to the health, safety, and welfare of the community in that it promotes a perception in the community that the laws protecting public and private property can be disregarded with impunity. This perception fosters a sense of disrespect of the law that results in an increase in crime; degrades the community and leads to urban blight; is detrimental to property values, business opportunities, and the enjoyment of life; is inconsistent with the City's property maintenance goals and aesthetic standards; and results in additional graffiti . . . [and] visual pollution and is hereby deemed a public nuisance. Graffiti must be abated as quickly as possible to avoid detrimental impacts.[44]

Similarly, the New York state legislature declared:

> The legislature hereby finds and declares that graffiti vandalism poses a serious problem for urban centers and especially the city of New York. . . . The legislature also finds that when unchecked, graffiti presents the image of a deteriorating community, a community that no longer cares about itself, a community that shows evidence of urban blight. Not only is graffiti an assault upon individual sensibilities, it is another reason for people to leave the city prompting a further downward spiral of economic and social conditions with severe consequences for the city of New York.[45]

The message is clear: graffiti and street art are criminal acts of vandalism that, if left unchecked, will quickly ruin the city.

Enforcement strategies and penalties quickly escalated to match the rhetoric. Laws in various cities prosecute graffiti and street art as vandalism, criminal mischief, malicious mischief, intentional destruction of property, or criminal trespass. Los Angeles eventually made it a felony if the damage exceeded four hundred dollars. In 2000, the state of California passed Proposition 21, which tied graffiti to gangs and made it a potential felony-level crime. Many cities organized vandalism enforcement teams such as L.A.'s GHOST (Graffiti Habitual Offenders Suppression Team), which placed undercover police on city buses, while property owners in many cities are coerced into paying for abatement. Penalties meted out to graffiti and street artists have included community service, revoking drivers' licenses, jail time, fines, giving property owners a civil claim against the writer, and sometimes worse.[46] Inevitably, more harsh surveillance and enforcement policies have led to more tags and throwups rather than the more stylistic, visually appealing pieces, since the penalties for getting caught are greater.

Despite the crackdowns, one is still left with the suspicion that buffing graffiti and street art does more to "catalyze . . . innovation and ingenuity" than to discourage them.[47] Abatement efforts have successfully squelched some graffiti and street art in some locations for some time. However, any stroll through a typical urban environment provides ample evidence that graffiti and street artists successfully and extensively circumvent the authorities. The widespread presence of graffiti and street art provides striking—and sometimes beautiful—visual evidence of a systematic failure of the state to enforce its own laws.

The ongoing efforts by graffiti and street artists to elude the authorities have produced the unintended effect of increasing the size and reach of the state. In attempting to successfully wage its war against graffiti and street art, the state has grown to counteract the threat to its existence, by increasing the funding of its surveillance and police force. The state cannot tolerate this ongoing insult to its authority, so it has grown in size and reach to counteract the threat. In short, graffiti and street art both destabilize the state by undermining its authority and, perversely, goad it into inflating its power and size.

Some graffiti and street artists challenge other forms of domination besides those represented by the state and capital. Yarn bombers again merit special mention. Knitting and crocheting have long been devalued precisely because they are considered domestic work and feminine.[48] They bring to mind fireside contemplation and domestic caring, evoking homely emotions of warmth, comfort, utility, and softness. For street artists who prefer to make a statement without damaging property, yarn bombing is the perfect choice since it is easy to remove and will not damage the surfaces to which it is applied. Yet, in the hands of yarn bombers, knitting and crocheting acquire an edge of subversion and rebuke. Like other forms of street art, yarn bombing counters dominant understandings of authority and ownership. With its references to feminine, female, and feminist, yarn bombing also counters masculinism by bringing "a conventionally female practice into conversation with a traditionally male movement."[49]

Yarn bombers colorfully subvert masculinist icons of public space. The traditional hero-on-a-horse public monument almost always portrays a heroic male figure whose fame derives from slaughter on the battlefield. This portrayal is emasculated by attaching a knitted pink tie around its hero's neck, as has been done on multiple occasions. Protesting Denmark's involvement in the Iraq War, Marianna Jørgensen in 2006 organized a team to crochet a tank cozy. Too big a project to do alone, she called for contributions through word of mouth, knitting clubs, and the Internet throughout Europe and the U.S. She and her collaborators created a pink crocheted blanket comprised of four thousand six-inch squares, and stitched it over an M24 Chaffee tank dating to World War II. Jørgensen named it "Pink M.24 Chaffee," and noted that when covered in pink yarn, a tank "becomes completely unarmed, and it loses its authority."[50] Theresa Honeywell similarly emasculated iconic masculine artifacts by knitting covers for a machine gun and a motorcycle.[51]

Whether one views them favorably or unfavorably, both graffiti and street art increase the capacity of ordinary people to challenge the power of the state and capital. They offer a tool for circumventing and challenging institutionalized powers governing access to public space and free expression. They help democratize urban space by contesting the terms governing access to it, terms that favor powerful commercial and state forces.

Equality

By emphasizing the importance of private property, and establishing a government to protect it, the liberal democratic social contract practically ensures that property owners wield power over those who own little or no property. Liberal democracies offer little remedy for this, resorting instead to fictions of political equality and equal opportunity. Although popular resentment occasionally surfaces, as it did during the Great Recession with the Occupy movement's 99 percent message, in general this formula remains an enduring and rarely challenged fact of life in liberal democracies.

Graffiti and street artists rebel against this status quo. If the walls of the city represent property and authority, graffiti and street artists attack both in a sustained, graphic assertion of equality. They assert their unwillingness to accede to the terms of a social contract that grants power and authority to property owners and the state institutions that protect them. They engage in a struggle for greater equality, pitting a ragtag army of artists against powerful, well-funded commercial and state forces intent on eliminating them. If this is a war, it is a war that graffiti and street artists can scarcely hope to win against such overwhelming odds. Graffiti and street artists remain marginalized, always subject to punitive responses by the authorities, their work vilified and buffed. On the other hand, most urban environments offer ample evidence of resilient graffiti and street artists, suggesting that powerful commercial and state forces can never fully win without resorting to an Orwellian police state.

Generally, mainstream media present the perspective from above; graffiti and street artists present the view from below, from people with little or no access to sanctioned means of communication. Graffiti and street art provide a way to speak back, to deny the terms imposed by dominant forces and to assert different terms.[52]

Most graffiti and street artists work outside the system of commodity production and exchange. They produce art for art's sake, for the sake of their inner muses, and for the sake of community members who share an affinity for it. Graffiti and street artists do their work with the expectation that their art may disappear quickly, buffed out by government workers or property owners. This ephemeral quality of graffiti and street art helps prevent its commodification. The "canvas"—concrete walls, steel beams, billboards, railroad cars—also defies commodification since, with rare exceptions, it cannot be purchased and moved into a gallery or private home. This makes graffiti and street art a truly public art, in which anyone with a spray can or enamel marker can contribute as an artist, and in which the art itself remains accessible to all, not just those who can purchase it.

Within the graffiti and street art communities, there are few significant barriers to entry. Costs of materials such as spray paint, markers, yarn, or stencils are minimal. Becoming a graffiti or street artist is a viable option for anyone who has a spray can and is willing to risk an encounter with the police. Talent and skill are recognized and valued, but beginners are welcome. Racial diversity is an acknowledged fact but, as we have seen, so is inequality of participation by gender. Even more so than punk or poetry slams, authority and power within the graffiti and street art scenes are horizontal and dispersed. There are no centralizations of power and authority within the graffiti and street art communities. Each graffiti and street artist, and each crew, is autonomous and self-determining. Although informal hierarchies of status according to skill and reputation develop, the populist, non-elitist nature of graffiti and street art ensures that beginners can add their voices to the mix. The result is a popular art form striking for its egalitarian character.

Freedom

As argued earlier, the kind of freedom embraced by anarchists requires a capacity for critical consciousness and autonomous choice. In liberal democracies, commercial and state forces often work systematically to undermine this capacity. People's everyday lives are saturated with commercial messages that increasingly define the character of everyday life. Sports arenas sell naming rights, teams adorn their uniforms with product logos, and half times and timeouts are named after corporate sponsors. Cinema and television are awash in corporate advertising and product placement. Even religion increasingly reflects corporate dominance, as seen in the newly resurgent "gospel of wealth" in the U.S., with its endorsement of getting rich and transformation of religious messaging into a product for sale. Everywhere you turn, billboards, flashing neon signs, storefront advertising, and humans dressed in bunny costumes assault the senses with invitations to consume. State authorities enable this corporatization of space by protecting advertisers' property rights and offering tax breaks to cover advertising costs. They also exacerbate it by emulating it: many cities and states sell public resources to the highest bidder in forms such as advertising on public buses and naming rights on sports arenas paid for by taxpayers.

The commercialization and commodification of culture thus represents a form of state-sanctioned propaganda on a massive scale. It is ubiquitous and naturalized and, naturally, most people take it for granted. The images we see repeatedly in an urban landscape become part of our individual and collective psyche. We scarcely see them after a time, but they nevertheless affect us at deep psychological levels. By acceding to the myriad instructions, and by normalizing the images in our field of vision, we are controlled in ways of which we are scarcely aware, if we are aware at all. We are induced to adopt certain routines and behaviors, molded into them by our sensory environment. To the degree this is true, it questions the notion of a free, autonomous chooser.

Public perception of graffiti and street art is heavily controlled by the same commercial and state interests that undermine autonomy in the first place. The public is thus informed by media conglomerates and public officials that graffiti and street art threaten cherished freedoms associated with property rights. Graffiti and street artists are often accused of polluting visual space and contributing to blight. The real blight, according to defenders of graffiti and street art, is the ubiquitous advertising that infiltrates every corner of public space. According to renowned street artist Banksy, "breaking into property and painting it might seem a little inconsiderate, but in reality the thirty square centimeters of your brain are trespassed upon every day by teams of marketing experts." Graffiti and street artists ask "Why . . . can Coke, Wells Fargo, the IRS or the Army inject themselves so easily into our public space, while artists and activists with a variety of critiques must stand on the sidelines or be accused of creating 'visual pollution'?"[53]

As also argued earlier, anarchist freedom requires that individuals have a direct say in determining the circumstances of their everyday lives. Graffiti and street artists add their voices to the public arena, claiming the right to help determine the character of everyday life. They challenge the "aesthetics of authority"[54] and the artificial order imposed by dominant state and commercial interests, as found in the visual landscape. Graffiti and street artists mar, subvert, and transform urban visual markers, in effect sabotaging the prevailing visual order. They bluntly refuse to accept corporate and state authority to create and impose a certain kind of order. In defacing property, graffiti and street artists challenge the authorities and their presumptive hegemony over public space and symbolic communication. They question to whom the streets belong, and to what uses they can and should be put. They are thus engaged in acts of rebellion against a prevailing way of life.

Some graffiti and street artists engage in their rebellion directly by "subvertising": by doctoring or replacing advertisements positioned in public space. Subvertisers mock the ads, transforming them into parodies of themselves and sometimes presenting entirely different messages. Sometimes they commandeer billboard space to place an anti-advertising message. At other times, and more commonly, subvertisers doctor an existing billboard, or other ad space, to alter its message.[55]

While inviting us to rebel against a prevailing order, graffiti and street artists also invite us to choose a different kind of life where "more important freedoms exist than the right and requirement to shop."[56] By challenging corporate and state dominance of symbolic communication in public spaces, graffiti and street artists help make possible the critical consciousness necessary for free, autonomous choice. By subverting the dominant trend of self-expression through consumption, graffiti and street artists open the possibility of genuine free expression, not one to which we are indoctrinated by corporate and state control over symbolic communication. They invite us to create, rather than to shop. They "talk back" to state and corporate authorities, inviting us to do the same and helping ensure, however marginally, that common people can add their voices to the public dialogue that helps determine the character of everyday life.

Operating for the most part outside the system of commodification and exchange, graffiti and street artists claim a level of autonomy not otherwise available to artists and other cultural workers whose livelihood depends on successful commodification and sale. In part because of its resistance to commodification, most graffiti and street art exist in a world very different from the world of gallery and museum art, and challenge some of the suppositions of gallery and museum art. Graffiti and street art are unsanctioned. No permission is requested or wanted. Graffiti and street artists relinquish control over their art once it has been installed. Whatever value these art forms carry, with few exceptions it cannot be measured in commercial or monetary terms. Given the transient, ephemeral nature of such art, and given that, for the most part, it cannot circulate as a commodity in a market, its dollar value tends to be zero. Access to graffiti and street art is unrestricted (except in cases where it has been installed in inaccessible places like abandoned subway tunnels or the underside of railroad trestles). All pedestrians, drivers, and urban dwellers have access to it, whether they want it or not. Finally, graffiti and street art are mediated by the sights and sounds of their physical environment, but not in a way directly controlled by authorities (though the need to elude police does partly determine its character). The mediation is not segregated from the urban experience; graffiti and street art are integral, organic parts of urban environments and derive their meaning in part from that urban environment.

This formula changes for graffiti and street art displayed in museums and exhibitions and that circulate as commercial commodities. Like punk music and poetry slams, some graffiti and street artists have taken advantage of commercial opportunities, and some have displayed and sold their work in gallery exhibitions. Despite official crackdowns and general elite art world indifference or hostility, fans and proponents of graffiti and street art have hosted gallery exhibitions since at least the early 1970s. Also, some gatekeepers within the world of elite art have found graffiti and street art worthy of display in galleries, and have attempted to promote and celebrate them as vibrant new forms of city art by hosting exhibitions. For the most part, these exhibitions have been held at relatively marginal galleries. However, some major galleries have hosted exhibitions. In 2011, for example, the Los Angeles Museum of Contemporary Art hosted a graffiti exhibition, much to the dismay of graffiti opponents.[57]

Having removed graffiti and street art from the streets and turned them into objects for display in galleries, it is inevitable that they would also begin circulating as commodities in a market, at an increasingly steep price. In one recent notorious example, a Hollywood, California, gas station owner dismantled a concrete wall on his property in order to encase graffiti art installed there by Banksy, and sold it at auction for $209,000.[58] Some graffiti and street artists now sell their art to corporations for marketing campaigns. Marketing executives and advertising agencies discovered that individuals in some coveted demographics viewed graffiti and street art as hip, and thus a potential hook with which to bait consumers, especially in fashion and sports marketing. Some graffiti and street artists also develop their own consumer products for sale, and have launched their own design companies for commercial work. By the late 1990s, graffiti and street art had become big business, with many ties to the corporate world, including corporate sponsorship of graffiti and street art festivals.[59]

Elite art patrons and proponents have generally frowned on the inclusion of graffiti and street art in gallery exhibitions. But so have many graffiti and street artists and their defenders. Viewers' experience of art in galleries and museums is circumscribed, framed, and mediated in a context drenched in wealth, power, and privilege. At stake is the definition of graffiti and street art, its social significance, and its power as a communicative medium. If graffiti and street art emerged in opposition to state and commercial power, what does inclusion in sanctioned gallery exhibitions do to its meaning and to its role? Inevitably, these ties to sanctioned galleries, and the commercialization of graffiti and street art, undermine their political potency. The example of Shepard Fairey's "Obey" campaign is instructive. The original campaign, started in 1988 by Fairey as an art student, featured a sinister rendition of the wrestler Andre the Giant, paired with the word "OBEY." He pasted his images around Charleston, South Carolina, and eventually in various other cities. He also sent his posters to collaborators abroad who pasted them up for him. As illegal interventions in various urban contexts, these "Obey" posters served as powerful reminders of the way we are controlled, manipulated, and directed by powerful commercial and state forces. By the late 1990s, however, Fairey had transformed his work into a clothing company and graphic design agency. This undermined the original power and significance of his "Obey" posters, transforming them from potent guerrilla interventions into logos for his merchandising empire. Similarly, in 1995 Kaws (aka Brian Donnelly) began subverting advertisements in bus shelters and phone booths by removing them, taking them home, doctoring them, and returning them to their original places. Calvin Klein models were redone getting groped from behind; children in Guise ads were made to look like aliens. These doctored billboards subverted corporate power and commodification. Eventually, though, recognizing the marketing potential of Kaws's work, corporations began paying him to doctor their ads.

While it is wholly understandable why graffiti or street artists would want to earn a living from their art, the commodification of graffiti and street art changes their meaning and function considerably from resistant and oppositional forces in urban culture to sanitized images in support of state and corporate power and authority. They begin serving the commercial and state forces that most graffiti and street artists challenge. In short, some graffiti and street art are used in support of the commercial and state forces that undermine freedom and autonomy.

Prefiguring Democracy

If graffiti and street artists contest the world offered by the state and capital in liberal democracies, what do they offer as an alternative? Critics argue that graffiti and street artists give us a world in which punks with no commitments other than their own narcissistic pleasure deface the visual environment, vandalize others' hard-earned possessions, create needless challenges for police forces, and strain the public budget to counter the vandalism. Graffiti and street art thus prefigure a world of asociality, ugliness, insecurity, and disorder. Defenders respond that the sociability—if the term even applies—of the current liberal democratic world is in fact profoundly individualistic, lacking in basic solidarity and community; that the visual world currently created and sustained by the liberal democratic state and capitalism is already ugly, marked by seemingly endless and often garish commercial messaging; that graffiti and street art add beauty to urban environments; that whatever security is enjoyed by owners of property does not extend to the billions worldwide who own little or no property; and that the current order, biased as it is in favor of people with exceptional power and wealth, must be destabilized and transformed.

Consistent with core anarchist principles, graffiti and street artists mount a sustained attack on liberal democratic understandings of property and the state that protects it. They assert a right of access to at least some of that property, use it to subvert commercial and state-sanctioned worldviews, and offer their own visions instead. What is that vision? Whether or not they draw their inspiration directly from anarchism, graffiti and street artists prefigure a world in which we defer less to authority, submit less to control, and conform less to others' expectations. They point to a world in which unsanctioned free thought, expression, and individuality are given more play. Graffiti and street artists prefigure a world in which property translates less into power and control; a world in which state authorities exert less control; and a world where the social contract less blatantly favors property owners.

Graffiti and street artists also proffer a vision in which average people become citizens who assert themselves against powerful forces that would control them. Rather than submit, they fight back. They act as engaged creators of the world around them rather than passive travelers through it and victims of it. They reclaim the public sphere from commercial and state authorities. Graffiti and street artists challenge the world in which money buys ownership and the right of public expression, and in which the state enforces the terms of this social contract. They graphically—and sometimes beautifully—portray their own alternative visions. Graffiti and street artists model a world less beholden to powerful state and commercial interests, and more committed to dispersed power, control, and authority.

The world proposed by graffiti and street artists contains more unmediated, uncontrolled beauty, creativity, spontaneity, and diversity; and more visual surprises in an environment that tends to be highly controlled. Graffiti and street art undermine the "Disneyfication" of public space[60] and replace it with a more disordered, uncontrolled, diversely creative vision. As written in vivid colors onto trains, underpasses, city walls, and glass towers, graffiti and street artists offer a more colorful, chaotic world, one less ordered and standardized.

Whether or not this is a more attractive, desirable world is open to debate. Property owners who stand to lose at least some control of their property are likely to oppose it. Critics of the current social contract and the liberal democratic world it represents are more apt to find it an attractive vision. The choice should not be posed as one between corporate domination and urban chaos. Rather, the choice is between a political economy dominated by corporate and state interests, on the one hand, and a more democratic urban space in which common people can partly determine the character of everyday life. Nor should the choice be posed as a stark opposition between private property and a property-less communalism. Following Proudhon, graffiti and street artists might suggest that the rights of property owners end where they become instruments of domination.

This assessment is incomplete so long as it remains focused on graffiti and street artists as renegades and rebels. As we have seen, at least some of these artists have joined forces with commercial and state interests. Graffiti and street artists who want to make a living from their art may have to play by at least some of the rules of capitalist markets. So graffiti and street art also prefigure a world in which capitalism continues to defuse rebellion by co-opting and incorporating some of the rebels. Most graffiti and street artists, however, earn no money from their art, and expect none. Their continued presence and ongoing rebellion ensure that cracks and margins endure where domination is challenged, and where visions of a different, more democratic world are kept vital.

6

Flash Mobs

Early use of the term "flash mob" emphasized lighthearted, even silly, happenings in public spaces in which several or more people, often summoned through social media, gathered to perform seemingly spontaneous actions lasting typically only a few minutes, and then dispersed as quickly as they had gathered. Since then, the term has gradually encompassed a more diverse array of events, making a single definition more problematic. Generic elements, all of which must be qualified, include an actual or apparent spontaneity in which participants assemble suddenly and randomly; a performance of some kind; an element of surprise for onlookers for whom the performance is unexpected; a generally short duration of approximately ten minutes or less; and a point or reason for organizing the flash mob. Some definitions include use of social media to organize the flash mob. The term remains contested.[1]

The spontaneity may be, and often is, illusory since tightly choreographed, scripted versions are generally planned—and often rehearsed—days or weeks in advance. Some events dubbed as flash mobs are heavily and widely publicized beforehand, effectively eliminating any element of surprise, and raising the question of whether or not they should be called flash mobs. The term "performance" must be flexible enough to encompass behavior not usually associated with it, including, for example, sudden and random gatherings of teenagers in public spaces to "act out." Some flash mobs last considerably longer than ten minutes. And the point of a flash mob is sometimes difficult to discern and must be surmised.

At least four different kinds of flash mobs can be identified.[2] Flash mobs for fun and entertainment include, for example, water fights, snowball or pillow fights, dancing, singing, No Pants Subway Ride, marriage proposals, zombie walks, laughing flash mobs, chirping like birds in New

York's Central Park, or acting like whirling dervishes on Market Street in San Francisco. Promotional (including commercial) flash mobs include singing Handel's "Hallelujah" chorus in a mall food court to promote an upcoming performance, dancing in a train station to promote a reality television show, or organizing flash mobs to sell a product or service. Flash mobs for specifically political purposes include spontaneous gatherings to protest government actions or policies, to poke fun at shallow consumerism, or to participate in broader social and political movements. Finally, flash mobs organized specifically for purposes that are criminal or perceived as criminal[3] include so-called "flash robs," where teenagers use social media to gather quickly at a convenience store to shoplift snacks, or spontaneous gatherings that disrupt street festivals or commercial normalcy. These four categories often overlap in practice. In various guises, they have been dubbed "spontaneous public performances,"[4] "performance art,"[5] "guerrilla theatre,"[6] "populist street theater,"[7] and "guerrilla street theatre."[8] All create a dramatic scene through performance and thus can be considered forms of popular art.

The roots of flash mobs include smart mobs, in which groups of people use social-networking technology to engage in collective action; the Situationist International, a group that viewed all space as potential performance space; performance art that began appearing in the 1960s; Allan Kaprow's "happenings," in which he assembled groups of people for spontaneous, often absurd celebratory actions; the sit-ins of the 1960s; Dadaism; and Surrealism, street theatre, yippie and Futurist pranks, raves, agitprop theatre, and protest movements using spectacle.[9] According to one popular narrative, flash mobs were invented in 2003 by Bill Wasik, known then only as "Bill," an editor at *Harper's Magazine*. Wasik himself was the source of that narrative, and others have repeated it.[10] However, flash mobs occurred well before 2003; they just were not called flash mobs. Prior to Wasik's first call for a flash mob, Charlie Todd in 2002 began organizing "missions" such as massive balloon fights and fake concerts. His group eventually became Improv Everywhere, which now organizes flash mobs globally. The first No Pants Subway Ride, organized by Improv Everywhere in January of 2002, featured six "agents" who boarded the same subway car at consecutive stops, dressed for winter but without pants.[11] Joung Yoon-soo describes a 2002 event in Seoul, Korea, in which scores of young people emerged suddenly in front of a shopping mall, handed out balloons and, at the sound of a whistle, dispersed as suddenly as they had appeared.[12] Paul Krassner describes two 1960s-era events organized by radio personalities with characteristics similar to flash mobs.

In one of them, radio personality Bob Fass in February 1967 organized a "fly-in" at Kennedy International Airport at which approximately seven thousand listeners showed up. A second radio personality, Jean Shepherd of WOR-AM, in New York City, issued a call for a "mill-in" to protest his firing. Approximately four hundred listeners showed up at the empty lot in Manhattan to which he had summoned them, listened to Shepherd's critique of consumerism, then dispersed.[13] The term "flash mob" itself was coined in 2003 by Sean Savage, a University of California, Berkeley, graduate student blogger.[14]

Regardless of its practical and etymological origins, Wasik did play an important role in the early development and popularization of the flash mob so-designated. In 2003, he organized his first flash mob in Manhattan by forwarding to acquaintances an email that he had earlier sent to himself from an anonymous source. The email invited people to converge on a retail store in Manhattan to mill about and confuse storekeepers and customers. This first attempt was thwarted by the police, however, who had been alerted by one of the recipients of Wasik's email summoning the flash mob. In subsequent attempts, Wasik adapted his design to reduce the likelihood of police preemption by instructing participants to gather at set locations where detailed instructions were distributed. His second, successful attempt occurred at Macy's in Midtown New York City in the rug department when approximately 130 people showed up seeking a "love rug" for their commune. His subsequent efforts brought two hundred participants to flood the lobby of the Hyatt Hotel for fifteen seconds of synchronized applause, and a crowd gathered at a shoe boutique in Soho pretending to be tourists on a bus tour. Wasik's motivation, he claimed in 2006 and later, was to spoof the hipsterism and scenesterism that he found rampant in New York City by creating an artificial and allegedly hip new trend.

This new happening was covered first by *Wired News*, and soon afterward by *USA Today*, *Newsweek*, *CNN*, and *People* magazine, which declared flash mobs one of the hottest fads of 2003.[15] Despite—or perhaps because of—the generally lighthearted and often dismissive quality of the reporting, flash mobs spread quickly and globally. The *New York Times* followed with an article on an alleged backlash against flash mobs as stupid and irrelevant.[16] In fact, if there was a backlash, it occurred among a minority of observers and participants. The rapid spread of the flash mob suggests instead a widespread interest and enthusiasm for it.

Despite the media's tendency to portray flash mobs as universally silly and innocuous, some early forms already took political and, sometimes, threatening shape. For example, Parisians were invited through a website on October 17, 2003, to participate in flash mobs to "react to the commodification of the world by attacking subway advertising posters." Hundreds of impromptu artists responded to the invitation and successfully "repainted" hundreds of posters.[17] Similarly, in 2004 thousands of Spaniards, summoned by a text message and email, organized in several hours in Barcelona, Madrid, Galicia, and other cities across Spain to protest a government cover-up of recent bombings.[18] In Prague, a flash mob protested laws prohibiting photographing or videotaping supermarkets and malls.[19] In 2003 in Singapore, flash mobbers organized to "break the monotony in a city that is used to a routine of shopping and consuming"; they referred to themselves as "urban misadventurers bent on breaking up the blah in city life."[20] Flash mobs have been used in Belarus since at least the early 2000s as a form of political dissent in the context of political repression. Using social media, activists have "experimented in organizing instantaneous demonstrations that appeared and disappeared in a flash, mobilizing thousands of people to demonstrate for a cause, such as solidarity with political prisoners."[21]

As early as 2003—ironically the same year Bill Wasik allegedly invented them—flash mobs were declared passé and declining. Since then, the media and other observers periodically declare that flash mobs are "a fading fad" or are "starting to lose their edge."[22] Despite these pronouncements of their demise, flash mobs continued to proliferate globally. A YouTube search conducted in March 2013 showed more than 9 million flash mob videos. Less than nine months later, a similar search yielded nearly 15 million. Each of these has been viewed multiple times; some have been viewed many millions of times. These numbers suggest that flash mobs are popular forms of performance art. The practice continues to flourish in all four of the categories identified above.

Social Organization

Anarchists have long argued that humans are capable of spontaneous organization, coordination, and cooperation without the intervention of a state or other centralized institution of power. Flash mobs vividly illustrate this claim. They prefigure new forms of social organization that involve partially random and spontaneous coordination and cooperation. Flash mobs can be described in the paradoxical terms of "organized spontaneity" and "precisely coordinated chaos."[23] The apparent spontaneity and chaos conceal organizational work done prior to the flash mob, and the coordination and cooperation that occurs in performance as the flash mob adapts and reacts to the circumstances of the scene and audience members (and sometimes police) at the scene.

According to a RAND Corporation report on digital networks of cyber-terrorists and cyber-criminals, "What all have in common is that they operate in small, dispersed units that can deploy nimbly—anywhere, anytime. . . . They know how to swarm and disperse, penetrate and disrupt, as well as elude and evade."[24] This description applies well to flash mobs. Most flash mobs organize and reorganize without warning or audience preparation. They appear almost anytime and anywhere. Like rhizomatic shoots, they appear suddenly on the scene, spontaneously and seemingly randomly. The spatial theatre in which flash mob performance occurs is practically limitless. Flash mob performances occur in public spaces including streets, plazas, parks, and public lobbies, and quasi-public or private spaces including shopping malls, auditoriums, marketplaces, corporate lobbies, churches, and anywhere else deemed appropriate for performance. This rhizomatic structure of flash mobs establishes one source of their power: they can spring up anywhere and anytime to surprise and disrupt, and authorities' responses will almost always lag. Flash mobs are reactive and adaptive in response to threats. If the police or other officials attempt to thwart a flash mob, it can disperse quickly and reappear elsewhere, aided by ready access to social media. Some can change shape and behavior, though others that are heavily choreographed are generally less adaptable. Individuals remain dispersed until they are summoned, usually via social media, to converge at a specific time and location; and they can disperse as rapidly as they converge.[25]

The random, spontaneous, even chaotic appearance of flash mobs conceals deeper layers of organization. Behind every flash mob lie one or more organizers. In preparing for a choreographed flash mob, organizers assume a leadership role in which they plan the event, map it out, scope the location, select the date, recruit participants, inform them about the details, recruit photographers and videographers to record the event, and supply the spark that begins the performance. For unscripted, unchoreographed flash mobs, the role of leadership sometimes ends with the summons. From there, the mob takes on a life of its own. However, as Mary Hawkesworth notes, it is a "facile notion" that flash mobs "organize without organizations." As demonstrated by the alterglobalization movements and "Revolution 2.0" in Belarus and the Middle East, organizers and participants relied extensively on "long-established networks" to organize effectively.[26] In short, the apparent randomness conceals hidden organization.

In the actual performance of a flash mob, "everyone is a leader and a follower, organizer and organized."[27] No one manages or directs the performance itself. This increases the threat to authorities who must deal with a swarm of performers rather than a central directing force or hub. In the actual performance of a flash mob, whether choreographed or not, individual performers cue off each other in a variety of ways. In scripted, choreographed flash mobs, performers react to each other's actions and expressions, albeit while still following the script and staying in their allotted roles. In unscripted flash mobs, performers are given more free rein to improvise and to spontaneously create their parts on the fly. Performers also must react spontaneously and creatively to audience cues, which can never be scripted. These cues—ranging from confusion and wonder to joy, irritation, and fear—become an integral part of the performance. The relation of performers to the audience is thus interactive and dialogic, to an extent that partially breaks down the distinction between performer and audience.

Even so-called criminal flash mobs do not behave completely chaotically. Individual performers respond to cues and signals from each other. Unofficial leaders emerge spontaneously, and patterns emerge. The result in each of these cases is, paradoxically, coordinated chaos.

Social media play a central role in the life span of flash mobs. Cell phones in particular enable disconnected individuals to organize quickly and spontaneously to form a collective actor capable of dispersing and reconvening as necessary. The crowd never need fully disconnect. Social media provide the primary means of maintaining a network of performers, choreographing the performance in space and time, and documenting the performance for dissemination on YouTube and via cell phone. Once the summons goes out, it takes on a life of its own, like shoots from a hub with little or no control over the directions they will take or the results. Yet, the immediacy of social media—especially text and cell phone—allows for last second adaptations ranging from change of scene to final notes on performance. Once the performance begins, social media is used to document the performance and to react to threats from police. Even some heavily choreographed flash mobs rely on social media for preparation and execution. Last-minute details can be arranged quickly via social media, and the shifting terrain of the performance theatre may require last-second changes in plans that social media enable. Social media, especially cell phones and YouTube, play a central role in magnifying, broadening, and broadcasting the performance beyond the immediate performance theatre. Social media also ensure the participation of a very diverse audience, basically anyone with access to the Internet.

As rhizomatic forms of social organization, flash mobs closely approximate anarchist forms of social organization. They prefigure decentralized social and political mobilization with little or no bureaucracy and minimal hierarchy. They hint at an activist model based on constant, loosely structured communication and networking that enables spontaneous uprising and collective action. Flash mobs bring to life the notion of "swarming"[28] as a political strategy for organizing in which individuals are dispersed until summoned for an action. Flash mobs flout the designs of city planners and managers who envision an ordered city mapped out and timed out to make it controllable and manageable. They demonstrate that people are capable of organized and coordinated cooperation without direction from above or from a center.

Political Action

Like graffiti and street artists, flash mobbers commandeer both public spaces (streets, parks, plazas) and quasi-public or private spaces (shopping malls, corporate lobbies, marketplaces), reframing them for the purpose of popular art. They open cracks in the everyday that prefigure anarchist norms of direct action and activism.

Like graffiti and street artists, many flash mobbers implicitly and explicitly ask why public visual and audio spaces are so dominated by commercial messages; and they insist on the right of citizens to express themselves, whether sanctioned by authorities or not. Flash mobbers take direct action to disrupt and destabilize the routine choreography of everyday life. They tell us in direct, exuberant, highly affective ways to color outside the lines; to integrate joy and passion into everyday experience; to shake off the mundane expectations of the status quo; and sometimes to take on the work of citizenship and political participation. Flash mob reconfiguration of space commands attention. The extra-ordinary use of ordinary space is impossible to ignore. Flash mobs challenge traditional and sanctioned understandings of public and private space, as well as the sanctioned, permissible uses of those spaces. They defy state and corporate control over spatial configurations and conceptualizations. As forms of direct action, flash mobs do their work in part by offering emotional interruptions of everyday life, giving us hints of the affective possibilities of life in the future. They illustrate the motivating power of art, captured in the experience of joy, anger, whimsy, amusement, surprise, curiosity, fear, and alarm.

Although condemned by the mass media and officialdom, flash mobs dubbed criminal (often performed by African American youth in various cities) hold great political potential as a means of destabilizing unjust structures, institutions, and orders. They create temporary mayhem and disorder, and this is a legitimate form of political action in a world that will not otherwise take notice.[29] All flash mobs are a disruption of the expected and the ordinary. Many are also direct challenges to authoritative choreographies of order. Public officials and authorities tend to view flash mobs as public nuisances or, worse, fearsome criminal outbreaks.

Access to a flash mob is relatively simple and straightforward. Anyone can organize one with minimal resources, and anyone can participate directly in the planning and execution of a flash mob. Many flash mobs reduce or eliminate the distinction between performer and audience. Even in highly choreographed flash mobs, audience members' reactions are typically recorded and become a part of the overall performance uploaded to the web. Sometimes their verbal reactions and comments are included as well as their visual and bodily reactions. Most flash mobs offer easy audience access to the performance, since most occur deliberately in public spaces or in private spaces made temporarily public in performance. Flash mob audiences become "participatory publics"[30] in viewing the performance, in their affective engagement, their direct physical participation in some performances, and in their integration in the video- and audiotaped record uploaded to the web.

By definition, a flash mob is a collective effort requiring concerted action. In a straightforward sense, flash mobs entail coordination and cooperation among participants in forms ranging from synchronized, highly choreographed performances to performances involving improvisation. Because a flash mob is a form of concerted effort does not make it sustainable as a form of collective political action. Most flash mobs are momentary interventions in everyday life, by design and intent. No effort is made to link them to ongoing collective action.

However, some flash mobs are linked to sustained collective political action in two ways. First, most flash mobs help create a collective identity in the practices of planning, organizing, and performing a flash mob. A collective identity also sometimes occurs affectively among performers and audience members. A "temporary community" forms.[31] This can dissipate rapidly and probably does for most flash mobs; however, for some, the effects may linger. For them, the affective dimension of flash mobs—the experience of being moved—may motivate participation in broader forms of collective action.

Second, flash mobs that are organized for specifically political reasons are often tied to sustained political efforts and movements. Several examples will illustrate. Nurses at St. Vincent Hospital in Worcester, Massachusetts, in 2011 organized a flash mob to press their claims of understaffing and patient safety. Another group of nurses organized a "flash mob choir" to protest service cuts. In both cases, the nurses' flash mobs were linked to ongoing struggles by medical support staff to maintain quality care and adequate pay and benefits.[32] As part of a larger movement addressing violence against women, students at the College of Brockport in 2013 organized flash mobs at three different locations on campus to draw attention to the issue.[33] As part of ongoing attempts to draw attention to injustices suffered by indigenous people of North America, native people in Canada organized flash mob–style circle dances that disrupted and blocked traffic.[34] Protesters organized a flash mob on July 11, 2011, to challenge the shooting by police of a homeless man; and protestors organized a series of flash mobs in August 2011 in London sparked by the police killing of a twenty-nine-year-old man in a botched arrest.[35] Finally, and perhaps most notoriously, participants in the Occupy movement and the "Arab Spring" have used social media and the flash mob as a means of mobilizing protest, occupation, and collective action. Each of these flash mobs links directly to broader forms of progressive collective action.

The rhizomatic nature of flash mobs and the constant threat of reappearance hang in the air for authorities to anticipate. The potential for outbreaks of collective action remains present. According to Bill Wasik, "What's really revolutionary about all these gatherings—what remains both dangerous and magnificent about them—is the way they represent a disconnected group getting connected, a mega-underground casting off its invisibility to embody itself, formidably, in physical space."[36] And once embodied, this collective actor can engage in direct action to challenge dominant forms of power.

Power

Prefiguring anarchist resistance to domination, flash mobs challenge the established, conventional order that is structured and controlled by state and corporate power. Flash mobs do this by destabilizing normalized expectations and routines, invading public spaces and changing their routine choreographies. This interrupts and challenges "the everyday order of things," making any public space "in continual danger of becoming unmanageable."[37] Larger flash mobs in particular threaten to spin out of control, to morph into something fearsome, like a virus, as performers swarm the event. This helps explain why authorities fear flash mobs and seek to contain them. Authorities also fear flash mobs and seek to contain and control them because they invoke spies or terrorists: they "combine secret plans, strict coordination, and swift action, and take self-conscious pleasure in the aura surrounding covert operations."[38] Improv Everywhere, one of the most prominent flash mob organizers, makes this resemblance explicit by calling their performers "agents" and their performances "missions" for which they synchronize their watches.

Ruth Carter notes that sometimes flash mobs "make a mess" and sometimes "they will get out of control."[39] Carter was writing about the mess created by pillow fight flash mobs, and she is clear throughout that she views losing control as undesirable. However, flash mobs hint at—and sometimes create—messes that are more serious than a cloud of feathers. Moreover, if the current regime of control is unjust, then a loss of control may be a good thing. Mayhem and confusion may play a valuable role in blowing up a social order that rests upon naturalized and routinized domination. Often the social order is maintained through indoctrination, propaganda, and disciplinary forces seeking to protect privileged political and commercial interests. Everyday reality is highly structured, in ways that enable thought and action but also thwart certain choices and behaviors. Flash mobs crack those structures, sometimes finely and sometimes in ways that open wide chasms. Destabilizing the social order opens the possibility of reconstructing it more justly.

Some flash mobbers sabotage the social order intentionally, registering their dissatisfaction with the status quo and a desire to change it. This sometimes takes the form of civil disobedience, where laws are deliberately broken in ways that range from the lighthearted to the deadly serious. Among the former are some of the flash mobs sponsored by Improv Everywhere. For example, they organized an "Offshore Gambling" flash mob in which performers rented boats, paddled out into a lake, put up a sign saying "Offshore Gambling," then illegally played poker for money. Similarly, in 2012 they organized a "Car Alarm Symphony" in which approximately one hundred "agents" parked near each other, walked behind a nearby wall, then started hitting the panic button on their car remotes, transgressing laws governing noise pollution and disturbing the peace. A less trivial example occurred on August 11, 2011, when flash mob organizers sought to disrupt the San Francisco Bay Area Rapid Transit (BART) system in order to protest police killing of a homeless man. BART officials learned of the attempt and blocked cell phone service at some train stations to thwart it. Hackers responded by breaking into the transit agency's website and forcing it offline.[40] The most prominent and visible flash mob civil disobediences occurred in the large-scale "Arab Spring" demonstrations, where the flash mob was used as a tool for sustained collective political action.

Power as a form of domination is made clearly visible by some of the flash mobs dubbed criminal. Highly publicized examples of these flash mobs began taking shape in 2009, achieving prominence in the spring and summer of 2010 in Philadelphia when thousands of predominately African American youth, summoned by social media, swarmed South Street and surrounding areas.[41] On March 20, 2010, approximately two thousand black teenagers took over South Street and surrounding areas. They were invited to converge via text, Twitter, Facebook, cell phone, and MySpace. "Come to South Street. South Street is poppin'," read one of the messages.[42] Car and store windows were broken, trashcans overturned, and some pedestrians were injured. Most businesses in the area closed by 9:30 p.m., leaving some shoppers outside to face the mob and others trapped inside. Police officers using mace curbed the violence by midnight. Several hundred youth were detained, and several dozen were prosecuted, most of them black teenagers from local public schools. Media accounts labeled them "crime mobs" or "violent flash mobs," and emphasized the chaos, violence, and fear.[43] The flash mobs on South Street continued in 2011, and the trend spread to other cities. Similar flash mobs—again incorporating primarily African American teenagers—were reported in Chicago, New York, Cleveland, London, Las Vegas, St. Paul, Milwaukee, and elsewhere, in addition to more of the same in Philadelphia. The language used to describe these flash mobs continued to emphasize "violent and uncontrollable mobs" that "terrorized metropolitan areas throughout several states," and the reporting continued to emphasize the racial composition consisting mostly of African American teenagers: these were "flash mobs of *black* teens."[44] A related form of flash mob soon took shape: the "flash mob robbery" in which youth use social media to converge on a store—usually a convenience store—enter it together so that the staff are overwhelmed by the sheer numbers, and make off with hundreds and sometimes thousands of dollars in food and other merchandise.[45]

The mainstream media and civil authorities variously characterized these flash mobs as melees,[46] wilding,[47] violent mobs composed of rampaging teens,[48] and "sinister" mobs composed of "young hoodlums" doing "acts of mayhem and violence."[49] New York City's Mayor Michael Bloomberg's invocation of the term "wilding" was especially loaded with meaning, given its association with the 1989 Central Park incident in which a jogger was beaten and raped, allegedly by black youth (later exonerated after six to thirteen years in jail). Critics of Bloomberg accused him of using it again as a scare tactic about black men and fears about them raping white women. Some have raised the possibility that the term "flash mob" has become code for young black teens; and that some residents and store owners who wish to respond with harsh punitive measures have a problem with racial diversity.[50]

Naturally, given these interpretations of events, official responses have emphasized condemnation, repression, and retaliation. Philadelphia's (African American) Mayor Michael Nutter, in a speech from the pulpit of his church, rhetorically addressed the participants in the flash mobs: "You've damaged yourself; you've damaged another person; you've damaged your peers; and quite frankly you've damaged your race."[51] Typifying a general trend, in 2011 the city of Philadelphia instituted tighter curfews and increased police presence on South Street and surrounding areas. Some cities began limiting access to public transit for youth, and various authorities, including the FBI, began increasing surveillance and monitoring of social networking sites both to anticipate flash mobs and to punish participants. Some cities targeted parents by penalizing them for repeat offenses by their children. Some police forces encouraged businesses and residents to register their surveillance cameras with the local police department. The Cleveland city council passed a bill making it illegal to use social media to organize violent, disorderly flash mobs, but the mayor vetoed it when the ACLU promised to challenge its constitutionality. In short, challenges by flash mobbers to concentrated power ironically have led to an increase in state power and reach.[52]

Mainstream media and public officials have attempted to explain these flash mobs in terms of bad parenting, disintegrating values, opportunist thrill-seeking, black racism against white people, bored and irresponsible youth, lack of recreational opportunities, and social media itself.[53] More informed and thoughtful explanations have emphasized their structured socioeconomic and racial roots, including stubborn inequities of class and race, persistent inequality, lack of educational and employment opportunities, and gentrification pressures pushing marginalized people further to the sidelines and deeper into poverty. In this narrative, black teenagers' actions are understood in terms of justifiable and wholly understandable black rage and resistance to domination. Black teenagers converge in "defiant gatherings" in reaction to their very real experience of oppression and shared sense of grievances. This narrative emphasizes "the exertion of political agency en masse by black youths" who seek to reshape urban life. Black youth send a vivid message of anger and frustration, however inchoate and fearsome, to city and corporate leaders that change is needed. As one teenage participant noted in quoting Martin Luther King, "People should remember . . . the riot is the language of the unheard."[54] They are making their presence known and their claims visible. These flash mobs help make institutionalized racism "legible," to borrow a term from political scientist James C. Scott, by exposing power relations and their dynamics.[55] Interpreted this way, these flash mobs can be seen as forms of civil disobedience by marginalized African American youth that threaten authority, destabilize the established order, and rip the veneer of normalcy off structured domination.

Commercial flash mobs have a mixed impact on power relations. On the one hand, many commercial flash mobs surprise and denaturalize everyday life in the same way as other flash mobs, and thus open the possibility of positive change. On the other hand, by definition commercial flash mobs promote commercial interests, and these are usually deeply and uncritically wedded to a capitalist political economy and the domination that entails. One of the best-known flash mobs, the "Do Re Mi" flash mob[56] performed in the train station in Antwerp, Belgium, on November 16, 2010, illustrates this dual role. This flash mob, viewed by over 30 million people on YouTube, surprises and delights. The scene opens with an overhead shot of the normal hubbub of a train station, some people hurrying to their train, others mingling, others paused in contemplation. The public address system is suddenly overridden by the voice of Julie Andrews singing the opening bars to "Do Re Mi" from the musical *The Sound of Music*. Some people stop what they are doing and look around in apparent confusion about the sudden interruption of the usual audiography of the train station. A middle-aged man suddenly begins dancing to the music. A young girl abruptly joins him. Others join, some pouring in from various side entries to the great hall. Soon there are dozens, then over a hundred, representing a wide range of age and dress, dancing in a choreographed performance that obviously includes skilled dancers. When the music ends, the audience applauds and cheers enthusiastically, and the dancers abruptly disperse.

On the one hand, the surprise, delight, and joy of performers and audience members alike are evident. It is a joyous interruption of the everyday, a brief destabilization of normal expectations. On the other hand, the flash mob was organized by a Belgium television station to promote a reality show featuring a search for an actress to play the part of Maria in an upcoming production of *The Sound of Music*. It was used to encourage more consumption of the sort of television that many critics view as the worst available for their sordid forays into cheap sensationalism and sentimentality. In other words, the flash mob promoted precisely the kind of mindless consumption of symbolic communication most likely to undermine critical thinking and overpower freedom and autonomy.

It is understandable why business interests would find flash mobs tempting as promotional tools.[57] They are perceived as hip, especially by younger generations. Generally they are organized and performed by a young demographic to whom most advertisers want to appeal. Like other forms of popular art considered in this book, flash mobs are thus "vulnerable to recuperation by consumer capitalism."[58] Several firms such as Flash Mob America and Big Hit Flash Mobs have formed to produce flash mobs for hire. Companies now routinely pay them to produce and sponsor a flash mob to promote their interests.

Flash mobs build capacity by giving common people a tool to reinvent and rewrite the rules of everyday life. Flash mobs create new meaning, stimulate the imagination, expand the horizons of the possible, and form new affective and practical connections, solidarities, and communities. Like graffiti and street artists, flash mobbers can never fully be repressed. This gives them a measure of grassroots power that authorities can never fully eradicate.

Equality

Most flash mobs model a type of political and economic equality characteristic of anarchism. In performance, the performers work together to create a scene apparently without hierarchical divisions. The flash mob itself appears to the unsuspecting audience member to be a creature of spontaneity, one that participants create by improvising without direction from a leader or director. Frequently a single individual will initiate the flash mob performance by, for example, suddenly breaking into song or dance, but typically that individual is quickly melded into a group performance. Others who appear at first to be bystanders join in the performance without apparent direction or cue. In some flash mobs, the performance begins simultaneously among all individuals. This is true, for example, of freeze flash mobs when everyone freezes simultaneously at the designated, synchronized time.

The apparently leaderless nature of flash mobs is often only that: apparent. Behind many flash mobs is at least one person who initiated, planned and, when appropriate, choreographed it. This can be true of every category of flash mob. Some flash mobs performed for fun and entertainment, such as a dance flash mob or a pillow fight flash mob, require hours and days of preparation in planning, choreographing, and perhaps rehearsing in advance. Organizers of overtly political flash mobs may similarly spend hours and days preparing signs, plotting strategy, and choreographing the event in time and space. Behind many promotional and commercial flash mobs lies an organizer, a staff person, or perhaps even a public relations firm doing the planning and preparation. Even a flash mob with criminal intent or criminal results may be planned and some attempt made to choreograph it in advance. This might be true, for example, of a so-called "flash rob." These organizers determine the rules and expectations for the performance, in effect wielding a form of pre-performance control.

Nevertheless, once the flash mob performance is set in motion, the leaders' control dissipates or disappears. Describing the initial flash mobs he organized in 2003, Bill Wasik said, "The project grew when people took it on as their own and forwarded the email; that was what made the idea work. . . . Other than when we handed out the flyers, the mobs basically did become leaderless."[59] Additionally, the performers necessarily must adapt at least somewhat to the idiosyncrasies of each performing space and audience, and this typically occurs randomly and spontaneously rather than as directed or controlled from above or from a center. In short, there is no maestro at the podium conducting this anarchist symphony as it unfolds.

Almost anyone can organize and perform in a flash mob and, judging by the countless examples on YouTube, a great many do so. This exemplifies the egalitarian spirit of DIY. If the flash mob requires music, some means of playing the music at sufficient volume is required. No special skills are needed, though some of the most popular flash mob videos are staged by groups that include at least some professional performers (usually singers or dancers). All that is required is an idea, a public space (or a private space with access), access to social media or other means of communication, and a group of willing accomplices. There are no significant class barriers to participating in a flash mob since most require little or nothing in financial investment. Aside from the obvious—for example, a flash mob organized by neo-Nazi homophobic misogynists—there are no significant racial, gender, or heterosexist barriers to organizing and participating. Some barriers inevitably arise for disabled populations when the flash mob performance occurs in spaces that are inaccessible for wheelchair users; but a web search reveals many flash mobs organized by and for disabled people, as well as flash mobs that include disabled performers.[60]

Many flash mobs create a distinction between performers and audience members. In these flash mobs, the performers come to the public space prepared to perform, while the surprised audience members remain on the sidelines. Most choreographed flash mobs reinforce this separation between performer and audience, since it would be difficult or impossible for most people to join a performance that has been choreographed and, especially, rehearsed in advance. That said, there are notable exceptions and qualifications to this separation between performer and audience. Many flash mobs are interactive and dialogic. Audience members often make an effort to participate by clapping along, moving to the rhythm of a flash mob using music, or in some other way visibly or audibly participating directly. Some flash mobs include an explicit attempt to draw audience members into direct participation. Flash mobs are often videotaped with the intention of uploading the recording to the Internet. These videotapes frequently make a point of including the crowd, and of focusing on specific audience members to record their reactions. Sometimes this includes an audio component to capture spoken reactions to the flash mob. In these cases of videotaping audience reaction, the audience becomes part of the overall flash mob performance, unwittingly or not. Many audience members participate affectively in the flash mob, as is often evident visibly and audibly. Finally, in some flash mobs the performers constitute much of the audience. This is true of protest flash mobs in which a general call is issued to gather somewhere for the purpose of performing protest, peaceful or otherwise. There is typically little if any advance choreographing. Participants show up and improvise. They perform, and they watch others performing.

Flash mobbers who perform without permission in private or quasi-private spaces such as shopping malls engage in an invasion that requires the disregard of property rules. Unauthorized performances in public spaces such as streets or parks also sometimes entail an invasion, and a willingness to claim public space without permission from the state and sometimes in direct violation of rules enacted and enforced by the state. These performers implicitly, and sometimes explicitly, assert an egalitarian right of access to public and private space.

Freedom

As argued in earlier chapters, critical consciousness is essential for anarchist and participatory democratic understandings of freedom and autonomy. Disruptions of normalized sensibilities, routines, and expectations sometimes make critical consciousness possible. Flash mobs disrupt and sabotage the everyday, sometimes in trivial ways and sometimes in more fundamental ways. They surprise and confuse. Flash mobbers hack into people's everyday realities, into their mundane, normalized, routine, everyday consciousness, opening cracks and fissures in everyday life. Hinting at a subversive quality, Alexander Halavais calls flash mobbers "metaphysical hooligans" and "vandals of the established order" whose actions "are absolutely designed to shake up the way people see things." And "when you shake things up, things will sometimes get broken."[61] Those "things" include people's everyday routines, expectations, and attitudes.

In a regimented, bureaucratized, temporally and physically controlled world, it becomes ever more important to create and encounter circumstances that surprise. Flash mobs force people to "establish a reflexive distance from the usual, routine 'choreography' " of public spaces, while proposing "alternative scenarios of behavior in public space."[62] By disrupting the everyday, flash mobs tear a hole in normalcy, however fleeting and trivial. They create hiccups in people's expectations and routines. As John Dewey put it about art in general, they break through the "crust of conventionalized and routine consciousness," allowing for the possibility of shifting sensibility and critical reflection.[63] This applies to all flash mobs that retain the element of surprise, including those organized strictly for fun, entertainment, and nonsense.

As also argued earlier, freedom and autonomy require that people have viable alternatives for choice and action. Sometimes it is difficult to know what those viable alternatives might be. Is our current everyday life the best we can do? Before we can make different choices and take alternative actions, we must be able to imagine them. Imagination is circumscribed if it is too long confined within parameters structured by cultural norms, expectations, and institutions. Many flash mobs liberate the spirit temporarily, and with it the imagination. Emma Goldman hinted at this when she insisted on the importance of dance, and art more generally, in the life she sought. Flash mobs offer a glimpse of that world she imagined in which beauty and joy are not sidelined in the regimented, controlled, work-obsessed everyday life that many take for granted in a liberal democracy. Robin Kelley argues that "the most radical art is not protest art but works that take us to another place, envision a different way of seeing, perhaps a different way of feeling."[64] Flash mobs, in this sense, are a form of radical art in their ability to transport participants and viewers to another place and to envision different worlds of feeling and experience. They help make us aware of alternatives to the status quo.

The liberating impact of some flash mobs on human emotion and imagination can best be understood by closely examining a particular performance. A videotaped flash mob opera in the Mercado Central de Valencia (Central Market of Valencia) on November 13, 2009, illustrates.[65] The video opens with shoppers mingling in the aisles, making purchases from vendors. Suddenly, music from the opera *La Traviata* begins to play. Moments later, a male opera singer, disguised as a shopkeeper working behind one of the counters, unexpectedly bursts into song. Shoppers pause and look for the singer. A woman, working behind a different counter, takes up the song in response to the first singer. The two singers leave their vending posts, and approach each other in the open aisle, still singing back and forth to each other and in harmony. A growing crowd gathers around the singers. A third male singer at the fringes of the crowd steps forward and begins singing. He is quickly joined by a fourth singer in harmony and response. The first couple steps aside while the new couple sings to each other and together. Throughout, the video camera pans across and through the crowd, sometimes closing in on individuals, all engrossed in the surprise performance and many smiling broadly. Soon the four are singing together. The first song ends, and the crowd—now numbering approximately two hundred—applauds enthusiastically. Seconds later, another song begins, and a fifth singer emerges from behind the crowd. Members of the crowd whirl around to locate him. He begins wandering through the parting crowd, still singing. An elderly couple marks time together; another young pair wraps arms and begins swaying to the music. The original singers join in and, singing separately and together, begin handing out glasses of champagne to random members of the audience. The singers begin choosing random dance partners from the audience, drawing them into a spirited waltz. As the music swells, some members of the crowd move in time to the music, while others stand riveted and deeply engrossed. The video ends with a close-up of a woman with tears streaming down her face and beaming happily. She looks directly at the camera, smiles broadly, nods, and points to her own tears as though affirming how the flash mob has moved her.

Shoppers in attendance that day and the 5 million online viewers since then (as of November, 2013) were treated to a spirited and joyous operatic performance that hacked into the everyday reality of the Mercado. Audience members at the event and subsequent viewers were moved, in several senses of the word. They were moved emotionally, some to tears. Others were moved physically to dance or otherwise keep time with the music. And all were moved out of their expectations of the routine experience of shopping. Judging from their faces and their body language, the flash mob temporarily lifted the spirits of those involved, however fleetingly. It hinted at more affectively rich and artful possibilities for everyday life.

Flash mobs model freedom in community perhaps more vividly and straightforwardly than previous art forms addressed in this book. By definition, a flash mob requires a group of individuals performing together, sometimes in tightly synchronized choreography. In tightly choreographed flash mobs, individual expression is relatively submerged within the synchronized sounds and motions of the group as a whole. Yet the individuals' expressive performances are essential to achieve the full effect of the flash mob. For other flash mobs, such as individualized dance mobs or spontaneous gatherings of teenagers in a Philadelphia street, individual participants improvise, while still contributing to the group performance. In either case, these flash mobs combine individual creative expression with communal formation and action.

At least some flash mobs produce a powerful affective union among the performers. An affective dimension pervades the scene, and actors are united by this affect, this sense of themselves as part of a collective "we." For non-criminal flash mobs, audience members are drawn into this affective union. As Dolan argues, live performances "inspire moments in which audiences feel themselves allied with each other" and where people "connect emotionally and spiritually."[66] Like other forms of art, they can produce a deeply engrossing affective experience where individual attentions are focused and united. In other words, flash mobs prefigure a world where individual expression is wedded to community connection. On the other hand, for at least some flash mobs that are dubbed criminal, it is likely that audience members feel repelled and threatened by the experience.

Flash mobs may also prefigure less desirable worlds than have been painted thus far. Choreographed flash mobs generally require that individuals sacrifice their ability to improvise for the sake of the group. One interpretation might be that flash mobs thus require "the willingness of individuals to become cogs within a preprogrammed machine,"[67] a future that will likely strike most people as the antithesis of freedom. At the same time that flash mobs represent a revolt against predictability and the status quo, they also "create potentially disturbing echoes of the sort of group-think exploited by the most controlling nations . . . the sort of communitas-through-synchronization encouraged by the mass choreography of authoritarian regimes, from drumming at fascist youth rallies to calisthenics in communist China."[68]

Flash mobs sponsored by business interests to promote consumerism may do so in terms that emphasize a faux freedom of expression. The message here, one that is ubiquitous in advertising, is that individuality and freedom are expressed by consuming a particular product. Anarchists and many others interested in issues of human freedom and ecological sustainability see advertising, including in the form of flash mobs, as potentially destructive of human freedom by binding us more and more to uncritical and apparently unlimited consumerism. These flash mobs encourage conformity of consumption. Yet sometimes the messages are mixed. A single flash mob organized to encourage and promote consumption may nevertheless achieve some of the effects described above of interrupting and interrogating the everyday, of liberating the spirit, and of creating an affective union.

Finally, it must be noted that at least some people would prefer not to experience flash mobs in any form. For them, a flash mob of any sort represents an imposition on their time and attention rather than a pleasurable intervention in everyday life. Flash mobs for them prefigure a world where others' understandings of art and pleasure are forced on them in public spaces, essentially undermining their freedom from such impositions.

Prefiguring Democracy

Flash mobs prefigure an everyday life marked by more surprise and spontaneity, and less routine and drudgery. This need not mean less social coordination and cooperation. As flash mobs artfully illustrate, individuals can organize and coordinate their actions without a central authority. As flash mobs also illustrate, increased surprise and spontaneity may sometimes mean disruption and sabotage of established orders. Destabilizing the established order may be a necessary prelude to critical consciousness. By challenging the routine, naturalized social and physical choreographies of public and private spaces, flash mobbers open the possibility of rethinking and re-creating everyday realities.

Flash mobs prefigure a world in which affect plays a critical role in heightening everyday pleasure and joy, and harnessing emotions for political purposes. Like Emma Goldman, flash mobbers tell us that a life worth living must integrate the pleasure and joy found in artful experience. Make more space in our lives for artful experience, they tell us, and less for mind-numbing work, drudgery, and routine. Flash mobbers also model an important practical dimension of artful experience and the affective conditions it creates: connection to collective action and social movement. Whether in the form of pleasure, joy, anger, or rage,[69] shared affective experience helps us recognize each other as members of a public with common interests. It binds us at least temporarily and sometimes durably, providing a basis for collective action and social movement. Affect also works as a motivator. The experience of being moved by artful performance motivates many people to participate as citizens in popular movements for change. As Leita Walker argues, "the mobs, with their abbreviated, nonsensical performances, are also a mix of fun, rebellion, collective action, and art." They are "glimpse[s] of future crowds—which could be more purposeful, and more powerful."[70] Like the other forms of popular art in this book, flash mobs prefigure more direct participation by common people in artful experience. And through art, common people are given more opportunities to rehearse and perform their roles as citizens.

Flash mobs also prefigure darker possibilities where individual freedom is submerged to the collective, not simply tied to it; where commercial interests co-opt artful performance to increase consumption and decrease critical consciousness; and where the synchronized community of a flash mob models fascism rather than participatory democracy. Flash mobbers interested in creating the conditions for greater democracy must be attuned to these darker possibilities. Like all forms of symbolic communication, flash mobs do not guarantee democratic outcomes. As the brief discussion of commercial flash mobs illustrates, they can be used to create and reinforce domination, as well as challenge it. Like the other forms of popular art addressed in this book, complex, disparate possibilities emerge.

7

Prefiguring Progressive Change

I have argued that DIY punk music, poetry slams, graffiti and street art, and flash mobs express anarchist values and practices in everyday cultural production, circulation, and reception, while pointing us toward a more democratic future. In this concluding chapter, I first summarize the case studies in terms of the anarchist values and practices they represent for everyday life, using the five analytical categories of social organization, political action, power, equality, and freedom, while also briefly sketching the implications for a democratic future. I then return to the theme raised in the introduction of prefiguration as a practical strategy for change.

Social Organization

DIY punk music, poetry slams, graffiti and street art, and flash mobs model decentralized, nonhierarchical social organization in which individuals and groups are linked in networks and communities. The main exception to this trend is poetry slam's PSI, formed to thwart commodification by corporate interests; and PSI retains elements of both representative and direct democracy. As noted earlier, many anarchists reject any form of representative democracy.

The art forms are organized and coordinated both at the local level and across levels. Organization and coordination overall comes from the bottom up, originating in local efforts to create opportunities for participation in popular art and the communities and networks that form around it. Flash mobs warrant special mention as models of how relatively spontaneous social organization can result in coordinated effort and collective action, as well as beauty and heightened affect. All four case studies offer evidence of successful work and accomplishment within a rhizomatic social model, without the hierarchy and centralized power of dominant forms of social organization in a liberal democracy. Dispersion and decentralization does not prevent cooperation and collective action.

The Internet and social media merit special mention for their key roles in linking the efforts of popular artists and other participants. Especially for flash mobs and graffiti and street art, the Internet prolongs the impact of art forms whose live public presence is often ephemeral. The Internet and social media function as public spaces where the art is made available for anyone with access to the appropriate technology, and where different individuals and groups share their work, communicate with each other, and coordinate collective action. For DIY punk musicians, the Internet and social media help arrange gigs, share art, and cement the social relationships that sustain the scene. Electronic media in each case study help form communities of interest and secure collective action.

Taken together, the four case studies prefigure forms of social organization less reliant on centralized, hierarchical authority structures taken for granted in liberal democracies. They model a more localized, federated form of democracy in which citizens take direct action to address shared concerns and problems.

Political Action

DIY punk musicians, poetry slammers, graffiti and street artists, and flash mobbers prefigure a world where common people identify shared concerns and problems, take direct action to address them, make change happen, and create the world they value. Circumventing reliance on existing institutions of state and capital, participants must of necessity take initiative and assume responsibility for the work of citizenship. They must "do it themselves." They must become citizen-artists.[1]

Each form of popular art opens multiple avenues for direct participation, both as artist and audience member. Each limits the barriers to participation found in liberal democracies, barriers erected and sustained by institutionalized class, gender, racial, and other differences. In many cases, barriers between artist and audience are also reduced or eliminated. Graffiti artists, who attempt little or no communication with a non-graffiti audience, are an exception. Many DIY punk musicians, poetry slammers, and flash mobbers intentionally break down barriers between artist and audience by incorporating audience participation, performing in accessible venues, and insisting that anyone can transition from audience to artist.

In some instances, "doing it yourself" means doing it illegally. This is particularly true of graffiti and street art, and flash mobs dubbed criminal. These instances can be viewed as a form of civil disobedience, a time-honored and sometimes-effective mode of political action in contexts where the law perpetuates injustice.

The case studies suggest that savvy use of the Internet and social media can increase the effectiveness of collective political action by helping participants identify common interests and coordinate effort. Flash mobs in particular also demonstrate that innovative, creative use of popular art can attract media attention when other efforts to do so fail.

The case studies also demonstrate the valuable role affect can play in motivating action, forming solidarities, attracting attention to a political agenda, and helping link individuals to social movement. Art has a unique capacity to generate and harness affect that routine speech and other forms of communication can rarely match.

Collective agency is made possible in part by creating spaces in which to gather. A key element in the political action of these four popular art forms is the claiming of spaces for public recognition and collective action. DIY punk musicians, poetry slammers, graffiti and street artists, and flash mobbers form TAZs, SPAZs, and sometimes PAZs where they rehearse and perform the anarchist values embedded in the beliefs and practices of each art form. The DIY ethos that pervades all four forms of popular art characterizes a world in which common people are expected to take responsibility for decision-making and direct action. In their emphasis on direct participation by common people in the creation and performance of popular art, the case studies prefigure direct, participatory democracy.

Power

DIY punk music, poetry slam, graffiti and street art, and flash mobs prefigure a world imagined by anarchists where power is more decentralized and dispersed than in liberal democracies. Concentrations of power within these art-worlds are undermined by their horizontal, rhizomatic social organization. Control and accountability for the most part exist in the nodes, and this ensures the dispersal and decentralization of political power. With few exceptions, such as poetry slam's PSI, no central locus of political power and authority exists. For the most part, power relations within the nodes themselves are horizontal and nonhierarchical, though some power gathers in the hands of strong individuals and organizers of punk festivals, poetry slams, graffiti crews, and flash mobs; and in the hands of the most prominent and successful artists.

These popular art forms also prefigure a world where concentrated economic power is systematically challenged. Graffiti and street art in particular threaten property, the ability of the state to protect it, and the domination represented by property and the state. Flash mobs also threaten the ability of the state to protect property by controlling the terms of access to it and to private and public space more generally. In all the case studies, economic barriers to access and participation are reduced or eliminated.

Each popular art form challenges domination. While graffiti and street art and flash mobs often confront state and capital directly, DIY punk music and poetry slams do so more indirectly by simply going off the grid to build alternatives that bypass or ignore the state and capital. In all cases, citizen-artists do most of their work in the cracks and on the margins of dominant structures of power. Ironically, in some cases the efforts to open and sustain liberatory cracks increases the power—but not necessarily the effectiveness—of the state as it mobilizes a punitive response. This is especially true of graffiti and street art, and some flash mobs. Sometimes, these popular art forms also challenge other forms of domination as found in racism, sexism, heterosexism, classism, and other structured inequalities. As we saw, this is especially true of poetry slam. On the other hand, DIY punk music and graffiti and street art fall short of successfully challenging male domination. Also, while these popular artists largely eliminate class domination within the cracks and margins they inhabit, most derive little if any financial support from their participation. For most this presents no problems since financial support is, for them, not a goal. For others who seek to earn an income from their participation, the case studies suggest overall a difficult challenge in building a basis for long-term financial sustainability.

The popular art forms addressed in this book build capacity by increasing critical consciousness, offering practical alternatives for action, and helping envision new horizons. Whether legally or illegally, citizen-artists make themselves seen and heard in a context where the laws, structures, and institutions of everyday life too often perpetuate domination.

Imagination and creativity are valuable skills of citizenship in identifying domination, understanding it, and challenging it. As the case studies show, popular art builds affective power, and it too is a potent form of democratic capacity in building affinities of solidarity and generating social movement.

DIY punk music, poetry slams, graffiti and street art, and flash mobs prefigure a form of democracy less defined by the dominant structures of power characteristic of liberal democracy. They model a world in which power is more horizontal and decentralized; and where structured class, racial, gender, and other forms of domination are recognized and addressed, and sometimes effectively reduced or eliminated.

Equality

In each form of popular art, power and authority are leveled. Each gives participants a direct experience of a relatively egalitarian world where common people take initiative, assume responsibility, and contribute as citizen-artists. They model political equality, where each person has access, voice, and a role in setting the terms of everyday life. They also for the most part model economic equality, though it is an equality of relative economic marginality within the spaces defined by the art forms. Also, in each case we saw that at least some artists take selective advantage of commercial opportunities. While understandable, it ensures distributive inequality.

The case studies are defined by an ethos of non-elitism characteristic of both anarchism and participatory democracy. As vividly illustrated by the DIY punk music exhortation "here's a chord, here's another, now go form a band," they invite and expect participation by common people. Access is open for the most part, requiring little or no formal training to get started. Participation is encouraged and in some cases expected. The gap between audience and artist is narrowed or eliminated. The art forms also largely eliminate class, gender, racial, and other hierarchies and barriers to participation, though they succeed to varying degrees in actually integrating diverse participation.

Taken together, these popular art forms prefigure a world less structured by systemic hierarchies and inequalities found in liberal democracies. They open vistas of a world less divided into haves and have-nots, privileged and unprivileged. They prefigure a democracy combining greater political and economic equality.

Freedom

In various ways and to varying degrees, the popular art forms addressed in this book prefigure a kind of freedom that goes well beyond liberal democratic understandings of freedom as freedom from interference. Each prefigures a freedom envisioned by anarchists marked by autonomy, independence, critical consciousness, and a capacity for effective action. By opening alternative spaces and new potential ways of life, these popular art forms increase people's choices and their viable options for thought and action. DIY punk music, poetry slams, graffiti and street art, and flash mobs help liberate the imagination; they help us see new, broader, more democratic possibilities and horizons.

I have argued that these art forms goad their participants to break through the "crust of conventionalized and routine consciousness."[2] To the degree that they succeed, they cultivate greater critical consciousness, an essential ingredient of genuine freedom and autonomy. They do this by offering both critique of existing forms of life and the outlines of alternatives shaped according to both anarchist and participatory democratic values.

DIY punk music, poetry slams, graffiti and street art, and flash mobs prefigure a kind of freedom that is empty if unaccompanied by deep social ties of solidarity and community. In each of the case studies, citizen-artists create their art in a social milieu made possible by the collective efforts of others, while at the same time helping sustain that collective milieu. Whether touring within the DIY punk network, writing and performing poetry for others to judge, reclaiming visual space with other graffiti and street artists, or opening spontaneous cracks in the everyday with coordinated dance and song, individual creative effort occurs within social ties of solidarity and communal connection. Participants experience their freedom because of community, not despite it.

The case studies also suggest a conception of freedom understood as having a meaningful say in determining the circumstances of everyday life. Participants engage in a "great refusal" to play by the rules of the larger mainstream society, while creating and following rules they set for themselves in coordination with other citizen-artists.

Finally, these popular art forms suggest that freedom of the imagination and spirit are integral to any democracy worthy of the name. Each emphatically demonstrates that imagination and creativity help us see new horizons and envision alternative worlds. Each also insists that affect—joy, anger, surprise, inspiration—has a role in public life for its own sake but also on practical grounds. Affect plays an important practical role in connecting the experience of "being moved" to social movement; in forming solidarities and affective communities; in drawing the attention of otherwise indifferent people; and in attracting the attention of the media.

Prefiguration and Social Movement

In closing, I focus on two practical dimensions of prefiguration as demonstrated by the case studies, and the prospects they offer for progressive change. These include the present opportunities offered by these forms of popular art to experience more democratic everyday lives within the cracks and on the margins, and the potential for spreading anarchist and democratic values outside the cracks and within the margins of mainstream society.

First, DIY punk music, poetry slams, graffiti and street art, and flash mobs all offer practical opportunities for performing anarchism and democracy in the present, within the cracks and on the margins of mainstream society. Many thousands of people spend parts of their lives in the cracks and marginal spaces opened by DIY punk music, poetry slams, graffiti and street art, and flash mobs. Whatever else you can say about these popular art forms, they cannot simply be dismissed as utopian.[3] They demonstrate convincingly that deeper experiences of democracy are possible than those offered by liberal democracy. DIY punk musicians, slam poets, graffiti and street artists, and flash mobbers engage collectively in the practical task of shaping an alternative world. They open spaces in which they perform anarchist and democratic values that reflect their political ideals, rather than waiting for a distant post-revolutionary, post-transformational period. They provide concrete evidence that people will work hard for reasons other than monetary gain; that ordinary people can organize relatively complete and satisfying lives based at least partly on anarchist and democratic values; that the domination experienced by many in their everyday lives can be at least partly mitigated; and that under some circumstances people are perfectly capable of ordering their lives peacefully and productively—and more democratically—apart from the dominating institutions of liberal democracy.

While struggling to escape the limits of the present and expand the realm of the possible, most DIY punk musicians, slam poets, graffiti and street artists, and flash mobbers necessarily straddle (at least) two worlds. They have to make a living, which may entail taking selective advantage of some of the rules and resources of liberal democracy while sometimes working to subvert them. Their participation in the alternative spaces created by popular art provides sustenance and respite from the alienation and struggle they experience in their lives outside the cracks and within the margins of liberal democratic society. In a time of neoliberal ascendancy, it would be easy for progressives to either succumb to despair or retreat to criticism unaccompanied by practical organizing. Knowing that popular artists continue to open and sustain cracks in neoliberal hegemony where alternative, more democratic forms of life flourish, helps sustain the hope and energy needed to resist and organize. Similarly, like Emma Goldman, DIY punk musicians, poetry slammers, graffiti and street artists, and flash mobbers insist that their everyday lives must include an element of beauty and joy that they find in their art. They make heightened aesthetic affect an integral, practical dimension in their lives.

By offering alternative views and horizons, these popular art forms encourage critical awareness of the limits of the present. They help us see more clearly and critically that democracy is diluted within liberal democracies. This is a necessary prelude to progressive movement and change. Operating within the cracks and on the margins, participants learn that other, more democratic worlds are possible. They give us hints of future possibilities, new ideas, new visions; and these motivate and guide us on the way toward whatever liberatory visions we may entertain. This integral dimension of prefiguration is deeply practical by giving us a foundation for imagining and creating alternatives, and for extending the realm of the possible.

Second, in addition to the daily practical experiences made possible within the cracks and on the margins, DIY punk music, poetry slams, graffiti and street art, and flash mobs are practically prefigurative in that they provide means of rehearsing the arts of citizenship for life outside the cracks and margins, where the democratic lessons learned within the alternative spaces can be applied, however tenuously at times. Most participants live only parts of their lives within the spaces created by the popular art forms addressed in this book. Most of necessity must earn a living outside these spaces and, more generally, live broader lives than can be sustained within any popular art form. Experiences of participants within these cracks and on the margins carry over to life outside them. As Martha Ackelsberg noted about alternative anarchist institutions, "*by participating* in communal, mutualist institutions . . . people learn how to participate in them."[4] Participation in the popular art forms addressed in this book helps develop skills and aptitudes that can be applied in other aspects of everyday life. At least some of the people who experience deeper democracy found in these forms of popular art are transformed. They learn that other, potentially more democratic everyday lives are possible. They take that awareness, and the skills and dispositions they have acquired, into mainstream liberal democratic society where they potentially become agents for change. If so, they make an impact beyond the cracks and marginal spaces. They resonate beyond, creating a ripple effect that expands outside the boundaries of specific popular art practices. This broadens their practical impact beyond the alternative spaces they open.

In addition to widening the cracks as a progressive strategy for change, these popular art forms thus suggest an alternative strategy of social contagion. In recent years, an "epidemiological imaginary"[5] has emerged, popularized especially by Malcolm Gladwell's *The Tipping Point*.[6] The "metaphorics of infection"[7] have been applied by Gladwell and others[8] to social phenomena ranging from crime waves to fashion trends to white flight, in addition to actual medical cases of infectious disease. Gladwell argues that much social change can be understood in terms of epidemics in which "ideas and products and messages and behaviors spread just like viruses do," as a process of contagion in which individuals with new ideas and behaviors infect others as though with a virus. This process of contagion initially produces small, incremental changes at the margins. Sometimes, the changes reach a "tipping point," described by Gladwell as "that one dramatic moment in an epidemic when everything can change all at once." It is "the moment of critical mass, the threshold, the boiling point." Whether or not social changes can reach a tipping point depends on the existing social context; they are "sensitive to the conditions and circumstances of the times and places in which they occur."[9]

While Gladwell's discussion is generally celebratory and uncritical—many of his illustrations are case studies of creating business opportunities—Chad Lavin and Chris Russill add a critical, progressive element to the discussion. They note, for example, the potential and actual use by the neoliberal state of the ideology of epidemics as a justification for increasing control and surveillance in order to control the spread of viruses and other infectious agents. We saw this occurring in the chapters on graffiti and street art, and flash mobs, as the state mobilized to control these infectious agents. Lavin and Russill also focus on the specifically progressive dimension of Gladwell's point about the importance of social context. They argue that a progressive deployment of the language and practice of epidemics requires accounting for social inequalities and inequities based, for example, on socioeconomic and racial differences.[10] The same can be said for graffiti and street art, and flash mobs dubbed criminal, as popular art forms that emerge primarily from marginalized populations. Understanding their role in making dominant forms of power legible requires in turn that we understand the social context in which they emerge.

Lavin and Russill are primarily interested in the value of the ideology of epidemics as a tool for explanation and interpretation, without addressing the progressive possibilities for political action and change. But the implications for political strategy and action are clear. Participants in the popular art forms addressed in this book would be seen as infectious agents who contaminate liberal democratic society with anarchist and participatory democratic values. These values potentially take root in the broader social body, infecting others in a process of contagion.

For example, DIY punk musicians accustomed to creating their own music and controlling the social milieus in which it circulates, and comfortable with circumventing the major labels to connect directly with fans, naturally take these attitudes and skills with them when they leave the scene, either temporarily or permanently. Their predisposition to "do it themselves" potentially infects their friends, family members, and neighbors, who mobilize to create community gardens, child-care cooperatives, and alternative housing options. Slam participants who learn that they are capable creators and judges of performance poetry carry this confidence in their creative, critical capacities outside the slam community into their respective homes and neighborhoods. There, they infect family members, friends, and neighbors with the confidence needed to push back against attempts by elites to foist inappropriate public art on their neighborhood, or against a proposed freeway expansion, or against an attempt by McDonald's Corporation to change local zoning laws to expand its hours of operation. Graffiti and street artists' challenge to liberal democratic rules of ownership and use of public visual space encourages a healthy questioning of attempts by the state and corporations to control the terms of access to, and behavior within, public and private space. This may emerge as attempts by others to organize against the installation of a billboard atop a local establishment, the privatization of public roads, or the hierarchical control exercised within corporations. Flash mobbers' embrace of surprise and spontaneity, and their willingness to revel in disruption, infects others with their willingness to go off the clock, to look with suspicion on further regimentation of work and leisure, to tolerate less efficiency and welcome more unpredictability and spontaneity, and to challenge the increase in surveillance at the workplace. In all four cases, popular artists inject anarchist and participatory democratic values into mainstream society, contaminate liberal democracy, and open the possibility of going viral.

Of course, there are no guarantees that any of this will actually happen. Any confidence in the inevitability of anarchist and democratic infection of the social body, not to mention the likelihood of nearing a tipping point, is misplaced. Like all progressive strategies for change, this one requires ongoing effort and struggle against long odds. The threat these popular art forms represent to liberal democratic domination is very real but also very limited overall, when measured in terms of their actual, immediate impact on dominant institutions and structures of liberal democracy. The prefigurative vision they offer is expansive, certainly more expansive than present circumstances can accommodate. With little exception, in none of the case studies did participants fundamentally threaten the entrenched power of privileged elites. If anything, some of the case studies suggest that attempts to open liberatory cracks may *increase* state power, as the state mobilizes a punitive response. This is especially true of graffiti and street art, and flash mobs viewed as criminal. These forms of popular art were under pressure and sometimes direct attack from powerful state forces. Moreover, all four popular art forms were under pressure to commodify, bringing with it the threat of co-optation. What does it say about the liberatory potential of graffiti and street art, for example, when large corporations begin using them to brand their products?

On the other hand, each case study also presents immediate practical alternatives to liberal democracy and the domination that constitutes it. Taken together, they present millions of people with very real opportunities for performing different, more anarchist and participatory democratic values in their everyday lives. By creating and sustaining concrete alternatives to liberal democracy, offering opportunities to develop and rehearse the values of anarchism and participatory democracy, expanding the horizons of the possible, mobilizing collective action, and sustaining both motivation and hope, these popular art forms challenge liberal democracy and the domination it represents. They send ripples of change outside the cracks and marginal spaces whose repercussions may be difficult to measure in immediate practical terms but are nevertheless felt at individual and social levels. As George McKay said of punk music, "small wonders have grand repercussions."[11]

DIY punk music, poetry slam, graffiti and street art, and flash mobs are each forms of collective action in their own right. They are also, as

Jeff Shantz writes of black blocs, "visible shorthands" for "a new type of social movement" that combines lifestyle politics and collective action.[12] DIY punk rockers, poetry slammers, graffiti and street artists, and flash mobbers recognize each other as sharing in a particular way of life—a culture—and the values and behaviors that constitute it. As Laura Portwood-Stacer argues about lifestyle politics, they constitute themselves as "both subculture and movement."[13] The lifestyle politics help make our means consistent with our ends—the essence of prefiguration, but they also move us toward the ends—the essence of social movement, assuming enough of us are participating. These artistic practices thus help create "a culture of democracy"[14] that supports and propels progressive social movement. Democracy requires citizens whose imaginations drive them toward creative solutions to systemic injustice, whose aversion to domination impels them to challenge power, and who are willing to harness their own efforts to collective democratic action. These dispositions and skills are made possible or not by the cultural milieu in which individuals are embedded.

Broadening and magnifying the democratic impact of the popular art forms addressed in this book through linkages with other social movements and progressive forces will require sustained attention and effort. Even if results fall short of hopes, we should not dismiss them as irrelevant or insignificant, any more than we should dismiss the Black Arts movement for failing to eliminate racism or the alterglobalization movement for failing to transform global political economy or feminism for not eradicating sexism. We should give credit for this: DIY punk music, poetry slam, graffiti and street art, and flash mobs make very real, concrete democratic differences in some people's lives, while keeping alive the possibility of broader social movement and change.

Notes

Chapter 1

1. Unbound Bookstore, Chicago, undated; quoted in Uri Gordon, *Anarchy Alive! Anti-Authoritarian Politics from Practice to Theory* (London: Pluto Press, 2008), 35.

2. Subcomandante Marcos, "First Declaration Against Neoliberalism and for Humanity," http://struggle.ws/mexico/ezln/ccri_1st_dec_real.html, January 30, 2006, accessed July 2010.

3. Emma Goldman, *My Disillusionment in Russia* (Mineola, N.Y.: Dover Publications, 2003 [1923]), 260–61; emphasis in original.

4. On anarchist prefiguration, see for example Benjamin Franks, *Rebel Alliances: The Means and Ends of Contemporary British Anarchisms* (Edinburgh, Scotland: AK Press, 2006); Benjamin Franks, "Vanguards and Paternalism," in Nathan J. Jun and Shane Wahl, eds., *New Perspectives on Anarchism* (Lanham, Md.: Rowman and Littlefield Publishers, Inc., 2010), 99–120, 112; Gordon, *Anarchy Alive!*, 5, 38; James Horrox, "Reinventing Resistance: Constructive Activism in Gustav Landauer's Social Philosophy," in Jun and Wahl, *New Perspectives on Anarchism*, 189–207, 200–02; Jeffrey S. Juris, "Anarchism, or the Cultural Logic of Networking," in Randall Amster, Abraham DeLeon, Luis A. Fernandez, Anthony J. Nocella, II, and Deric Shannon, eds., *Contemporary Anarchist Studies: An introductory anthology of anarchy in the academy* (New York: Routledge, 2009), 213–23, 219; and Marianne Maeckelbergh, *The Will of the Many: How the Alterglobalisation Movement is Changing the Face of Democracy* (London: Pluto Press, 2009), 66–68.

5. Wright, *Envisioning Real Utopias* (London and New York: Verso, 2010), 303.

6. James Buccellato, "Sign of the Outlaw: Liberal Boundaries, Social Banditry and the Political Act," *New Political Science: A Journal of Politics and Culture* 34.3 (September 2012), 271–94.

7. Pattrice Jones, "Free as a bird: natural anarchism in action," in Amster, et al., *Contemporary Anarchist Studies*, 236–46, 236.

8. Wright, *Envisioning Real Utopias*, 337.

9. Ibid., 322.

10. Colin Ward, *Anarchy in Action* (London: Allen and Unwin, 1973), 18.

11. Wright, *Envisioning Real Utopias,* 324.

12. John Holloway, *Crack Capitalism* (London and New York: Pluto Press, 2010), 11, 4.

13. Ibid., 11. See also Michael Hardt and Antonio Negri, *Empire* (Cambridge, Mass.: Harvard University Press, 2000), p. 204, who argue that "Refusal certainly is the beginning of a liberatory politics, but it is only a beginning. . . . We need to create a new social body, a project that goes well beyond refusal. Our lines of flight, our exodus must be constituent and create a real alternative. Beyond the simple refusal, or as part of that refusal, we need also to construct a new mode of life."

14. Holloway, *Crack Capitalism*, 11.

15. Max Horkheimer, *Eclipse of Reason* (London and New York: Continuum, [1946] 2004), 25.

16. Holloway, *Crack Capitalism*, 35. See also Holloway's *Change the World Without Taking Power* (London: Pluto Press, 2002), in which he explores some of these same themes.

17. Horrox, "Reinventing Resistance," 202.

18. Ruth Kinna, *Anarchism: A Beginner's Guide* (Oxford: One World Publications, 2005), 144–55.

19. My understanding of art is indebted especially to John Dewey, *Art as Experience*, in *John Dewey: The Later Works, 1925–1953*, volume 10: 1934, edited by Jo Ann Boydston (Carbondale, Ill.: Southern Illinois University Press, 1989 [1934]). Dewey characterized distinctions between high and low art bluntly as "out of place and stupid." Dewey, *Art as Experience*, 231.

20. Antonio Gramsci, *Selections from the Prison Notebooks of Antonio Gramsci*, edited and trans. by Quintin Hoare and Geoffrey Nowell Smith (New York: International Publishers, 1971).

21. See for example Tony Bennett, "Popular Culture and the 'Turn to Gramsci,'" in John Storey, ed., *Cultural Theory and Popular Culture: A Reader* (Harlow, England: Pearson Longman, 2009), 81–87; Stuart Hall, "Notes on Deconstructing 'The Popular,'" in Raphael Samuel, ed., *Peoples' History and Socialist Theory* (London: Routledge and Kegan Paul Ltd., 1981), 227–40; Stuart Hall, "Cultural Studies and Its Theoretical Legacies," in Lawrence Grossberg, Cary Nelson, and Paula Treichler, eds., *Cultural Studies* (New York: Routledge, 1992), 277–94; Dick Hebdige, "From Culture to Hegemony," in Simon During, ed., *The Cultural Studies Reader* (London: Routledge, 1993), 357–67; Mark Mattern, "Cajun music, cultural revival: theorizing political action in popular music," *Popular Music and Society* 22:2 (Summer 1998), 31–48; Tim Patterson, "Notes on the Historical Application of Marxist Cultural Theory," *Science and Society* 34:3 (1975), 257–91; and Manuel Peña, *The Texas-Mexican Conjunto: History of a Working Class Music* (Austin, Tex.: University of Texas Press, 1985).

22. Dewey, "Liberty and Social Control," in *John Dewey: The Later Works, 1925–1953*, volume 11: 1935–1937, edited by Jo Ann Boydston (Carbondale, Ill.: Southern Illinois University Press, 1991 [1935]), 360–63, 362.

23. Dewey, "Individualism, Old and New," in *John Dewey: The Later Works, 1925–1953*, volume 5: 1929–1930, edited by Jo Ann Boydston (Carbondale, Ill.: Southern Illinois University Press, 1988 [1929/30]), 41–144.

24. Dewey, "Freedom and Culture," in *John Dewey: The Later Works, 1925–1953*, volume 13: 1938–1939, edited by Jo Ann Boydston (Carbondale, Ill.: Southern Illinois University Press, 1991 [1939]), 65–188, 70.

25. Dewey, *Art as Experience*, 110, 275.

26. Dewey, "The Public and Its Problems," in *John Dewey: The Later Works, 1925–1953*, volume 2: 1925–1927, edited by Jo Ann Boydston (Carbondale, Ill.: Southern Illinois University Press, 1988 [1927]), 235–372, 349.

27. Dewey, *Art as Experience*, 328.

28. Allan Antliff, *Anarchy and Art: From the Paris Commune to the Fall of the Berlin Wall*, 2007, 11.

29. Pierre Proudhon, *Du principe de l'art et de sa destination social* (Paris: Garnier Frères, 1865), 43, 84; italics in original.

30. Peter Kropotkin, "Appeal to the Young," in *Kropotkin's Revolutionary Pamphlets*, Roger N. Baldwin, ed. (New York: Dover Press, 1970 [1880]), 273.

31. Emma Goldman, *The Social Significance of Modern Drama* (New York: Applause Theater Book Publishers, 1987 [1914]), 1–2.

32. Anarchist historian Peter Marshall renders this as, "If I can't dance, it's not my revolution." Marshall, *Demanding the Impossible: A History of Anarchism* (Oakland, Calif.: PM Press, 2010 [1992]), 409.

33. Emma Goldman, *Living My Life*, volume I (New York: Alfred Knopf, 1931) and volume II (Hempstead, N.Y.: Garden City Publishing Company, 1934); volume I, 56.

34. Goldman, Foreword to *Social Significance of Modern Drama*, http://sunsite3.berkeley.edu/Goldman/Writings/Drama/foreword.html).

35. David Graeber, "Anarchism, academia, and the avant-garde," in Amster, et al., *Contemporary Anarchist Studies*, 103–12, 110–11. See also Wilhelm von Humboldt on the relation between art and unalienated labor: In a condition of freedom, "all peasants and craftsmen might be elevated into artists; that is, men who love their own labor for its own sake, improve it by their own plastic genius and inventive skill, and thereby cultivate their intellect, ennoble their character, and exalt and refine their pleasures." Humboldt, quoted in Noam Chomsky, "Introduction," in Daniel Guérin, *Anarchism: From Theory to Practice* (New York: Monthly Review Press, 1970), vii–xx, xi.

36. According to ongoing surveys conducted by Gallup since 2000, most workers are disengaged from their work. Gallup's June 2013 report found that 70 percent of American workers are either "not engaged" or "actively disengaged." The number of American workers who say they are "actively engaged" in their work has never exceeded 30 percent since Gallup began the survey in 2000. These figures vividly demonstrate the deeply alienating character of work in a capitalist political economy. See Ricardo Lopez, "Most 'not engaged' at work, poll finds," *The Cleveland Plain Dealer*, Thursday, June 20, 2013.

37. Antliff, *Anarchy and Art*, 46.

38. Deric Shannon, "Raising the Curtain: Anarchist Economics, Resistance, and Culture," *Peace Studies Journal* 4:2 (July 2011), 47–56, 47, 48, 52, 54, 52, 53.

39. Josh MacPhee and Erik Reuland, "Introduction: Towards Anarchist Art Theories," in Josh MacPhee and Erik Reuland, eds., *Realizing the Impossible: Art Against Authority* (Oakland, Calif.: AK Press, 2007), 3–5, 5.

40. Jill Dolan, *Utopia in Performance: Finding Hope at the Theater* (Ann Arbor, Mich.: The University of Michigan Press, 2005), 5, 6.

41. Ian McEwan, quoted in Dolan, *Utopia in Performance*, title pages.

42. Dolan, *Utopia in Performance*, 15.

Chapter 2

1. David Held, for example, identifies nine different variants. David Held, *Models of Democracy* (Cambridge, Mass.: Polity Press, 1987). Held does not address so-called deliberative democracy, a relatively new entrant on the terrain of democratic theory and practice. On deliberative democracy, which emphasizes rational public deliberation among citizens to discover or create a common will, see for example James Bohman, *Public Deliberation: Pluralism, Complexity, and Democracy* (Cambridge, Mass.: MIT Press, 1996); Jurgen Habermas, *Between Facts and Norms*, trans. William Rehg (Cambridge, Mass.: MIT Press, 1996); Diana C. Mutz, *Hearing the Other Side: Deliberative versus Participatory Democracy* (Cambridge: Cambridge University Press, 2006); and Ian Shapiro, *The State of Democratic Theory* (Princeton, N.J.: Princeton University Press, 2003).

2. Democratic theorists further distinguish between different kinds of liberal democracy. See for example Held, *Models of Democracy*, especially chapters 3, 5, and 6; William Hudson, *American Democracy in Peril: Eight Challenges to America's Future* (Washington, D.C.: CQ Press, 2010), "Introduction," pp. 1–24; and C. B. Macpherson, *The Life and Times of Liberal Democracy* (Oxford: Oxford University Press, 1977).

3. Participatory democratic theory was relatively submerged by the prominence of deliberative democratic theory in the 1990s and 2000s, but interest in participatory democratic theory and practice has again begun to emerge. On both its submergence and reemergence, see especially Jeffrey Hilmer, "The State of Participatory Democratic Theory," *New Political Science: A Journal of Politics and Culture* 32:1 (March 2010), 43–63; and Carole Pateman, "Participatory Democracy Revisited," *Perspectives on Politics* 10:1 (March 2012), 7–19. As Hilmer argues (54), the aims and goals of participatory democratic theory are much broader than those of deliberative democratic theory, which can be viewed as a necessary, but insufficient component of participatory democratic theory. For classic and contemporary examples of seminal texts in participatory democratic theory and practice, see for example Aristotle, *Politics*, trans. Ernest Barker (Oxford: Oxford University Press, 1998), 6.1317b–1318a; Benjamin Barber, *Strong Democracy: Participatory Politics for a New Age* (Berkeley, Calif.: University of California

Press, 1984); Dewey, especially *The Public and Its Problems*; Thomas Jefferson, "Letter to Samuel Kercheval" [1816], in Adrienne Koch and William Peden, eds., *The Life and Selected Writings of Thomas Jefferson* (New York: Random House, 1944), 615; Jefferson, "Letter to James Madison" [1787], in Koch and Peden, *The Life and Selected Writings of Thomas Jefferson*, 407; Macpherson, *Life and Times of Liberal Democracy*, "Model 4: Participatory Democracy," 93–115; Jane Mansbridge, *Beyond Adversary Democracy* (New York: Basic Books, 1980); Carole Pateman, *Participation and Democratic Theory* (Cambridge: Cambridge University Press, 1970); Jean Jacque Rousseau, especially *The Social Contract*, in Alan Ritter and Julia Conaway Bondanella, eds., *Rousseau's Political Writings*, trans. by Julia Conaway Bondanella (New York: W. W. Norton, 1988 [1762]), 84–173; and Pericles's "funeral oration" in Thucydides, *History of the Peloponnesian War*, trans. by Richard Crawley (New York: E. P. Dutton, 1910), 2.37–40. For introductions to participatory democracy, see for example Terrence Cook and Patrick Morgan, eds., *Participatory Democracy* (San Francisco: Canfield Press, 1971); and Dimitrios Roussopoulos and C. George Benello, eds., *Participatory Democracy: Prospects for Democratizing Democracy* (Montreal: Black Rose Books, 2005 [1970]).

4. See, for example, Dave Morland and John Carter, "Anarchism and Democracy," in Malcolm Todd and Gary Taylor, eds., *Democracy and Participation: Popular protest and new social movements* (London: Merlin Press, 2004), 78–95; John Wakeman, *Anarchism and Democracy*, Freedom Pamphlet (London: Freedom Press, 1920), 6–7, 15; and Charlotte Wilson, "Social Democracy and Anarchism," in The Dark Star Collective, *Quiet Rumours: An Anarcha-Feminist Reader* (Edinburgh: AK Press/Dark Star, 2002), 69–80, 70.

5. See, for example, Randall Amster, Abraham DeLeon, Luis A. Fernandez, Anthony J. Nocella, II, and Deric Shannon, "Introduction," in Amster et al., *Contemporary Anarchist Studies*, 1–7; Graeber, "Anarchism, academia, and the avant-garde"; David Graeber, *The Democracy Project: A History, a Crisis, a Movement* (London: Allen Lane, 2013); Elena Loizidou, "'This Is What Democracy Looks Like,'" in Jimmy Casas Klausen and James Martel, eds., *How Not to Be Governed: Readings and Interpretations from a Critical Anarchist Left* (Lanham, Md.: Lexington Books, 2011), 167–87; Maeckelbergh, *The Will of the Many*, 224–27; Todd May, "Anarchism from Foucault to Rancière," in Amster, et al., *Contemporary Anarchist Studies*, 11–25, 15–17; Cindy Milstein, "Reappropriate the Imagination!," in MacPhee and Reuland, *Realizing the Impossible*, 296–307; and Jeff Shantz, *Living Anarchy: Theory and Practice in Anarchist Movements* (Bethesda, Md.: Academica Press, 2009), 2, 91.

6. See Murray Bookchin, *Social Anarchism or Lifestyle Anarchism: An Unbridgeable Chasm* (Edinburgh and San Francisco: AK Press, 1995); Kinna, *Anarchism*, 15; Colin Ward, *Anarchism: A Very Short Introduction* (Oxford: Oxford University Press, 2004), 2–3; and Leonard Williams, "Anarchism Revived," *New Political Science* 29:3 (September 2007), 297–312. The claim that "there are as many varieties of anarchism as there are anarchists" may be only a slight exaggeration. Amster, et al., "Introduction," 2.

7. For an intellectual and practical history of anarchism, see Marshall, *Demanding the Impossible*. For introductions to anarchist theory and practice, see for example Guérin, *Anarchism*; Kinna, *Anarchism*; and Ward, *Anarchism*. Seminal anarchist thinkers include, for example, William Godwin (1756–1836), Pierre-Joseph Proudhon (1809–1865), Michael Bakunin (1814–1876), Peter Kropotkin (1842–1921), and Emma Goldman (1869–1940). See Marshall's "Select Bibliography," in *Demanding the Impossible*, 759–92 for selected works by these and other anarchist thinkers.

8. See, for example, Richard Hofstadter, *The American Political Tradition and the Men Who Made It* (New York: Vintage Books, 1989 [1948]), 6, 7, 9 for selected anti-democratic quotes by American founders.

9. Madison, "Federalist No. 39" [1788], in Alexander Hamilton, James Madison, and John Jay, *The Federalist Papers* (Toronto: Bantam Books, 1982), 190; John Adams, "Letter to Samuel Adams" [1790], in *The Political Writings of John Adams*, ed. George W. Carey (Washington, D.C.: Regnery, 2000), 665.

10. Daniel Kemmis, *Community and the Politics of Place* (Norman, Okla.: University of Oklahoma Press, 1990), 12.

11. See for example John Rawls, "A Well-Ordered Society," in *In Defense of Human Dignity*, ed. Robert Kraynak and Glenn Tinder (Notre Dame, Ind.: University of Notre Dame Press, 2003), in which he pointedly excludes private ownership of the means of production from his list of basic liberties. The social democracies of western and northern Europe, with their high rates of taxation and extensive social welfare spending, represent at least partial challenges to laissez-faire capitalism.

12. Bakunin, in Sam Dolgoff, ed., *Bakunin On Anarchy: Selected Works of the Activist-Founder of World Anarchism* (London: Allen & Unwin, 1973), 270.

13. Kropotkin, in Nicolas Walter, ed., *Anarchism and Anarchist Communism* (London: Freedom Press, 1987), 7.

14. Goldman, "What I Believe," in *Red Emma Speaks*, ed. Alix Kates Shulman (London: Wildwood House, 1979 [1908]), 36.

15. On anarchist economics, see for example Eric Buck, "The flow of experiencing in anarchic economies," in Amster, et al., 57–69; Peter Gelderloos, *Anarchy Works* (San Francisco: Ardent Press, 2010), 76–133; Deric Shannon, Anthony J. Nocella II, and John Asimakopoulos, eds., *The Accumulation of Freedom: Writings on Anarchist Economics* (Oakland, Calif.: AK Press, 2012); and Chris Spannos, ed., *Real Utopia: Participatory Society for the 21st Century* (Oakland, Calif.: AK Press, 2008).

16. See Todd May, "Introduction," in Jun and Wahl, *New Perspectives on Anarchism*, 1–5, 3 on the distinction between rhizomatic and arboreal social organization. See also Gordon, *Anarchy Alive!*, 14–17, for a discussion of contemporary anarchists' models of organization. See especially Juris, "Anarchism, or the Cultural Logic of Networking," 213–23 for a discussion of anarchist models of social organization as found in contemporary social movements, especially

the alterglobalization movement. See also Franks, *Rebel Alliances*, chapter 4 on "Organisation," 196–259.

17. Rousseau, *Social Contract*, book IV, chapter 1, para. 1, 149.

18. On workplace and economic democracy, see for example Robin Archer, *Economic Democracy: The Politics of Feasible Socialism* (Oxford: Clarendon Press, 1995); Samuel Bowles and Herbert Gintis, "A Political and Economic Case for the Democratic Enterprise," in *The Idea of Democracy*, eds., David Copp, Jean Hampton, and John Roemer (Cambridge: Cambridge University Press, 1993), 375–99; Robert Dahl, *A Preface to Economic Democracy* (Berkeley, Calif.: University of California Press, 1985); Gregory Dow, *Governing the Firm: Workers' Control in Theory and Practice* (Cambridge: Cambridge University Press, 2003); David Ellerman, *The Democratic Worker-Owned Firm: A New Model for the East and West* (London: Unwin Hyman, 1990); Donald George, *Economic Democracy: The Political Economy of Self-Management and Participation* (London: Macmillan Press, 1993); Edward Greenberg, *Workplace Democracy: The Political Effects of Participation* (Ithaca, N.Y.: Cornell University Press, 1986); and Tom Malleson, "Economic Democracy: The Left's Big Idea for the Twenty-First Century?," *New Political Science: A Journal of Politics and Culture* 35.1 (March 2013), 84–108.

19. See, for example, Barber, *Strong Democracy*, 1984; Harry Boyte, *Community Is Possible: Repairing America's Roots* (New York: Harper & Row, 1984); Boyte, *CommonWealth: A Return to Citizen Politics* (New York: Free Press, 1989); Dewey, *The Public and Its Problems*; and Dewey, *Individualism, Old and New*.

20. Dewey, *The Public and Its Problems*.

21. According to Peter Marshall, Kropotkin's "most important insight was that only a genuine community can allow the full development of the free individual" (Marshall, *Demanding the Impossible*, 338).

22. Michael Albert and Robin Hahnel, *Looking Forward: Participatory Economics for the Twenty First Century* (Boston: South End Press, 1991).

23. Bakunin, "Letter to a Frenchman on the Present Crisis," (1870) http://marxists.org/reference/archive/bakunin/works/1870/letter-frenchman.htm.

24. Gustav Landauer, *For Socialism*, trans. David J. Parent (St. Louis, Mo.: Telos Press, 1978 [1911]), and Landauer, *Revolution and Other Writings: A Political Reader*, ed. and trans. by Gabriel Kuhn (Oakland, Calif.: PM Press, 2010).

25. Richard Day, *Gramsci Is Dead: Anarchist Currents in the Newest Social Movements* (London: Pluto Press, 2005), 126.

26. See, for example, David Graeber, *Direct Action: An Ethnography* (Edinburgh: AK Press, 2009), 203, 207; and Benjamin Franks, *Rebel Alliances*, chapter 5 on "Anarchist Tactics," 260–347.

27. Hakim Bey, *T.A.Z.: The Temporary Autonomous Zone, Ontological Anarchy, Poetic Terrorism* (Brooklyn, N.Y.: Automedia, 1991).

28. Day, *Gramsci Is Dead*, 164.

29. See for example Jesse Cohn, *Anarchism and the crisis of representation: Hermeneutics, aesthetics, politics* (Cranbury, N.J.: Rosemont Publishing & Printing

Corp., 2006), especially chapter 9, "The Critique of Democracy as Representation," 199–215; Brian Martin, "Democracy without Elections," in Howard J. Ehrlich, ed., *Reinventing Anarchy, Again* (Edinburgh: AK Press, 1996), 123–36; Morland and Carter, "Anarchism and Democracy"; and Robert Paul Wolff, *In Defense of Anarchism* (Berkeley, Calif.: University of California Press, 1998 [1970]), "Preface to the 1998 Edition," vii–xxv.

30. See Guérin, *Anarchism*, 19 on the "inconsistency of anarchist doctrine" on the matter of voting and elections.

31. Staughton Lynd and Andrej Grubacic, *Wobblies & Zapatistas: Conversations on Anarchism, Marxism and Radical History* (Oakland, Calif.: PM Press, 2008), 87.

32. Macpherson, *Life and Times of Liberal Democracy*, 95.

33. Proudhon, *Solution du problème social* (Paris: Éditions Lacroix, 1868), 56, trans. Jesse Cohn. Unlike most of his nineteenth-century peers, Bakunin accepted a limited form of majoritarianism. He argued that decision-making in communes would occur by majority vote, with universal suffrage of both men and women. He also advised fellow anarchists to become deputies or otherwise help the socialist parties in Parliament. See Marshall, *Demanding the Impossible*, 278, 297. Proudhon himself was elected to Parliament in June 1848.

34. On consensus decision-making and other aspects of anarchist group process and decision making, see especially David Graeber, "The New Anarchists," *New Left Review* 13, January-February 2002, newleftreview.org/11/13/david-graeber-the-new-anarchists, accessed 5/24/12; Graeber, "Anarchism, academia, and the avant-garde," 104; and Graeber, *The Democracy Project*, esp. chapter 4, "How Change Happens," 208–70.

35. Hilmer, "The State of Participatory Democracy," 43.

36. Herman Daly, Thomas Prugh, and Robert Costanza, *The Local Politics of Global Sustainability* (Washington, D.C.: Island Press, 2000), 112.

37. Cohn, *Anarchism and the crisis of representation*, 208.

38. Lynd and Grubacic, *Wobblies & Zapatistas*, 86. For more on the differences between delegates and representatives, see Murray Bookchin, *Remaking Society: Pathways to a Green Future* (Boston: South End Press, 1990), 174–75; and Punkerslut, "Delegation, Not Representation: On the Practical Methods of Anarchism for Decentralized, Anti-Authoritarian Organizing," http://www.punkerslut.com/articles/delegation_not_representation.html, accessed 9/24/12.

39. Uri Gordon, "Power and Anarchy: In/equality + In/visibility in Autonomous Politics," in Jun and Wahl, *New Perspectives on Anarchism*, 39–66, 40.

40. Gordon, *Anarchy Alive!*, 50; and Gordon, "Power and Anarchy," 40–45. Gordon credits the eco-feminist writer Starhawk for this distinction.

41. Power-over, or domination, has been dissected in the so-called faces of power debate. For a summary of this discussion see Peter Digeser, "The Fourth Face of Power," *Journal of Politics* 54, no. 4 (November 1992), 977–1007. Todd May argues that domination represents to anarchism what exploitation represents

to Marxism: the central form of oppression around which liberatory theory and practice are organized. May, "Anarchism from Foucault to Rancière," 11.

42. Gordon, *Anarchy Alive!*, 50, quoting the eco-feminist writer Starhawk; Gordon, "Power and Anarchy," 40.

43. Bakunin, in *Bakunin On Anarchy*, 330.

44. Kropotkin, *The State: Its Historic Role*, trans. Vernon Richards (London: Freedom Press, 1969 [1897]), 10.

45. Charles Lindblom, "The Market As Prison," *Journal of Politics* 44:2 (1982), 324–36.

46. See Deric Shannon, Anthony J. Nocella, II, and John Asimakopoulos, "Anarchist Economics: A Holistic View," in Shannon, et al., *The Accumulation of Freedom*, 11–39, for a summary of anarchists' critique of capitalism.

47. John Locke, *The Second Treatise on Civil Government* (Buffalo, N.Y.: Prometheus Books, 1986 [1690]), 49.

48. Thomas Hobbes, *Leviathan* (New York: Penguin Books, 1968 [1651]), part 1, chapter 13, 183–88.

49. Goldman, "What I Believe," 36.

50. Pierre-Joseph Proudhon, "The System of Economic Contradictions," in *No Gods, No Masters: An Anthology of Anarchism*, ed. Daniel Guerín, trans. Paul Sharkey (Oakland, Calif.: AK Press, 2005 [1840]), 55–76, 55–56.

51. At least some earlier anarchists recognized gender domination and sought to challenge it. Kropotkin favored liberating women from household drudgery to free that "half humanity subjected to the slavery of the hearth" (Kropotkin, *The Conquest of Bread* (London: Elephant Editions, 1985 [1906]), p. 128). Goldman argued in favor of women's reproductive and sexual freedom, and against treating women as "sex commodities" and servants. (Goldman, "Woman Suffrage," in *Anarchism and Other Essays*, ed. Richard Drinnon (New York: Dover, 1969), 211.

52. Rousseau, *Discourse on Inequality* [1755], in Ritter and Bondanella, *Rousseau's Political Writings*, 43.

53. Godwin, in Peter Marshall, ed., *The Anarchist Writings of William Godwin* (London: Freedom Press, 1986), 140, 100.

54. See for example Jefferson, "Letter to James Madison [October 28, 1785]," in Philip Foner, ed., *Basic Writings of Thomas Jefferson* (New York: Willey Book Company, 1944), 520; and Jefferson, "Letter to Samuel Kercheval [July 12, 1816]," in Foner, *Basic Writings of Thomas Jefferson*, 746, 749.

55. Plato, *The Republic*, trans. Desmond Lee (New York: Penguin Books, 1987), paras. 421d–422a, p. 188.

56. Proudhon, *What Is Property?* trans. Benjamin Tucker (New York: Dover Publications, 1970 [1840]), 89; Proudhon, *Justice in the Revolution and the Church*, 4 volumes (Paris, 1858), III, 174.

57. Bakunin, in *Bakunin On Anarchy*, 125. See also May, "Anarchism from Foucault to Rancière"; and May, "Introduction." May argues that anarchism presupposes equality.

58. David Graeber, *The Democracy Project*, 183–84.

59. Jefferson, letter to James Madison, October 28, 1785, The Founders' Constitution, volume 1, chapter 15, document 32, http://press-pubs.uchicago.edu/founders/documents/v1ch15s32.html, The University of Chicago Press.

60. On this distinction between two kinds of freedom, see Benjamin Constant, "The Liberty of the Ancients Compared with That of the Moderns" [1816], in David Boaz, *The Libertarian Reader: Classic and Contemporary Readings from Lao-Tzu to Milton Friedman* (New York: Free Press, 1997), 65–70; and Isaiah Berlin, *Two Concepts of Liberty* (Oxford: Clarendon Press, 1958).

61. William Connolly, *The Terms of Political Discourse*, 2nd ed. (Princeton, N.J.: Princeton University Press, 1983), chapter 4, 140–78, 172. See also S. I. Benn and W. L. Weinstein, "Being Free to Act and Being a Free Man," *Mind* 80 (1971), 194–211, who argue that "underlying and presupposed by the concept of freedom of action there is another but related concept, that of autonomy—of the free man as chooser" (194).

62. The exceptions generally represent a radical individualist strain of anarchism. See for example Max Stirner, *The Ego and His Own* (London: A. C. Fifield, 1912 [1845]) and Murray Rothbard, *For a New Liberty: The Libertarian Manifesto* (New York: Collier, 1978).

63. Bakunin, quoted in Noam Chomsky, "Introduction," x; Bakunin, quoted in Guérin, *Anarchism*, 33; Bakunin, in *Bakunin On Anarchy*, 257; and Bakunin, in G. P. Maximoff, ed., *The Political Philosophy of Bakunin* (New York: The Free Press, 1953), 165.

64. Rudolf Rocker, *Anarcho-Syndicalism: Theory and Practice* (London: Secker and Warburg, 1938), 31.

65. Wilhelm von Humboldt, *On the Limits of State Action*, trans. J. W. Burrow (Indianapolis, Ind.: Liberty Fund, 1993), 100.

66. Rudolf Rocker, *Anarcho-Syndicalism*, 31.

67. Bakunin, in *The Political Philosophy of Bakunin*, 267.

68. Max Nettlau, "Anarchist: Communist or Individualist? Both," http://theanarchistlibrary.org/library/Max_Nettlau__Anarchism__Communist_or_Individualist__Both.pdf., 3, 5.

69. Vernon Richards, ed., *Errico Malatesta: His Life and Ideas*, (London: Freedom Press, 1977), 23, 24. See also Andrew Hemingway, "Individualism and/or Solidarity? 'Anarchist Modernism' in the U.S.," *Oxford Art Journal* 25:2 (2002), 165–70.

70. Bookchin, *Social Anarchism or Lifestyle Anarchism*, 9–10. For responses to Bookchin, see for example the debate in *Anarchist Studies* 4:2 (1996) and 6:1 (1998) among L. Susan Brown, Janet Biehl, and Thomas Martin; and Bob Black, *Anarchy after Leftism* (Columbia, Mo.: C.A.L. Press, 1997). See also Bookchin's "Whither Anarchism: A Reply to Recent Anarchist Critics," in Bookchin, *Anarchism, Marxism, and the Future of the Left: Interviews and Essays, 1993–1998* (Oakland, Calif.: AK Press, 1999). Laura Portwood-Stacer's *Lifestyle Politics and Radical Activism* (New York: Bloomsbury, 2013) can be read as an extended

defense of so-called lifestyle anarchism against Bookchin's "binary view . . . based on a premise that there are two kinds of anarchists—those who are interested in radical social transformation and those who are interested only in their own lives" (135).

71. On "effective freedom," see for example Dewey, "Liberty and Social Control"; Dewey, *Liberalism and Social Action* [1935], in *John Dewey:The Later Works, 1925–1953*, volume 11, ed. Jo Ann Boydston (Carbondale, Ill.: Southern Illinois University Press, 1991), 1–66, 27; and Dewey, *Ethics*, in *John Dewey: The Middle Works, 1899–1924*, volume 5, ed. Jo Ann Boydston (Carbondale, Ill.: Southern Illinois University Press, 1978 [1908]), 392.

Chapter 3

1. Gordon, *Anarchy Alive!*, 19.

2. Tom Buechele, "DIY Masculinity: Masculine Identity in DIY Punk Subculture," Presentation at the 2006 Annual Meeting of the American Sociological Association, Montreal, Canada, 4–5.

3. George McKay, "DiY Culture: notes towards an intro," in George McKay, ed., *DiY Culture: Party & Protest in Nineties Britain* (London: Verso, 1998), 1–53, 2, 14.

4. Julia Downes, "Riot Grrrl: The Legacy and Contemporary Landscape of DIY Feminist Cultural Activism," in Nadine Monem, ed., *Riot Grrrl: Revolution Girl Style Now!* (London: Black Dog Publishing, 2007), 11–49, 13.

5. George McKay, *Senseless Acts of Beauty: Cultures of Resistance since the Sixties* (London: Verso, 1996), 11.

6. Downes, "Riot Grrrl," 13.

7. Craig O'Hara, *The Philosophy of Punk: More Than Noise* (London: AK Press, 1999), 21.

8. McKay, "DiY Culture," 1.

9. Quoted in McKay, "DiY Culture," 2, 1.

10. Quoted in Paul Rosen, "'It was easy, it was cheap, go and do it!': Technology and Anarchy in the UK Music Industry," in Jon Purkis and James Bowen, eds., *Twenty-First Century Anarchism* (London: Cassell, 1997), 99–116, 104.

11. See the Do DIY website at http://www.dodiy.org/ for a sense of size and diversity of the contemporary U.S. scene. It includes a state-by-state listing of houses and other DIY venues in the U.S.

12. See especially David Hesmondhalgh, "Post-Punk's attempt to democratise the music industry: the success and failure of Rough Trade," *Popular Music* 16:3 (1997), 255–74; and Rosen, "'It was easy, it was cheap, go and do it!'"

13. Pete Dale, "It was easy, it was cheap, so what?: Reconsidering the DIY principle of punk and indie music," *Popular Music History* 3:2 (2008), 171–93, 174.

14. See especially Hesmondhalgh's history of Rough Trade, "Post-Punk's attempt to democratise the music industry," 1997.

15. Rosen, " 'It was easy, it was cheap, go and do it!' " 108.

16. O'Hara, *The Philosophy of Punk*, 158.

17. Robert Strachan, "Micro-independent record labels in the UK: Discourse, DIY cultural production and the music industry," *European Journal of Cultural Studies* 10:2 (2007), 245–65, 247.

18. See especially Evan Landon Wendel, "New Potentials for 'Independent' Music: Social Networks, Old and New, and the Ongoing Struggles to Reshape the Music Industry," M.S. Thesis (Comparative Media Studies), Massachusetts Institute of Technology, June 2008, for a discussion of the benefits and limitations of social media in DIY musical production and distribution.

19. For histories of Crass, see especially McKay, *Senseless Acts of Beauty*; and Emilie Hardman, "Before You Can Get Off Your Knees: Profane Existence and Anarcho-Punk as a Social Movement," paper presented at the annual meeting of the American Sociological Association, New York City, August 11, 2007.

20. Dave Laing, quoted in McKay, *Senseless Acts of Beauty*, 77.

21. Crass, "Punk Is Dead," from *The Feeding of the 5000* LP, Small Wonder Records, 1978.

22. Crass/Poison Girls, "Persons Unknown/Bloody Revolutions," Crass Records, 1980.

23. Crass, "Big A, little a," from *Christ—The Album*, Crass Records, 1982.

24. Crass, "How Does It Feel To Be the Mother of 1000 Dead?/The Immortal Death," Crass Records, 1983.

25. Letter from Pete Wright, quoted in McKay, *Senseless Acts of Beauty*, 100.

26. Quoted in Hardman, "Before You Can Get Off Your Knees," 4.

27. Quoted in Hardman, "Before You Can Get Off Your Knees," 5. See also http://profanexistence.com/, accessed 12/7/14.

28. Joel [no last name provided], *Profane Existence* #11/12, Autumn 1991, 10.

29. See http://www.bereafest.org/, accessed 7/01/10.

30. O'Hara, *The Philosophy of Punk*, 15.

31. See Tim Gosling, " 'Not for Sale': The Underground Network of Anarcho-Punk," in Andy Bennett and Richard Peterson, eds., *Music Scenes: Local, Translocal, and Virtual* (Nashville, Tenn.: Vanderbilt University Press, 2004), 168–83, especially 170 on the accessibility of DIY music.

32. Dale, "It was easy, it was cheap, so what?," 190.

33. http://dodiy.org/index.php?n=Main.Ohio, accessed 6/23/10; http://www.bereafest.org/, accessed 8/14/10.

34. Strachan, "Micro-independent record labels in the UK," 247.

35. Reprinted in Downes, "Riot Grrrl," 24.

36. Reprinted in Downes, "Riot Grrrl," 40.

37. O'Hara, *The Philosophy of Punk*, 160, 162. See O'Hara's full discussion, 160–65, on the difficulties of making a living in the DIY punk music scene.

38. http://dodiy.org/index.php?n=Main.Ohio, accessed 6/23/10.

39. See the 2010 list of corporate sponsors at http://www.afropunk.com/page/afropunk-10-nyc, accessed 7/14/10.

40. Wendel, "New Potentials for 'Independent' Music," 57. Earlier, in a similar vein, George McKay proposed to call the scene DiO (Do it Ourselves), rather than DIY. McKay, "DiY Culture," 27. Neither Wendel nor McKay extensively developed the insight, nor did either develop it specifically in terms of its implications for freedom.

41. Hardman, "Before You Can Get Off Your Knees," 3.

42. Strachan, "Micro-independent record labels in the UK," 248.

43. McKay, *Senseless Acts of Beauty,* 101.

Chapter 4

1. On the roots of slam poetry, see for example Cristin Aptowicz, *Words in Your Face: A Guided Tour Through Twenty Years of the New York City Poetry Slam* (New York: Soft Skull, 2008), 4; Mark Eleveld, ed., *The Spoken Word Revolution: slam, hip hop & the poetry of a new generation* (Naperville, Ill.: sourcebooks mediaFusion, 2003), 80; Gary Mex Glazner, "Poetry Slam: An Introduction," in Gary Mex Glazner, ed., *Poetry Slam: The Competitive Art of Performance Poetry* (San Francisco: Manic D Press, 2000), 11; Gregory Harms, "Performance Art: Blood, Ice Skates, and Coyotes in the 20th Century," in Eleveld, *The Spoken Word Revolution*, 76–78; Terry Jacobus, "Poetic Pugilism," in Eleveld, *The Spoken Word Revolution*, 81–89, 85–88; Anne MacNaughton, "The Taos Poetry Circus," in Eleveld, *The Spoken Word Revolution*, 101–04, 101–02; Daniel Nester, "Foreword," in Aptowicz, *Words in Your Face*, xiii–xiv, xiv; Richard Prince, "Once a 'virgin, virgin' at the Green Mill," in Eleveld, *The Spoken Word Revolution*, 139–41; Marc Kelly Smith and Joe Kraynak, *The Complete Idiot's Guide to Slam Poetry* (Indianapolis, Ind.: Alpha Books, 2004), 4–7, 22; Susan Somers-Willett, *The Cultural Politics of Slam Poetry: Race, Identity, and the Performance of Popular Verse in America* (Ann Arbor, Mich.: The University of Michigan Press, 2009), 16, 52–67; and Cecily von Ziegesar, ed., *Slam* (New York: Alloy Books, 2000), 3.

2. On the genesis of poetry slam in its modern form, see for example Aptowicz, *Words in Your Face*, 94–96; Glazner, *Poetry Slam*, 11–12; Guy Le Charles Gonzalez, "The Revolution Will Be," in Mark Eleveld, ed., *The Spoken Word Revolution, Redux* (Naperville, Ill.: Sourcebooks MediaFusion, 2007), 23–27, 23; Jean Howard, "Performance Art, Performance Poetry—The Two Sisters," in Eleveld, *The Spoken Word Revolution*, 64–67, 65; Jeff Kass, "The 'Youuuuths': 'At base, we humans want to connect with each other . . . ,'" in Eleveld, *The Spoken Word Revolution, Redux*, 198–200, 198; Susan Somers-Willett, "Can Slam Poetry Matter?," *RATTLE* 13, no. 1 (2007), 85–90, 85; Marc Smith, "About Slam Poetry,"

in Eleveld, *The Spoken Word Revolution*, 116–20, 117–18; Smith and Kraynak, *The Complete Idiot's Guide*, 17, 31, 297, 304–13.

3. For examples see Smith and Kraynak, *The Complete Idiot's Guide*, 304–13.

4. Smith and Kraynak, *The Complete Idiot's Guide*, 17. For a very partial list of slam venues, see www.poetryslam.com, which also hosts a listserv.

5. On slam variations, see especially Bob Holman, "The Room," in Glazner, *Poetry Slam*, 15–21; and Smith and Kraynak, *The Complete Idiot's Guide*, 290.

6. http://www.poetryslam.com/content/what-poetry-slam-inc.

7. See www.poetryslam.com for information about PSI. See Smith and Kraynak, *The Complete Idiot's Guide*, 23–26, 42, 275–82 for additional discussion of the organization and functioning of PSI.

8. A full set of rules can be found at www.poetryslam.com.

9. Aptowicz, *Words in Your Face*, 38, 149–150. On slam touring, see also Jeffrey McDaniel, "Slam and the Academy," in Gary Mex Glazner, ed., *Poetry Slam: The Competitive Art of Performance Poetry* (San Francisco: Manic D Press, 2000), 35–37, 35; and Mikaela Renz, "Aftermath: Organizing Community," in Susan McAllister, Don McIver, Mikaela Renz, and Daniel S. Solis, eds., *A Bigger Boat: The Unlikely Success of the Albuquerque Poetry Slam Scene* (Albuquerque, N.Mex.: University of New Mexico Press, 2008), 319–21.

10. Aptowicz, *Words in Your Face*, 97.

11. Susan McAllister, "Slam Poetry Demystified," in McAllister, et al., *A Bigger Boat*, 29–30, 29.

12. The list of groups, businesses, political agencies, politicians, cities, counties, arts centers, radio stations, charitable groups, nonprofits, and a generic "all our fabulous volunteers" acknowledged for their role in helping sponsor the 2005 Albuquerque National Poetry Slam covers three single-spaced pages. See McAllister, et al., *A Bigger Boat*, 271–73.

13. Jacobus, "Poetic Pugilism," 89.

14. Smith, "About Slam Poetry," 119.

15. Luis J. Rodriguez, "Crossing Boundaries, Crossing Cultures: Poetry, Performance, and the New American Revolution," in Eleveld, *The Spoken Word Revolution*, 208–22, 210.

16. McAllister, et. al., *A Bigger Boat*, 19. Virginia Hampton estimated that the black population of Albuquerque doubled during the four days of NPS. Hampton, "Forty-Eight-Hour Poetry Jook Joint . . . Out ch'Yonda," in McAllister, et al., *A Bigger Boat*, 2008, 182–83, 183.

17. Marc Kelly Smith and Joe Kraynak, *Take the Mic: The Art of Performance Poetry Slam, and the Spoken Word* (Naperville, Ill.: Sourcebooks, Inc., 2009), 25. Smith and Kraynak refer to slam as a "rainbow coalition" (25).

18. Somers-Willett, *The Cultural Politics of Slam Poetry*, 11, 69.

19. Somers-Willett, *The Cultural Politics of Slam Poetry*, 7.

20. For example, the Albuquerque Slam Team was invited to perform at a National Democratic fundraiser in 2006, and at the city of Albuquerque's Fourth

of July celebration. See Daniel S. Solis, "Aftermath: The Wider Community," in McAllister, et al., *A Bigger Boat*, 313–14.

21. Somers-Willett, "Can Slam Poetry Matter?," 88.

22. Dana Gioia, *Can Poetry Matter? Essays on Poetry and American Culture*, Tenth Anniversary Edition (St. Paul, Minn.: Graywolf Press, 2002 [April, 1991]), 17.

23. Aptowicz, *Words in Your Face*, 249.

24. Dewey, *Art as Experience*, and Dewey, *The Public and Its Problems.*

25. Joseph Epstein, "Who Killed Poetry?" *Commentary* 86, no. 2 (1988): 14–15.

26. Dana Gioia, *Can Poetry Matter?*, 10, 19, 1. The titles of these Brahmin poets' and critics' ruminations themselves reveal a disregard or unawareness of slam poetry.

27. John Barr, "American Poetry in the New Century," *Poetry* 188, no. 5 (2006), 433–41, 433, 434.

28. Harold Bloom, "The Man in the Back Row Has a Question," *Paris Review* 154 (Spring 2000), 379.

29. Smith and Kraynak, *The Complete Idiot's Guide*, 8.

30. Jacobus, "Poetic Pugilism," 83.

31. Alix Olson, "Diary of a Slam Poet," *Ms.*, December 2000/January 2001, 66–73, 68.

32. Smith and Kraynak, *The Complete Idiot's Guide*, 9–10, 15, 20.

33. Glazner, *Poetry Slam*, 14.

34. Smith and Kraynak, *The Complete Idiot's Guide*, 22.

35. Aptowicz, *Words in Your Face*, 197–98.

36. John Dewey's *Art as Experience* emphasized these aspects of aesthetic and artistic experience in his own approach to determining good from bad art.

37. On this point, see especially Eleveld, *The Spoken Word Revolution*, 11–12.

38. Tori Amos, quoted in von Ziegesar, *Slam*, 5.

39. Billy Collins, "Poems on the page, Poems in the air," in Eleveld, *The Spoken Word Revolution*, 3–5, 4. See also Aptowicz, *Words in Your Face*, xx; Renz, "Aftermath," 320; and Daniel S. Solis, "Letter from the Chair of NPS 2005 (from the Event Program)," in McAllister, et al., *A Bigger Boat*, 168–69, 169.

40. Mike Henry, Karyna McGlynn, Danny Solis, Susan B. Anthony Somers-Willett, Genevieve Van Cleve, Hilary Thomas, Phil West, and Wammo, "Group Discussion on the Group Piece," in Glazner, *Poetry Slam*, 214–20, 216.

41. Genevieve Van Cleve, "Tour," in Glazner, *Poetry Slam*, 139. See again Dewey (*Art as Experience*), who emphasized the community-creating role of successful art.

42. Aptowicz interview with Somers-Willett, in Aptowicz, *Words in Your Face*, 336. On the commercial pressures within the slam community, see also Aptowicz, *Words in Your Face*, 240–63; McDaniel, "Slam and the Academy," 35; Jerry Quickley, "hip hop Poetry," in Eleveld, *The Spoken Word Revolution*, 42;

Smith, "About Slam Poetry," 116; and Somers-Willett, *The Cultural Politics of Slam Poetry*, 9–13.

43. Dolan, *Utopia in Performance*, 6.

Chapter 5

1. Joe Austin, *Taking the Train: How Graffiti Art Became an Urban Crisis in New York City* (New York: Columbia University Press, 2001), 271.

2. Jeffrey Deitch, Roger Gastman, and Aaron Rose, *Art in the Streets* (New York: Skira Rizzoli Publications, Inc./Museum of Contemporary Art, Los Angeles, 2011), 10.

3. Austin, *Taking the Train*, 5.

4. Daniel J. D'Amico, "Thou Shall Not Paint: A Libertarian Understanding of the Problems Associated with Graffiti on Public v. Private Property," http://www.graffiti.org/faq/d_amico.html, 2003, 1, accessed 2/26/2012. D'Amico's libertarian analysis predictably condones graffiti when sprayed on public property, in which case he views it as "liberation of stolen property from a coercive government" (2). On the other hand, when sprayed on private property, it is a criminal act of vandalism and should be punished accordingly.

5. Richard S. Christen, "Hip Hop Learning: Graffiti as an Educator of Urban Teenagers," *Educational Foundations* 17:4 (Fall 2003), 57–82, 3; and Anna Wacławek, *Graffiti and Street Art* (London: Thames and Hudson, 2011), 43.

6. C. Noble, "City Space: A Semiotic and Visual Exploration of Graffiti and Public Space in Vancouver," http://www.graffiti.org/faq/noble_semiotic_warfare2004.html, 2004, downloaded 2/26/2012, 2.

7. Austin, *Taking the Train*, 4–5, quoting the New York City Metropolitan Transportation Authority.

8. New York City mayor Michael Bloomberg, quoted in Jeff Chang, "American Graffiti," *Village Voice*, September 10, 2002, http://www.villagevoice.com/2002-09-10/books/american-graffiti/1/, downloaded 2/26/12.

9. Cedar Lewisohn, *Street Art: The Graffiti Revolution* (New York: Harry N. Abrams, Inc., 2008), 99.

10. Denver resident Charles A. Hillestad, in an interview with *Rocky Mountain News*, July 7, 1989; and New York City parks commissioner Hubert Stern, quoted in Austin, *Taking the Train*, 269.

11. Mayor Bloomberg, quoted in Chang, "American Graffiti," 1.

12. Mayor Bloomberg, quoted in Chang, "American Graffiti," 1. According to one surreal assessment by Federico Pena, mayor of Denver from 1982 to 1998, "No matter how good it looks, graffiti is ugly." Quoted in Jeff Ferrell, *Crimes of Style: Urban Graffiti and the Politics of Criminality* (Boston: Northeastern University Press, 1996), 179.

13. On the different graffiti forms see, for example, Nicholas Ganz, *Graffiti World: Street Art from Five Continents* (London: Thames and Hudson, 2004), 8–10;

Steve Grody, *Graffiti L.A.: Street Styles and Art* (New York: Harry N. Abrams, Inc., 2006), 15–18; and Wacławek, *Graffiti and Street Art*, 13–19.

14. For a firsthand account of the dangers sometimes faced by graffiti and street artists, see Dan Witz, *In Plain View: 30 Years of Artworks Illegal and Otherwise* (Berkeley, Calif.: Gingko Press, 2010), 35.

15. On the history of graffiti and street art, see for example Deitch, Gastman, and Rose, *Art in the Streets*, 296–303; Ganz, *Graffiti World*, 8–10; Grody, *Graffiti L.A.*, 9–11; Russell Howze, *Stencil Nation: graffiti, community, and art* (San Francisco: Manic D. Press, 2008), 12–17; Lewisohn, *Street Art*, 26–27; and James Prigoff, "Foreword," in Grody, *Graffiti L.A.*, 7–8. For early accounts of graffiti and its social significance, see for example Henry Chalfant and Martha Cooper, *Subway Art* (New York: Holt, Rinehart, and Winston, 1984); Norman Mailer, Jon Naar, and Mervyn Kurlansky, *Faith of Graffiti* (New York: Praeger, 1974); and Allan Schwartzman, *Street Art*, (New York: The Dial Press, Doubleday & Co., 1985).

16. Henry Chalfant, quoted in Lewisohn, *Street Art*, 7; Deitch, Gastman, and Rose, *Art in the Streets*, 10.

17. See for example Lewisohn, *Street Art*, 31; and Wacławek, *Graffiti and Street Art*, 12.

18. [No author listed], "'TAKI 183' Spawns Pen Pals," *New York Times*, July 21, 1971.

19. Prigoff, "Foreword," 7.

20. @149st, "Female Writers," The Cyber Bench: Documenting New York City Graffiti, 2001, http://www.at149st.com/women.html, accessed 2/26/2012, 2.

21. Nancy Macdonald, quoted in Nicholas Ganz, *Graffiti Women: Street Art from Five Continents* (London: Thames and Hudson, Ltd., 2006), 12. See @149st, "Female Writers," for a list of female writers from various periods beginning in the early 1970s and extending into the 2000s. On women's participation in the graffiti and street art scenes, see for example Ganz, *Graffiti Women*, 2006; Grody, *Graffiti L.A.*, 203; and Lewisohn, *Street Art*, 46.

22. Lewisohn, *Street Art*, 46; Grody, *Graffiti L.A.*, 203.

23. Mandy Moore and Leanne Prain, *Yarn Bombing: The Art of Crochet and Knit Graffiti* (Vancouver, B.C.: Arsenal Pulp Press, 2009), 17.

24. Ganz, *Graffiti World*, 18.

25. Caleb Neelon and Sonik, "Ten Years [1994–2004] of Art Crimes: The Effects and Educational Functions of the Internet in Graffiti," http://www.graffiti.org/faq/ten_years_of_art_crimes.html, 2004, accessed 2/26/2012, 1; Ethel Seno, ed., with Banksy, Carlo McCormick, Anne Pasternak, Marc & Sara Schiller, and J. Tony Serra, *Trespass: A History of Uncommissioned Urban Art* (Berlin: Teschen GmbH, 2010), 11.

26. Ganz, *Graffiti World*, 10. See also Neelon and Sonik, "Ten Years of Art Crimes," 2. For other examples of websites featuring graffiti and street art, see at149st.com, barcelonastreetart.net, bombingscience.com, craftster.org, craftsanity.com, craftzine.com, crochetville.org/forum, ffffound.com, flickr.com,

graffiti-art center, graffitiresearchlab.com, JustSeeds.org, StencilArchive.org, StencilRevolution.com, stitchnbitch.org/snb_groups.htm, streetsy.com, supernaturale.com, visualorgasm.com, whipup.net, and woostercollective.com.

27. Wacławek, *Graffiti and Street Art*, 178.

28. See, for example, Sam Parker, "Artist Uses Flowers to Tackle Homophobic Abuse," April 19, 2013, http://www.buzzfeed.com/samjparker/artist-uses-flowers-to-tackle-homophobic-abuse, accessed 8/15/2013; and Seno, *Trespass*, 113.

29. Seno, *Trespass*, 115. See http://urbanprankster.com/2009/06/nazi-petting-zoo/ for a video rendition, accessed 8/15/2013.

30. See the images at http://arts.guardian.co.uk/pictures/0,,1543331,00.html, accessed 8/15/2013; and http://www.stencilrevolution.com/banksy-art-prints/girl-and-soldier/, accessed 8/15/2013.

31. Witz, *In Plain View*, 164; http://www.danwitz.com/index.php?article_id=45, accessed 8/15/2013.

32. http://www.stencilrevolution.com/profiles/blek-le-rat/.

33. On reclaiming public space using performance art, see Josh MacPhee and Nato Thompson, "The Department of Space and Land Reclamation [DSLR]," in MacPhee and Reuland, *Realizing the Impossible*, 220–27. MacPhee and Thompson describe DSLR "street interventions" in Chicago beginning in 2001 that included rolling a giant ball of trash down Michigan Avenue from the Chicago Museum of Contemporary Art to the Art Institute of Chicago, and "neighborhood sonification modules" in which loud compact disc players placed inside camp coolers were chained in front of gentrification sites such as Starbucks and expensive lofts.

34. Lewisohn, *Street Art*, 75.

35. Quoted in Moore and Prain, *Yarn Bombing*, 69.

36. Seno, *Trespass*, 10–11.

37. Seno, *Trespass*, 130.

38. Shannon Holopainen, "Six Theses on the Tag," http://www.graffiti.org/faq/holopainen.html, 2006, 2, accessed 2/26/2012.

39. Chang, "American Graffiti," 4.

40. Noble, "City Space," 2.

41. Chang, "American Graffiti," 6–7; Robert Lederman, "It's All Under Control," http://www.graffiti.org/faq/control.html, 1997, 1, accessed 2/26/2012.

42. Kevin Element, "Hard Hitting Modern Perspective on Hip Hop Graffiti," http://www.graffiti.org/faq/element.html, 1996, 1, accessed 2/26/2012; Seno, *Trespass*, 311.

43. Quoted in Howze, *Stencil Nation*, 106.

44. Quoted in Seno, *Trespass*, 311.

45. Ibid., 311.

46. Chaka, a prolific tagger arrested in 1991 for graffiti vandalism, was sentenced to one year in jail and 1,500 hours of graffiti cleanup. Gkae, arrested in 1997 for the same infraction, spent seventeen months in jail for a three-year sentence, and was charged $100,000 in fines. London writer Enzo received a three-year prison term for his graffiti work. In 1983, Michael Stewart was killed

by transit police while writing on a 14th Street station wall. On sanctions against graffiti and street artists, see for example Chang, "American Graffiti," 4; Grody, *Graffiti L.A.*, 36–38; Howze, *Stencil Nation*, 107; Noble, "City Space," 7; and Seno, *Trespass*, 311.

47. Chang, "American Graffiti," 7.

48. The Aids Memorial Quilt merits special mention as another example of public art that builds upon traditionally feminine artwork. See http://www.aidsquilt.org/about/the-aids-memorial-quilt for a history.

49. Wacławek, *Graffiti and Street Art*, 72.

50. Jørgensen, quoted in Moore and Prain, *Yarn Bombing*, 205–06.

51. http://theresahoneywell.com/home.html. For these and many other illustrations of yarn bombing, see for example craftivism.com, freddierobins.com, incogknito.com, Knitta Please, and magdasayeg.com.

52. On graffiti and street art as providing a voice for the relatively marginalized, see for example Sarah Giller, "Graffiti: Inscribing Transgression on the Urban Landscape," http://www.graffiti.org/faq/giller.html, 1997, 1, 5, accessed 2/26/2012; Grody, *Graffiti L.A.*, 180; Howze, *Stencil Nation*, 8; and Wacławek, *Graffiti and Street Art*, 43.

53. Banksy, in Seno, *Trespass*, 6; Jeremiah McNichols, "Visualizing Dissent: Graffiti As Art," http://thinkingpictures.blogspot.com/2006/07/visualizing-dissent-graffiti-as-art.html, July 26, 2006, accessed 2/26/2012, 4.

54. Ferrell, *Crimes of Style*, 178.

55. For examples of subvertising, see *Adbusters* magazine, a nonprofit that runs no ads, whose slogan reads "We are a global network of culture jammers and creatives working to change the way information flows, the way corporations wield power, and the way meaning is produced in our society." http://www.adbusters.org/magazine.

56. D. S. Black, quoted in Howze, *Stencil Nation*, 82.

57. For discussions of gallery exhibitions of graffiti and street art, see for example Grody, *Graffiti L.A.*, 41, 284–85; Lewisohn, *Street Art*, 42, 93; and Wacławek, *Graffiti and Street Art*, 7, 58–59.

58. See the story in Allan Kozinn, "Gas Station Banksy Brings $209,000 at Auction," *New York Times*, December 9, 2013.

59. On the commercialization of graffiti and street art, see for example Deitch, Gastman, and Rose, *Art in the Streets*, 287–88; Howze, *Stencil Nation*, 96–97; Lewisohn, *Street Art*, 41, 81, 120; and Wacławek, *Graffiti and Street Art*, 170–71.

60. Noble, "City Space," 15.

Chapter 6

1. For various definitions, see [no author listed], "Dadaist lunacy or the future of protest?," SIRC: Social Issues Research Centre, 2003, http://www.sirc.org/

articles/flash_mob.shtml, accessed 9/27/2013; [no author listed], "Get Ready for a Flash Mob!," *People Magazine* 60:8, 8/25/2003; Ruth Carter, *Flash Mob Law: The Legal Side of Planning and Participating in Pillow Fights, No Pants Rides, and Other Shenanigans* (Chicago: American Bar Association, 2013), 1; Michelle Delio, "Flash Mobs Get a Dash of Danger," *Wired.com,* September 10, 2003, http://www.wired.com/culture/lifestyle/news/2003/09/60364?currentPage=all, accessed 9/10/2013; Philip Stanley Grant, Anjali Bal, and Michael Parent, "Operatic flash mob: Consumer arousal, connectedness and emotion," *Journal of Consumer Behaviour* 11 (2012), 244–51, 244; Amy Harmon, "Ideas & Trends: Flash Mobs; Guess Some People Don't Have Anything Better to Do," *New York Times*, August 17, 2003; Ruud Kaulingfreks and Samantha Warren, "SWARM: Flash mobs, mobile clubbing and the city," *Culture and Organization* 16:3 (September 2010), 211–27, 211; and Ronald Williamson and J. Howard Johnston, *The School Leader's Guide to Social Media* (Larchmont, N.Y.: Eye on Education, Inc., 2012), 20.

2. Others have proposed flash mob categories. According to Georgiana Gore, while the earliest flash mobs may have been about fun and play, more recent flash mob dances fall into three categories: celebration, political, and commercial (Gore, "Flash Mob Dance and the Territorialisation of Urban Movement," *Anthropological Notebooks* 16:3 (2010), 125–31, 126–127). Virág Molnár distinguished between five different kinds of flash mobs based on sociality or function: 1) atomised flash mobs, 2) interactive flash mobs, 3) performance flash mobs, 4) political flash mobs, and 5) advertising. See Virág Molnár, "Reframing Public Space Through Digital Mobilization: Flash Mobs and the Futility of Contemporary Urban Youth Culture," 2009, http://isites/harvard.edu/fs/docs/icb.topic497840.files/Molnar_Reframing-Public-Space.pdf.

3. Some flash mob enthusiasts wish to exclude this last "criminal" form from the category of flash mob. Others use different or modified terminology such as "flash mob crime," "flash mob assault," or "flash rob" to distinguish them from legal and unthreatening flash mobs. Whatever the validity of their arguments, the media routinely refer to "criminal" flash mobs as flash mobs, and I will follow suit.

4. Carter, *Flash Mob Law*, xiii.

5. Lauren Claycomb, "Regulating Flash Mobs: Seeking a Middle Ground Approach that Preserves Free Expression and Maintains Public Order," *University of Louisville Law Review*, volume 51 (2013), 375–405, 378.

6. Carter, *Flash Mob Law*, 3.

7. Charles Shaw, organizer of an August 2003 flash mob in Chicago, quoted in Claycomb, "Regulating Flash Mobs," 387.

8. [no author], "Waterfight in Stanley Park, but are flash mobs starting to lose their edge?," *Vancouver Sun*, July 12, 2008.

9. On the roots of flash mobs, see Carter, *Flash Mob Law*, 2; Claycomb, "Regulating Flash Mobs," 380, 388; Gloria Goodale, "'Tis the season for flash mobs, you say? They're just getting started," *Christian Science Monitor*, December 23, 2010; Gore, "Flash Mob Dance," 128; Jekaterina Lavrinec, "From a 'Blind Walker' to an 'Urban Curator': Initiating 'Emotionally Moving Situations' in Pub-

lic Spaces," *Borderland Studies* 4:1 (2011), 54–63, 58; John Muse, "Flash Mobs and the Diffusion of Audience," *Theater* 40:3 (2010), 9–23, 11; and Howard Rheingold, *Smart mobs, the next social revolution* (Cambridge, Mass.: Basic Books, 2002).

10. Bill Wasik, "My Crowd: Or, Phase 5: A report from the inventor of the flash mob," *Harper's Magazine*, March 2006, 56–66. For examples of others who credit Wasik with the invention of flash mobs, see Claycomb, "Regulating Flash Mobs," 375; Delio, "Flash Mobs Get a Dash of Danger"; and Eric Tucker and Thomas Watkins, "Flash Mobs, No Longer Just Dance Parties and Pillow Fights, Pose Growing Criminal Threat: Cops," in *Cybercrime*, ed. Louise I. Gerdes (Farmington Hills, Mich.: Greenhaven Press, 2013), 92–97, 93.

11. See a full description in Muse, "Flash Mobs," 16–17. The No Pants Subway Ride is now an annual event, attracting thousands of participants in multiple cities around the world.

12. Joung Yoon-soo, "Flash Mobs: The Younger Generation Declares Its Cultural Independence," *Koreana*, Spring 2005, 74–77, 75.

13. See Paul Krassner, "Corporations co-opted the flash mob," *Salon*, September 23, 2013.

14. Bill Wasik, "#Riot: Self-Organized, Hyper-Networked Revolts—Coming to a City Near You," *Wired*, December 16, 2011, http://www.wired.com/magazine/2011/12/ff_riots/all/1, accessed 9/13/2013, 5.

15. [no author], "Fads of the Year," *People* 60:26, 12/29/2003.

16. Harmon, "Ideas & Trends."

17. Richard Leydier, "The New Underground," *Art Press* no. 296 (December 2003), 5.

18. Andrew Losowsky, "A 21st-century protest," *The Guardian*, March 24, 2004.

19. Delio, "Flash Mobs Get a Dash of Danger."

20. Ibid.

21. Mary Hawkesworth, *Political Worlds of Women: Activism, Advocacy, and Governance in the Twenty-First Century* (Boulder, Colo.: Westview Press, 2012), 286.

22. John Saunders, "Flash Mobs," in *Acts of Citizenship*, eds. Engin F. Isin and Greg M. Nielsen (London: Zed Books, 2008), 295–96, 295; [no author], "Waterfight in Stanley Park."

23. Gloria Goodale, "Art Attack! Random acts of culture," *Christian Science Monitor*, December 21, 2010; Muse, "Flash Mobs," 14.

24. Quoted in Kaulingfreks and Warren, "SWARM," 222.

25. See especially Kaulingfreks and Warren, "SWARM," on the rhizomatic, unmanaged structure of flash mobs.

26. Hawkesworth, *Political Worlds of Women*, 287.

27. Kaulingfreks and Warren, "SWARM," 220.

28. See Kaulingfreks and Warren, "SWARM"; and Michael Hardt and Antonio Negri, *Multitude: War and Democracy in the Age of Empire* (New York: The Penguin Press, 2004). See also Jeff Shantz's discussion of black blocs that "form,

dissolve and re-form as the situation requires, re-constituting themselves on a different basis for each political demonstration." Shantz, *Living Anarchy*, 74.

29. Shantz, *Living Anarchy*, 69, calls for a "criminology of resistance" that "would take seriously the criminalized activities undertaken by anarchists" in order to appreciate the ways that behaviors dubbed criminal actually represent attempts to realize human dignity and self-determination.

30. Dolan, *Utopia in Performance*, 10–12.

31. Dolan, *Utopia in Performance*, 10. See also Lavrinec, "From a 'Blind Walker' to an 'Urban Curator,'" 59, on the creation of "new solidarities" through performance in public space; Lawrence Grossberg, *We Gotta Get Out of This Place: Political Conservatism and Popular Culture* (New York: Routledge, 1992) on the creation of "affective communities" through music; and John Dewey, especially his *Art as Experience*, on the capacity of art to break through walls separating worlds of experience, creating new possibilities for solidarity and community.

32. [no author], "St. Vincent nurses organize flash mob for safe staffing," *Massachusetts Nurse*, February/March 2011, 7; [no author], "Flash Mob Choir in Protest at Cuts to NHS Services," *Nursing Standard* 27:23 (February 6, 2013), 33.

33. [no author], "WMS 421 Spring 2013 Activism Videos: V-Day Brockport Dances in Opposition to Violence Against Women," *Dissenting Voices* 2:1, Article 10, http://digitalcommons.brockport.edu/dissentingvoices/vol2/iss1/10/.

34. Bilbo Poynter, "Idle No More: Canada's indigenous 'Occupy' movement," *Christian Science Monitor*, January 10, 2013.

35. Michael J. Fitzpatrick, "The Constitutionality of Restricting the Use of Social Media: Flash Mob Protests Warrant First Amendment Protections," *Seton Hall Law Review*, 2013; Wasik, "#Riot," 6.

36. Ibid., 12.

37. Saunders, "Flash Mobs," 295; Kaulingfreks and Warren, "SWARM," 214.

38. Muse, "Flash Mobs," 14.

39. Carter, *Flash Mob Law*, 44, 109.

40. Elizabeth Dias, Katy Steinmetz, and Mark Thompson, "High-Tech Crackdown," *Time International (Atlantic Edition)* 178:8 (August 29, 2011).

41. See Marcus Anthony Hunter, *Black Citymakers: How the Philadelphia Negro Changed Urban America* (Oxford: Oxford University Press, 2013); and Patrik Jonsson, "Philadelphia 'flash mobs': black mayor takes aim at black community," *Christian Science Monitor*, August 15, 2011.

42. Hunter, *Black Citymakers*, 205.

43. "Flash Mobs Step from Dancing to Crimes," 2011, http://criminal.lawyers.com/Criminal-Law-Basics/Flash-Mobs-Step-From-Dancing-to-Crimes.html, accessed 1/27/14. See also Cyril Josh Barker, "Fear Factor: Does NYC have a mob problem?," *The New York Amsterdam News*, April 8–April 14, 2010, 3; Jonsson, "Philadelphia 'flash mobs'"; Hunter, *Black Citymakers*, 205; Ian Urbina, "Mobs are born as word grows by text message," *New York Times*, March 24, 2010.

44. Claycomb, "Regulating Flash Mobs," 375; Pat Galbincea and Peter Krouse, "More than 200 turn out for meeting on flash mobs," *Cleveland Plain*

Dealer, July 14, 2011, emphasis added; and Steve Lasky, "The Medium is the Message," *Security Technology Executive*, October 2011, 8.

45. See for example Pat Murphy, "7-11 flash mob: Maryland police investigate store robbery," *Christian Science Monitor*, August 16, 2011; and Tucker and Watkins, "Flash Mobs," 94. For other examples of criminalized flash mobs, see Eoin O'Carroll's account of criminalized water pistol fights in Colchester, England and Tehran, respectively (Eoin O'Carroll, "Flash mobs or splash mob? UK man arrested for planning water pistol fight," *Christian Science Monitor*, August 15, 2011); Norman Oder et al.'s description of police intervention in a flash mob of students at the University of Tennessee Chattanooga on April 23, 2009 (Norman Oder, Andrew Albanese, Lynn Blumenstein, and Josh Hadro, "'Flash Mob' at UTC Library Dispersed with Mace," *Library Journal*, May 15, 2009, 13–14; and Bill Wasik's description of a flash mob in greater London on August 7, 2011 involving extensive police intervention (Wasik, "#Riot," 6).

46. Tom Feran, "Sheriff, local groups to seek answers at flash-mob forums," *Cleveland Plain Dealer*, July 9, 2011.

47. New York City mayor Michael Bloomberg, quoted in Barker, "Fear factor," 3.

48. Patrik Jonsson, " 'Flash mob' crimes: How good are police at tracking down culprits?," *Christian Science Monitor*, August 22, 2011.

49. Lasky, "The Medium is the Message," 8.

50. Stan Donaldson, "'Flash Mob' fears spur a rush to judgment," *Cleveland Plain Dealer*, December 19, 2011.

51. BBC News, "Mixed feelings over Philadelphia's flash-mob curfew," August 12, 2011, http://www.bbc.co.uk/news.world-us-canada-14509831?print=true, accessed 9/13/2013.

52. See especially Claycomb, "Regulating Flash Mobs," 382–86 for a discussion of legislative attempts in three states to criminalize and curb flash mobs.

53. [no author], "Social-media-organized violence is scary, dangerous and intolerable," letters to the editor, *Cleveland Plain Dealer*, August 28, 2011; [no author], "To fight crime, focus on the mob," 2011; Patrik Jonsson, "Flash mob attacks: Rising concern over black teen involvement," *Christian Science Monitor*, August 9, 2011; and Tucker and Watkins, "Flash Mobs," 97.

54. Hunter, *Black Citymakers*, 207.

55. James C. Scott, *Seeing Like A State* (New Haven, Conn.: Yale University Press, 1999), 9.

56. http://www.youtube.com/watch?v=7EYAUazLI9k

57. See especially Carter, *Flash Mob Law*, Ch. 8: "Using Flash Mobs as a Marketing Tool," 69–75; and Krassner, "Corporations co-opted the flash mob."

58. Gore, "Flash Mob Dance," 128.

59. Wasik, quoted in Francis Heaney, "The Short Life of Flash Mobs: Interview with Bill Wasik," *Stay Free! Magazine* (June 2005), http://www.stayfreemagazine.org/archives/24/flash-mobs-history.html.

60. See for example http://vimeo.com/30156652, http://www.youtube.com/watch?v=hp3gz56fyRs, and http://www.youtube.com/watch?v=Vnf8ZQNRZIo.

61. Halavais, quoted in Gloria Goodale, "'Tis the season for flash mobs."

62. Lavrinec, "From a 'Blind Walker' to an 'Urban Curator,'" 54.

63. Dewey, *The Public and Its Problems*, 349. See also Augusto Boal, *Theatre of the Oppressed* (London: Pluto Press, 1993), who envisioned audience members as "spect-actors" who participate in performance, liberating themselves from social restrictions and opening the possibility of thinking and acting autonomously.

64. Robin Kelley, *Freedom Dreams: The Black Radical Imagination* (Boston: Beacon Press, 2002), 11.

65. http://www.youtube.com/watch?v=Ds8ryWd5aFw. For a similar video of an opera flash mob, this one performed in a Philadelphia market, see http://www.youtube.com/watch?v=_zmwRitYO3w.

66. Dolan, *Utopia in Performance*, 2, 92.

67. Muse, "Flash Mobs," 19.

68. Ibid., 21.

69. On anger and rage as vital components of social movements and powerful motivators for activism, see for example Jeff Goodwin, James M. Jasper, and Francesca Polletta, eds., *Passionate Politics: Emotions and Social Movements* (Chicago: Chicago University Press, 2001); David Ost, "Politics as the Mobilization of Anger: Emotions in Movements and in Power," *European Journal of Social Theory* 7:2 (2004), 229–44; and Robert Solomon, *A Passion for Justice: Emotions and the Origins of the Social Contract* (New York: Addison Wesley, 1990).

70. Leita Walker, "Synchronized, collective, and so far pointless," *Christian Science Monitor*, August 4, 2003.

Chapter 7

1. On this notion of citizen-artist, see Linda Frye Burnham and Steven Durland, eds., *The Citizen Artist: 20 Years of Art in the Public Arena* (Gardiner, N.Y.: Critical Press, 1998); and Mark Mattern and Nancy Love, "Activist Arts, Community Development, and Democracy," in Love and Mattern, eds., *Doing Democracy: Activist Art and Cultural Politics* (Albany, N.Y.: SUNY Press, 2013), 339–66, especially 355–56.

2. Dewey, *The Public and Its Problems*, 349.

3. On this criticism of anarchism as utopian, and responses against it, see for example Randall Amster, "Anarchy, utopia, and the state of things to come," in Amster, et al., *Contemporary Anarchist Studies*, 290–301; and Gelderloos, *Anarchy Works*. For a critique of participatory democracy as utopian, see especially Mark Warren, "What Should We Expect from More Democracy? Radically Democratic Responses to Politics," *Political Theory* 24:2 (1996), 241–70.

4. Martha Ackelsberg, *Resisting Citizenship: Feminist Essays on Politics, Community, and Democracy* (New York and London: Routledge, 2010), 103;

emphasis in original. On the practical learning that occurs within autonomous spaces, see also Chris Carlsson, *Nowtopia: How Pirate Programmers, Outlaw Bicyclists, and Vacant-Lot Gardeners Are Inventing the Future Today* (Oakland, Calif.: AK Press, 2008), 53; Joel Olson, "The problem with infoshops and insurrection: US anarchism, movement building, and the racial order," in Amster, et al., *Contemporary Anarchist Studies*, 35–45; and Shantz, *Living Anarchy*, 24.

5. Chad Lavin and Chris Russill, "The Ideology of the Epidemic," *New Political Science: A Journal of Politics and Culture* 32:1 (March 2010), 65–82, 65.

6. Malcolm Gladwell, *The Tipping Point: How Little Things Can Make a Big Difference* (New York: Back Bay Books/Little Brown and Company, 2002 [2000]).

7. Lavin and Russill, "The Ideology of the Epidemic," 65.

8. As Lavin and Russill point out, Gladwell built on the work of precursors already working with the tropes of epidemiology. These include, for example, Richard Brodie, *Virus of the Mind: The New Science of the Meme* (Seattle: Integral Press, 1996); Thomas Friedman, *The Lexus and the Olive Tree: Understanding Globalization* (New York: Farrar Strauss, and Giroux, 1999), pp. xi–xv, who compared the 1997 Asian financial crisis to a virus; Hardt and Negri, *Empire*, 136, who wrote that "the age of globalization is the age of universal contagion"; and Douglas Rushkoff, *Media Virus!* (New York: Ballantine, 1994). More recently, a literature on "biopolitics" derived in part from Michel Foucault and Gilles Deleuze employs the terms of immunology and epidemics. See for example Roberto Esposito, *Bios: Biopolitics and Philosophy* (St. Paul, Minn.: University of Minnesota Press, 2008); Miguel Vatter, "Biopolitics: From Surplus Value to Surplus Live," *Theory & Event* 12:2 (2009); and Jan Wright and Valeria Harwood, eds, *Biopolitics and the "Obesity Epidemic"* (New York: Routledge, 2009).

9. Gladwell, *The Tipping Point*, 7, 9, 12, 139.

10. Lavin and Russill, "The Ideology of the Epidemic," 82, 79.

11. George McKay, *Senseless Acts of Beauty*, 101.

12. Shantz, *Living Anarchy*, 92. A black bloc is a group of anarchists organized for direct action.

13. Portwood-Stacer, *Lifestyle Politics and Radical Activism*, 7.

14. Shantz, *Living Anarchy*, 91.

Bibliography

"Dadaist lunacy or the future of protest?" SIRC: Social Issues Research Centre, 2003. http://www.sirc.org/articles/flash_mob.shtml.

"Fads of the Year." *People* 60:26, 12/29/2003.

"Flash Mob Choir in Protest at Cuts to NHS Services." *Nursing Standard* 27:23 (February 6, 2013): 33.

"Flash Mobs Step from Dancing to Crimes," 2011. http://criminal.lawyers.com/Criminal-Law-Basics/Flash-Mobs-Step-From-Dancing-to-Crimes.html.

"Get Ready for a Flash Mob!" *People Magazine* 60:8, 8/25/2003.

"Social-media-organized violence is scary, dangerous and intolerable." Letters to the editor. *Cleveland Plain Dealer*, August 28, 2011.

"St. Vincent nurses organize flash mob for safe staffing." *Massachusetts Nurse*, February/March 2011, 7.

"'TAKI 183' Spawns Pen Pals," *New York Times*, July 21, 1971.

"Waterfight in Stanley Park, but are flash mobs starting to lose their edge?" *Vancouver Sun*, July 12, 2008.

"WMS 421 Spring 2013 Activism Videos: V-Day Brockport Dances in Opposition to Violence Against Women." *Dissenting Voices* 2:1, article 10. http://digitalcommons.brockport.edu/dissentingvoices/vol2/iss1/10/.

@149st. "Female Writers." The Cyber Bench: Documenting New York City Graffiti, 2001. http://www.at149st.com/women.html.

Ackelsberg, Martha. *Resisting Citizenship: Feminist Essays on Politics, Community, and Democracy*. New York and London: Routledge, 2010.

Adams, John. *The Political Writings of John Adams*. Edited by George W. Carey. Washington, D.C.: Regnery, 2000.

Albert, Michael, and Robin Hahnel. *Looking Forward: Participatory Economics for the Twenty First Century*. Boston: South End Press, 1991.

Amster, Randall. "Anarchy, utopia, and the state of things to come." In *Contemporary Anarchist Studies: An introductory anthology of anarchy in the academy*. Edited by Randall Amster, Abraham DeLeon, Luis A. Fernandez, Anthony J. Nocella, II, and Deric Shannon. New York: Routledge, 2009, 290–301.

Amster, Randall, Abraham DeLeon, Luis A. Fernandez, Anthony J. Nocella, II, and Deric Shannon. *Contemporary Anarchist Studies: An introductory anthology of anarchy in the academy*. New York: Routledge, 2009.

Antliff, Allan. *Anarchy and Art: From the Paris Commune to the Fall of the Berlin Wall*. Vancouver: Arsenal Pulp Press, 2007.

Aptowicz, Cristin. *Words in Your Face: A Guided Tour Through Twenty Years of the New York City Poetry Slam*. New York: Soft Skull, 2008.

Archer, Robin. *Economic Democracy: The Politics of Feasible Socialism*. Oxford: Clarendon Press, 1995.

Aristotle. *Politics*. Translated by Ernest Barker. Oxford: Oxford University Press, 1998.

Austin, Joe. *Taking the Train: How Graffiti Art Became an Urban Crisis in New York City*. New York: Columbia University Press, 2001.

Bakunin, Michael. In *Bakunin On Anarchy: Selected Works of the Activist-Founder of World Anarchism*. Edited by Sam Dolgoff. London: Allen & Unwin, 1973.

———. In *The Political Philosophy of Bakunin*. Edited by G. P. Maximoff. New York: The Free Press, 1953.

———. "Letter to a Frenchman on the Present Crisis," (1870), http://marxists.org/reference/archive/bakunin/works/1870/letter-frenchman.htm.

Barber, Benjamin. *Strong Democracy: Participatory Politics for a New Age*. Berkeley, Calif.: University of California Press, 1984.

Barker, Cyril Josh. "Fear Factor: Does NYC have a mob problem?" *The New York Amsterdam News*, April 8–14, 2010.

Barr, John. "American Poetry in the New Century." *Poetry* 188, no. 5 (2006): 433–41.

BBC News. "Mixed feelings over Philadelphia's flash-mob curfew." August 12, 2011. http://www.bbc.co.uk/news.world-us-canada-14509831?print=true.

Benn, S. I., and W. L. Weinstein. "Being Free to Act and Being a Free Man." *Mind* 80 (1971): 194–211.

Bennett, Tony. "Popular Culture and the 'Turn to Gramsci.'" In *Cultural Theory and Popular Culture: A Reader*. Edited by John Storey. Harlow, England: Pearson Longman, 2009, 81–87.

Berlin, Isaiah. *Two Concepts of Liberty*. Oxford: Clarendon Press, 1958.

Bey, Hakim (aka Peter Lamborn Wilson). *T.A.Z.: The Temporary Autonomous Zone, Ontological Anarchy, Poetic Terrorism*. Brooklyn, N.Y.: Automedia, 1991.

Black, Bob. *Anarchy after Leftism*. Columbia, Mo.: C.A.L. Press, 1997.

Bloom, Harold. "The Man in the Back Row Has a Question." *Paris Review* 154 (Spring 2000): 379.

Boal, Augusto. *Theatre of the Oppressed*. London: Pluto Press, 1993.

Bohman, James. *Public Deliberation: Pluralism, Complexity, and Democracy*. Cambridge, Mass.: MIT Press, 1996.

Bookchin, Murray. *Remaking Society: Pathways to a Green Future*. Boston: South End Press, 1990.

———. *Social Anarchism or Lifestyle Anarchism: An Unbridgeable Chasm*. San Francisco: AK Press, 1995.

———. *Anarchism, Marxism, and the Future of the Left: Interviews and Essays, 1993–1998*. San Francisco: AK Press, 1999.

Bowles, Samuel, and Herbert Gintis. *Democracy and Capitalism*. New York: Basic Books, 1986.

———. "A Political and Economic Case for the Democratic Enterprise." In *The Idea of Democracy*. Edited by David Copp, Jean Hampton, and John Roemer. Cambridge: Cambridge University Press, 1993, 375–99.

Boyte, Harry. *Community Is Possible: Repairing America's Roots*. New York: Harper & Row, 1984.

———. *CommonWealth: A Return to Citizen Politics*. New York: Free Press, 1989.

Buccellato, James. "Sign of the Outlaw: Liberal Boundaries, Social Banditry and the Political Act." *New Political Science: A Journal of Politics and Culture* 34.3 (September 2012): 271–94.

Buck, Eric. "The flow of experiencing in anarchic economies." In *Contemporary Anarchist Studies: An introductory anthology of anarchy in the academy*. Edited by Randall Amster, Abraham DeLeon, Luis A. Fernandez, Anthony J. Nocella, II, and Deric Shannon. New York: Routledge, 2009, 57–69.

Buechele, Tom. "DIY Masculinity: Masculine Identity in DIY Punk Subculture." Presentation at the 2006 Annual Meeting of the American Sociological Association, Montreal, Canada.

Burnham, Linda Frye, and Steven Durland, eds. *The Citizen Artist: 20 Years of Art in the Public Arena*. Gardiner, N.Y.: Critical Press, 1998.

Carlsson, Chris. *Nowtopia: How Pirate Programmers, Outlaw Bicyclists, and Vacant-Lot Gardeners Are Inventing the Future Today*. Oakland, Calif.: AK Press, 2008.

Carter, Ruth. *Flash Mob Law: The Legal Side of Planning and Participating in Pillow Fights, No Pants Rides, and Other Shenanigans*. Chicago: American Bar Association, 2013.

Chalfant, Henry, and Martha Cooper. *Subway Art*. New York: Holt, Rinehart, and Winston, 1984.

Chang, Jeff. "American Graffiti." *Village Voice*, September 10, 2002. http://www.villagevoice.com/2002-09-10/books/american-graffiti/1/.

Chomsky, Noam. "Introduction." In *Anarchism: From Theory to Practice*. Edited by Daniel Guérin. New York: Monthly Review Press, 1970, vii–xx.

Christen, Richard S. "Hip Hop Learning: Graffiti as an Educator of Urban Teenagers." *Educational Foundations* 17:4 (Fall 2003): 57–82.

Claycomb, Lauren. "Regulating Flash Mobs: Seeking a Middle Ground Approach that Preserves Free Expression and Maintains Public Order." *University of Louisville Law Review*, volume 51 (2013): 375–405.

Cohn, Jesse. *Anarchism and the crisis of representation: Hermeneutics, aesthetics, politics*. Cranbury, N.J.: Rosemont Publishing & Printing Corp, 2006.

Collins, Billy. "Poems on the page, Poems in the air." In *The Spoken Word Revolution: slam, hip hop & the poetry of a new generation*. Edited by Mark Eleveld. Naperville, Ill.: sourcebooks mediaFusion, 2003, 3–5.

Connolly, William. *The Terms of Political Discourse*, 2nd ed. Princeton, N.J.: Princeton University Press, 1983.

Constant, Benjamin. "The Liberty of the Ancients Compared with That of the Moderns" [1816]. In *The Libertarian Reader: Classic and Contemporary Readings from Lao-Tzu to Milton Friedman*. Edited by David Boaz. New York: Free Press, 1997, 65–70.

Cook, Terrence, and Patrick Morgan, eds. *Participatory Democracy*. San Francisco: Canfield Press, 1971.

Dahl, Robert. *A Preface to Economic Democracy*. Berkeley, Calif.: University of California Press, 1985.

Dale, Pete. "It was easy, it was cheap, so what?: Reconsidering the DIY principle of punk and indie music." *Popular Music History* 3:2 (2008): 171–93.

Daly, Herman, Thomas Prugh, and Robert Costanza. *The Local Politics of Global Sustainability*. Washington, D.C.: Island Press, 2000.

D'Amico, Daniel J. "Thou Shall Not Paint: A Libertarian Understanding of the Problems Associated with Graffiti on Public v. Private Property," 2003. http://www.graffiti.org/faq/d_amico.html.

Day, Richard. *Gramsci Is Dead: Anarchist Currents in the Newest Social Movements*. London: Pluto Press, 2005.

Deitch, Jeffrey, Roger Gastman, and Aaron Rose. *Art in the Streets*. New York: Skira Rizzoli Publications, Inc./Museum of Contemporary Art, Los Angeles, 2011.

Delio, Michelle. "Flash Mobs Get a Dash of Danger." *Wired.com*, September 10, 2003. http://www.wired.com/culture/lifestyle/news/2003/09/60364?currentPage=all.

Dewey, John. *Ethics*. In *John Dewey: The Middle Works, 1899–1924*, volume 5. Edited by Jo Ann Boydston. Carbondale, Ill.: Southern Illinois University Press, 1978 [1908].

———. *The Public and Its Problems*. In *John Dewey: The Later Works, 1925–1953*, volume 2: 1925–1927. Edited by Jo Ann Boydston. Carbondale, Ill.: Southern Illinois University Press, 1988 [1927], 235–372.

———. *Individualism, Old and New*. In *John Dewey: The Later Works, 1925–1953*, volume 5: 1929–1930. Edited by Jo Ann Boydston. Carbondale, Ill.: Southern Illinois University Press, 1988 [1929/30], 41–144.

———. *Art as Experience*. In *John Dewey: The Later Works, 1925–1953*, volume 10: 1934. Edited by Jo Ann Boydston. Carbondale, Ill.: Southern Illinois University Press, 1989 [1934]).

———. *Liberalism and Social Action*. In *John Dewey: The Later Works, 1925–1953*, volume 11. Edited by Jo Ann Boydston. Carbondale, Ill.: Southern Illinois University Press, 1991 [1935], 1–66.

———. "Liberty and Social Control." In *John Dewey: The Later Works, 1925–1953*, volume 11: 1935–1937. Edited by Jo Ann Boydston. Carbondale, Ill.: Southern Illinois University Press, 1991 [1935], 360–63.

———. *Freedom and Culture*. In *John Dewey: The Later Works, 1925–1953*, Volume 13: 1938–1939. Edited by Jo Ann Boydston. Carbondale, Ill.: Southern Illinois University Press, 1991 [1939], 65–188.

Dias, Elizabeth, Katy Steinmetz, and Mark Thompson. "High-Tech Crackdown." *Time International (Atlantic Edition)* 178:8 (August 29, 2011).

Digeser, Peter. "The Fourth Face of Power." *Journal of Politics* 54, no. 4 (November 1992): 977–1007.

Dolan, Jill. *Utopia in Performance: Finding Hope at the Theater*. Ann Arbor, Mich.: The University of Michigan Press, 2005.

Donaldson, Stan. " 'Flash Mob' fears spur a rush to judgment," *Cleveland Plain Dealer*, December 19, 2011.

Dow, Gregory. *Governing the Firm: Workers' Control in Theory and Practice*. Cambridge: Cambridge University Press, 2003.

Downes, Julia. "Riot Grrrl: The Legacy and Contemporary Landscape of DIY Feminist Cultural Activism." In *Riot Grrrl: Revolution Girl Style Now!* Edited by Nadine Monem. London: Black Dog Publishing, 2007, 11–49.

Element, Kevin. "Hard Hitting Modern Perspective on Hip Hop Graffiti," 1996. http://www.graffiti.org/faq/element.html.

Eleveld, Mark, ed. *The Spoken Word Revolution: slam, hip hop & the poetry of a new generation*. Naperville, Ill.: Sourcebooks MediaFusion, 2003.

———, ed. *The Spoken Word Revolution, Redux*. Naperville, Ill.: Sourcebooks MediaFusion, 2007.

Ellerman, David. *The Democratic Worker-Owned Firm: A New Model for the East and West*. London: Unwin Hyman, 1990.

Epstein, Joseph. "Who Killed Poetry?" *Commentary* 86, no. 2 (1988): 14–15.

Feran, Tom. "Sheriff, local groups to seek answers at flash-mob forums." *Cleveland Plain Dealer*, July 9, 2011.

Ferrell, Jeff. *Crimes of Style: Urban Graffiti and the Politics of Criminality*. Boston: Northeastern University Press, 1996.

Fitzpatrick, Michael J. "The Constitutionality of Restricting the Use of Social Media: Flash Mob Protests Warrant First Amendment Protections." *Seton Hall Law Review*, 2013.

Franks, Benjamin. *Rebel Alliances: The Means and Ends of Contemporary British Anarchisms*. Edinburgh: AK Press, 2006.

———. "Vanguards and Paternalism." In *New Perspectives on Anarchism*. Edited by Nathan J. Jun and Shane Wahl. Lanham, Md: Rowman and Littlefield Publishers, Inc., 2010, 99–120.

Galbincea, Pat, and Peter Krouse. "More than 200 turn out for meeting on flash mobs." *Cleveland Plain Dealer*, July 14, 2011.

Ganz, Nicholas. *Graffiti World: Street Art from Five Continents*. London: Thames and Hudson, 2004.

———. *Graffiti Women: Street Art from Five Continents*. London: Thames and Hudson, 2006.

Gelderloos, Peter. *Anarchy Works*. San Francisco: Ardent Press, 2010.

George, Donald. *Economic Democracy: The Political Economy of Self-Management and Participation*. London: Macmillan Press, 1993.

Giller, Sarah. "Graffiti: Inscribing Transgression on the Urban Landscape," 1997. http://www.graffiti.org/faq/giller.html.

Gioia, Dana. *Can Poetry Matter? Essays on Poetry and American Culture*, Tenth Anniversary Edition. St. Paul, Minn.: Graywolf Press, 2002 [1991].

Gladwell, Malcolm. *The Tipping Point: How Little Things Can Make a Big Difference*. New York: Back Bay Books/Little Brown and Company, 2002 [2000].

Glazner, Gary Mex, ed. *Poetry Slam: The Competitive Art of Performance Poetry*. San Francisco: Manic D Press, 2000.

Goldman, Emma. "What I Believe." In *Red Emma Speaks*. Edited by Alix Kates Shulman. London: Wildwood House, 1979 [1908].

———. *The Social Significance of Modern Drama*. New York: Applause Theater Book Publishers, 1987 [1914].

———. *My Disillusionment in Russia*. Mineola, N.Y.: Dover Publications, 2003 [1923].

———. *Living My Life*, volume I. New York: Alfred Knopf, 1931.

———. *Living My Life*, volume II. Hempstead, N.Y.: Garden City Publishing Company, 1934.

Gonzalez, Guy Le Charles. "The Revolution Will Be." In *The Spoken Word Revolution, Redux*. Edited by Mark Eleveld. Naperville, Ill.: Sourcebooks MediaFusion, 2007, 23–27.

Goodale, Gloria. "Art Attack! Random acts of culture." *Christian Science Monitor*, December 21, 2010.

———. "'Tis the season for flash mobs, you say? They're just getting started." *Christian Science Monitor*, December 23, 2010.

Goodwin, Jeff, James M. Jasper, and Francesca Polletta, eds. *Passionate Politics: Emotions and Social Movements*. Chicago: Chicago University Press, 2001.

Gordon, Uri. *Anarchy Alive! Anti-Authoritarian Politics from Practice to Theory*. London: Pluto Press, 2008.

———. "Power and Anarchy: In/equality + In/visibility in Autonomous Politics." In *New Perspectives on Anarchism*. Edited by Nathan J. Jun and Shane Wahl. Lanham, Md.: Rowman and Littlefield Publishers, Inc., 2010, 39–66.

Gore, Georgiana. "Flash Mob Dance and the Territorialisation of Urban Movement." *Anthropological Notebooks* 16:3 (2010): 125–31.

Gosling, Tim. "'Not for Sale': The Underground Network of Anarcho-Punk." In *Music Scenes: Local, Translocal, and Virtual*. Edited by Andy Bennett and Richard Peterson. Nashville, Tenn.: Vanderbilt University Press, 2004, 168–83.

Graeber, David. "The New Anarchists." *New Left Review* 13, January–February 2002, newleftreview.org/11/13/david-graeber-the-new-anarchists, accessed 5/24/12.

———. "Anarchism, academia, and the avant-garde." In *Contemporary Anarchist Studies: An introductory anthology of anarchy in the academy*. Edited by

Randall Amster, Abraham DeLeon, Luis A. Fernandez, Anthony J. Nocella, II, and Deric Shannon. New York: Routledge, 2009, 103–12.

———. *Direct Action: An Ethnography*. Edinburgh: AK Press, 2009.

———. *The Democracy Project: A History, a Crisis, a Movement*. London: Allen Lane, 2013.

Gramsci, Antonio. *Selections from the Prison Notebooks of Antonio Gramsci*. Edited and translated by Quintin Hoare and Geoffrey Nowell Smith. New York: International Publishers, 1971.

Grant, Philip Stanley, Anjali Bal, and Michael Parent. "Operatic flash mob: Consumer arousal, connectedness and emotion." *Journal of Consumer Behaviour* 11 (2012): 244–51.

Greenberg, Edward. *Workplace Democracy: The Political Effects of Participation*. Ithaca, N.Y.: Cornell University Press, 1986.

Grody, Steve. *Graffiti L.A.: Street Styles and Art*. New York: Harry N. Abrams, Inc., 2006.

Grossberg, Lawrence. *We Gotta Get Out of This Place: Political Conservatism and Popular Culture*. New York: Routledge, 1992.

Guérin, Daniel. *Anarchism: From Theory to Practice*. New York: Monthly Review Press, 1970.

Habermas, Jurgen. *Between Facts and Norms*. Translated by William Rehg. Cambridge, Mass.: MIT Press, 1996.

Hall, Stuart. "Notes on Deconstructing 'The Popular.'" In *Peoples' History and Socialist Theory*. Edited by Raphael Samuel. London: Routledge and Kegan Paul Ltd., 1981, 227–40.

———. "Cultural Studies and Its Theoretical Legacies." In *Cultural Studies*. Edited by Lawrence Grossberg, Cary Nelson, and Paula Treichler. New York: Routledge, 1992, 277–94.

Hampton, Virginia. "Forty-Eight-Hour Poetry Jook Joint . . . Out ch'Yonda." In *A Bigger Boat: The Unlikely Success of the Albuquerque Poetry Slam Scene*. Edited by Susan McAllister, Don McIver, Mikaela Renz, and Daniel S. Solis. Albuquerque, N.Mex.: University of New Mexico Press, 2008, 182–83.

Hardman, Emilie. "Before You Can Get Off Your Knees: Profane Existence and Anarcho-Punk as a Social Movement." Paper presented at the annual meeting of the American Sociological Association, New York City, August 11, 2007.

Hardt, Michael, and Antonio Negri. *Empire*. Cambridge, Mass.: Harvard University Press, 2000.

———. *Multitude: War and Democracy in the Age of Empire*. New York: The Penguin Press, 2004.

Harmon, Amy. "Ideas & Trends: Flash Mobs; Guess Some People Don't Have Anything Better to Do." *New York Times*, August 17, 2003.

Harms, Gregory. "Performance Art: Blood, Ice Skates, and Coyotes in the 20th Century." In *The Spoken Word Revolution: slam, hip hop, & the poetry of a new generation*. Edited by Mark Eleveld. Naperville, Ill.: Sourcebooks MediaFusion, 2003, 76–78.

Hawkesworth, Mary. *Political Worlds of Women: Activism, Advocacy, and Governance in the Twenty-First Century*. Boulder, Colo.: Westview Press, 2012.

Heaney, Francis. "The Short Life of Flash Mobs: Interview with Bill Wasik." *Stay Free! Magazine* (June 2005). http://www.stayfreemagazine.org/archives/24/flash-mobs-history.html.

Hebdige, Dick. "From Culture to Hegemony." In *The Cultural Studies Reader*. Edited by Simon During. London: Routledge, 1993, 357–67.

Held, David. *Models of Democracy*. Cambridge: Polity Press, 1987.

Hemingway, Andrew. "Individualism and/or Solidarity? 'Anarchist Modernism' in the U.S." *Oxford Art Journal* 25:2 (2002): 165–70.

Henry, Mike, Karyna McGlynn, Danny Solis, Susan B. Anthony Somers-Willett, Genevieve Van Cleve, Hilary Thomas, Phil West, and Wammo. "Group Discussion on the Group Piece." In *Poetry Slam: The Competitive Art of Performance Poetry*. Edited by Gary Mex Glazner. San Francisco: Manic D Press, 2000, 214–20.

Hesmondhalgh, David. "Post-Punk's attempt to democratise the music industry: the success and failure of Rough Trade." *Popular Music* 16:3 (1997): 255–74.

Hilmer, Jeffrey. "The State of Participatory Democratic Theory." *New Political Science: A Journal of Politics and Culture* 32:1 (March 2010): 43–63.

Hofstadter, Richard. *The American Political Tradition and the Men Who Made It*. New York: Vintage Books, 1989 [1948].

Holloway, John. *Change the World Without Taking Power*. London: Pluto Press, 2002.

———. *Crack Capitalism*. London and New York: Pluto Press, 2010.

Holman, Bob. "The Room." In *Poetry Slam: The Competitive Art of Performance Poetry*. Edited by Gary Mex Glazner. San Francisco: Manic D Press, 2000, 15–21.

Holopainen, Shannon. "Six Theses on the Tag," 2006. http://www.graffiti.org/faq/holopainen.html.

Horkheimer, Max. *Eclipse of Reason*. London and New York: Continuum, [1946] 2004.

Horrox, James. "Reinventing Resistance: Constructive Activism in Gustav Landauer's Social Philosophy." In *New Perspectives on Anarchism*. Edited by Nathan J. Jun and Shane Wahl. Lanham, Md.: Rowman and Littlefield Publishers, Inc., 2010, 189–207.

Howard, Jean. "Performance Art, Performance Poetry—The Two Sisters." In *The Spoken Word Revolution*. Edited by Mark Eleveld. Naperville, Ill: Sourcebooks MediaFusion, 2003, 64–67.

Howze, Russell. *Stencil Nation: graffiti, community, and art*. San Francisco: Manic D. Press, 2008.

Hudson, William. *American Democracy in Peril: Eight Challenges to America's Future*. Washington, D.C.: CQ Press, 2010.

Hunter, Marcus Anthony. *Black Citymakers: How the Philadelphia Negro Changed Urban America*. Oxford: Oxford University Press, 2013.

Jacobus, Terry. "Poetic Pugilism." In *The Spoken Word Revolution: slam, hip hop, & the poetry of a new generation*. Edited by Mark Eleveld. Naperville, Ill.: Sourcebooks MediaFusion, 2003, 81–89.

Jefferson, Thomas. *The Life and Selected Writings of Thomas Jefferson*. Edited by Adrienne Koch and William Peden. New York: Random House, 1944.

———. *Basic Writings of Thomas Jefferson*. Edited by Philip Foner. New York: Willey Book Company, 1944.

———. Letter to James Madison, October 28, 1785. In The Founders' Constitution. Chicago: The University of Chicago Press. Volume 1, chapter 15, document 32. Available at http://press-pubs.uchicago.edu/founders/documents/v1ch15s32.html.

Jones, Pattrice. "Free as a bird: natural anarchism in action." In *Contemporary Anarchist Studies: An introductory anthology of anarchy in the academy*. Edited by Randall Amster, Abraham DeLeon, Luis A. Fernandez, Anthony J. Nocella, II, and Deric Shannon. New York: Routledge, 2009, 236–46.

Jonsson, Patrik. "Flash mob attacks: Rising concern over black teen involvement." *Christian Science Monitor*, August 9, 2011.

———. "Philadelphia 'flash mobs': black mayor takes aim at black community." *Christian Science Monitor*, August 15, 2011.

———. "'Flash mob' crimes: How good are police at tracking down culprits?" *Christian Science Monitor*, August 22, 2011.

Jun, Nathan J. and Shane Wahl, eds. *New Perspectives on Anarchism*. Lanham, Md.: Rowman and Littlefield Publishers, Inc., 2010.

Juris, Jeffrey S. "Anarchism, or the Cultural Logic of Networking." In *Contemporary Anarchist Studies: An introductory anthology of anarchy in the academy*. Edited by Randall Amster, Abraham DeLeon, Luis A. Fernandez, Anthony J. Nocella, II, and Deric Shannon. New York: Routledge, 2009, 213–23.

Kass, Jeff. "The 'Youuuuths': At base, we humans want to connect with each other." In *The Spoken Word Revolution, Redux*. Edited by Mark Eleveld. Naperville, Ill.: Sourcebooks MediaFusion, 2007, 198–200.

Kaulingfreks, Ruud, and Samantha Warren. "SWARM: Flash mobs, mobile clubbing and the city." *Culture and Organization* 16:3 (September 2010): 211–27.

Kelley, Robin. *Freedom Dreams: The Black Radical Imagination*. Boston: Beacon Press, 2002.

Kemmis, Daniel. *Community and the Politics of Place*. Norman, Okla.: University of Oklahoma Press, 1990.

Kinna, Ruth. *Anarchism: A Beginner's Guide*. Oxford: One World Publications, 2005.

Kozinn, Allan. "Gas Station Banksy Brings $209,000 at Auction." *New York Times*, December 9, 2013.

Krassner, Paul. "Corporations co-opted the flash mob." *Salon*, September 23, 2013.

Kropotkin, Peter. "Appeal to the Young." In *Kropotkin's Revolutionary Pamphlets*. Edited by Roger N. Baldwin. New York: Dover Press, 1970 [1880].

Landauer, Gustav. *For Socialism*. Translated by David J. Parent. St. Louis, Mo.: Telos Press, 1978 [1911].

———. *Revolution and Other Writings: A Political Reader*. Edited and translated by Gabriel Kuhn. Oakland, Calif.: PM Press, 2010.

Lasky, Steve. "The Medium is the Message." *Security Technology Executive*, October 2011, 8.

Lavin, Chad, and Chris Russill. "The Ideology of the Epidemic." *New Political Science: A Journal of Politics and Culture* 32:1 (March 2010): 65–82.

Lavrinec, Jekaterina. "From a 'Blind Walker' to an 'Urban Curator': Initiating 'Emotionally Moving Situations' in Public Spaces." *Borderland Studies* 4:1 (2011): 54–63.

Lederman, Robert. "It's All Under Control," 1997. http://www.graffiti.org/faq/control.html.

Lewisohn, Cedar. *Street Art: The Graffiti Revolution*. New York: Harry N. Abrams, Inc., 2008.

Leydier, Richard. "The New Underground." *Art Press* 296 (December 2003): 5.

Loizidou, Elena. "'This Is What Democracy Looks Like.'" In *How Not to Be Governed: Readings and Interpretations from a Critical Anarchist Left*. Edited by Jimmy Casas Klausen and James Martel. Lanham, Md: Lexington Books, 2011, 167–87.

Lopez, Ricardo. "Most 'not engaged' at work, poll finds." *The Cleveland Plain Dealer*, June 20, 2013.

Losowsky, Andrew. "A 21st-century protest." *The Guardian*, March 24, 2004.

Lynd, Staughton, and Andrej Grubacic. *Wobblies & Zapatistas: Conversations on Anarchism, Marxism and Radical History*. Oakland, Calif.: PM Press, 2008.

MacNaughton, Anne. "The Taos Poetry Circus." In *The Spoken Word Revolution: slam, hip hop, & the poetry of a new generation*. Edited by Mark Eleveld. Naperville, Ill.: Sourcebooks MediaFusion, 2003, 101–04.

MacPhee, Josh, and Erik Reuland, eds. *Realizing the Impossible: Art Against Authority*. Oakland, Calif.: AK Press, 2007.

MacPhee, Josh, and Nato Thompson. "The Department of Space and Land Reclamation." In *Realizing the Impossible: Art Against Authority*. Edited by Josh MacPhee and Erik Reuland. Oakland, Calif.: AK Press, 2007, 220–27.

Macpherson, C. B. *The Life and Times of Liberal Democracy*. New York: Oxford University Press, 1977.

Madison, James. "Federalist No. 39" [1788]. In Alexander Hamilton, James Madison, and John Jay, *The Federalist Papers*. Toronto: Bantam Books, 1982.

Maeckelbergh, Marianne. *The Will of the Many: How the Alterglobalisation Movement is Changing the Face of Democracy*. London: Pluto Press, 2009.

Mailer, Norman, Jon Naar, and Mervyn Kurlansky. *Faith of Graffiti*. New York: Praeger, 1974.

Malatesta, Errico. *Errico Malatesta: His Life and Ideas*. Edited by Vernon Richards. London: Freedom Press, 1977.

Malleson, Tom. "Economic Democracy: The Left's Big Idea for the Twenty-First Century?" *New Political Science: A Journal of Politics and Culture* 35.1 (March 2013): 84–108.

Mansbridge, Jane. *Beyond Adversary Democracy*. New York: Basic Books, 1980.

Marcos, Subcomandante. "First Declaration Against Neoliberalism and for Humanity," January 30, 2006. http://struggle.ws/mexico/ezln/ccri_1st_dec_real.html.

Marshall, Peter. *Demanding the Impossible: A History of Anarchism*. Oakland, Calif.: PM Press, 2010 [1992].

Martin, Brian. "Democracy without Elections." In *Reinventing Anarchy, Again*. Edited by Howard J. Ehrlich. Edinburgh: AK Press, 1996, 123–36.

Mattern, Mark. "Cajun music, cultural revival: theorizing political action in popular music." *Popular Music and Society* 22:2 (1998): 31–48.

Mattern, Mark, and Nancy S. Love. "Activist Arts, Community Development, and Democracy." In *Doing Democracy: Activist Art and Cultural Politics*. Edited by Nancy S. Love and Mark Mattern. Albany, New York: SUNY Press, 2013, 339–66.

May, Todd. "Anarchism from Foucault to Rancière." In *Contemporary Anarchist Studies: An introductory anthology of anarchy in the academy*. Edited by Randall Amster, Abraham DeLeon, Luis A. Fernandez, Anthony J. Nocella, II, and Deric Shannon. New York: Routledge, 2009, 11–25.

———. "Introduction." In *New Perspectives on Anarchism*. Edited by Nathan J. Jun and Shane Wahl. Lanham, MD: Rowman and Littlefield Publishers, Inc., 2010, 1–5.

McAllister, Susan. "Slam Poetry Demystified." In *A Bigger Boat: The Unlikely Success of the Albuquerque Poetry Slam Scene*. Edited by Susan McAllister, Don McIver, Mikaela Renz, and Daniel S. Solis. Albuquerque, N.Mex.: University of New Mexico Press, 2008, 29–30.

McAllister, Susan, Don McIver, Mikaela Renz, and Daniel S. Solis, eds. *A Bigger Boat: The Unlikely Success of the Albuquerque Poetry Slam Scene*. Albuquerque, N.Mex.: University of New Mexico Press, 2008.

McDaniel, Jeffrey. "Slam and the Academy." In *Poetry Slam: The Competitive Art of Performance Poetry*. Edited by Gary Mex Glazner. San Francisco: Manic D Press, 2000, 35–37.

McKay, George. *Senseless Acts of Beauty: Cultures of Resistance since the Sixties*. London: Verso, 1996.

McKay, George, ed. *DiY Culture: Party & Protest in Nineties Britain*. London: Verso, 1998.

McNichols, Jeremiah. "Visualizing Dissent: Graffiti As Art," July 26, 2006. http://thinkingpictures.blogspot.com/2006/07/visualizing-dissent-graffiti-as-art.html.

Milstein, Cindy. "Reappropriate the Imagination!" In *Realizing the Impossible: Art Against Authority*. Edited by Josh MacPhee and Erik Reuland. Oakland, Calif.: AK Press, 2007, 296–307.

Molnár, Virág. "Reframing Public Space Through Digital Mobilization: Flash Mobs and the Futility of Contemporary Urban Youth Culture," 2009. http://isites/harvard.edu/fs/docs/icb.topic497840.files/Molnar_Reframing-Public-Space.pdf.

Moore, Mandy, and Leanne Prain. *Yarn Bombing: The Art of Crochet and Knit Graffiti*. Vancouver: Arsenal Pulp Press, 2009.

Morland, Dave, and John Carter. "Anarchism and Democracy." In *Democracy and Participation: Popular protest and new social movements*. Edited by Malcolm Todd and Gary Taylor. London: Merlin Press, 2004, 78–95.

Murphy, Pat. "7-11 flash mob: Maryland police investigate store robbery." *Christian Science Monitor*, August 16, 2011.

Muse, John. "Flash Mobs and the Diffusion of Audience." *Theater* 40:3 (2010): 9–23.

Mutz, Diana C. *Hearing the Other Side: Deliberative versus Participatory Democracy*. Cambridge: Cambridge University Press, 2006.

Neelon, Caleb, and Sonik. "Ten Years [1994–2004] of Art Crimes: The Effects and Educational Functions of the Internet in Graffiti," 2004. http://www.graffiti.org/faq/ten_years_of_art_crimes.html.

Nester, Daniel. "Foreword." In *Words in Your Face: A Guided Tour Through Twenty Years of the New York City Poetry Slam*. Edited by Cristin Aptowicz. New York: Soft Skull, 2008, xiii–xiv.

Nettlau, Max. "Anarchist: Communist or Individualist? Both." http://theanarchistlibrary.org/library/Max_Nettlau__Anarchism__Communist_or_Individualist__Both.pdf.

Noble, C. "City Space: A Semiotic and Visual Exploration of Graffiti and Public Space in Vancouver," 2004. http://www.graffiti.org/faq/noble_semiotic_warfare2004.html.

O'Carroll, Eoin. "Flash mobs or splash mob? UK man arrested for planning water pistol fight." *Christian Science Monitor*, August 15, 2011.

Oder, Norman, Andrew Albanese, Lynn Blumenstein, and Josh Hadro. "'Flash Mob' at UTC Library Dispersed with Mace." *Library Journal*, May 15, 2009, 13–14.

O'Hara, Craig. *The Philosophy of Punk: More Than Noise*. London: AK Press, 1999.

Olson, Alix. "Diary of a Slam Poet." *Ms.*, December 2000/January 2001, 66–73.

Olson, Joel. "The problem with infoshops and insurrection: US anarchism, movement building, and the racial order." In *Contemporary Anarchist Studies: An introductory anthology of anarchy in the academy*. Edited by Randall Amster, Abraham DeLeon, Luis A. Fernandez, Anthony J. Nocella, II, and Deric Shannon. New York: Routledge, 2009, 35–45.

Ost, David. "Politics as the Mobilization of Anger: Emotions in Movements and in Power." *European Journal of Social Theory* 7:2 (2004): 229–44.

Parker, Sam. "Artist Uses Flowers to Tackle Homophobic Abuse," April 19, 2013. http://www.buzzfeed.com/samjparker/artist-uses-flowers-to-tackle-homophobic-abuse.

Pateman, Carole. *Participation and Democratic Theory*. Cambridge: Cambridge University Press, 1970.

———. "Participatory Democracy Revisited." *Perspectives on Politics* 10:1 (March 2012): 7–19.

Patterson, Tim. "Notes on the Historical Application of Marxist Cultural Theory." *Science and Society* 34:3 (1975): 257–91.

Peña, Manuel. *The Texas-Mexican Conjunto: History of a Working Class Music*. Austin, Tex.: University of Texas Press, 1985.

Portwood-Stacer, Laura. *Lifestyle Politics and Radical Activism*. New York: Bloomsbury, 2013.

Poynter, Bilbo. "Idle No More: Canada's indigenous 'Occupy' movement." *Christian Science Monitor*, January 10, 2013.

Prigoff, James. "Foreword." In *Graffiti L.A.: Street Styles and Art*. Edited by Steve Grody. New York: Harry N. Abrams, Inc., 2006, 7–8.

Prince, Richard. "Once a 'virgin, virgin' at the Green Mill." In *The Spoken Word Revolution: slam, hip hop, & the poetry of a new generation*. Edited by Mark Eleveld. Naperville, Ill.: Sourcebooks MediaFusion, 2003, 139–41.

Proudhon, Pierre. *Du principe de l'art et de sa destination social*. Paris: Garnier Frères, 1865.

———. *Solution du problème social*. Translated by Jesse Cohn. Paris: Éditions Lacroix, 1868.

Punkerslut. "Delegation, Not Representation: On the Practical Methods of Anarchism for Decentralized, Anti-Authoritarian Organizing. http://www.punkerslut.com/articles/delegation_not_representation.html.

Quickley, Jerry. "hip hop Poetry." In *The Spoken Word Revolution: slam, hip hop & the poetry of a new generation*. Edited by Mark Eleveld. Naperville, Ill.: Sourcebooks MediaFusion, 2003, 38–42.

Rawls, John. "A Well-Ordered Society." In *In Defense of Human Dignity*. Edited by Robert Kraynak and Glenn Tinder. Notre Dame, Ind.: University of Notre Dame Press, 2003.

Renz, Mikaela. "Aftermath: Organizing Community." In *A Bigger Boat: The Unlikely Success of the Albuquerque Poetry Slam Scene*. Edited by Susan McAllister, Don McIver, Mikaela Renz, and Daniel S. Solis. Albuquerque, N.Mex.: University of New Mexico Press, 2008, 319–21.

Rheingold, Howard. *Smart mobs, the next social revolution*. Cambridge, Mass.: Basic Books, 2002.

Rocker, Rudolf. *Anarcho-Syndicalism: Theory and Practice*. London: Secker and Warburg, 1938.

Rodriguez, Luis J. "Crossing Boundaries, Crossing Cultures: Poetry, Performance, and the New American Revolution." In *The Spoken Word Revolution:*

slam, hip hop, & the poetry of a new generation. Edited by Mark Eleveld. Naperville, Ill.: Sourcebooks MediaFusion, 2003, 208–22.

Rosen, Paul. "'It was easy, it was cheap, go and do it!': Technology and Anarchy in the UK Music Industry." In *Twenty-First Century Anarchism*. Edited by Jon Purkis and James Bowen. London: Cassell, 1997, 99–116.

Rothbard, Murray. *For a New Liberty: The Libertarian Manifesto*. New York: Collier, 1978.

Rousseau, Jean Jacque. *Rousseau's Political Writings*. Edited by Alan Ritter and Julia Conaway Bondanella. Translated by Julia Conaway Bondanella. New York: W. W. Norton, 1988 [1762].

Roussopoulos, Dimitrios, and C. George Benello, eds. *Participatory Democracy: Prospects for Democratizing Democracy*. Montreal: Black Rose Books, 2005 [1970].

Saunders, John. "Flash Mobs." In *Acts of Citizenship*. Edited by Engin F. Isin and Greg M. Nielsen. London: Zed Books, 2008, 295–96.

Schwartzman, Allan. *Street Art*. New York: The Dial Press, Doubleday & Co., 1985.

Scott, James C. *Seeing Like A State*. New Haven, Conn.: Yale University Press, 1999.

Seno, Ethel, ed., with Banksy, Carlo McCormick, Anne Pasternak, Marc & Sara Schiller, and J. Tony Serra. *Trespass: A History of Uncommissioned Urban Art*. Berlin: Teschen GmbH, 2010.

Shannon, Deric. "Raising the Curtain: Anarchist Economics, Resistance, and Culture." *Peace Studies Journal* 4:2 (2011): 47–56.

Shannon, Deric, Anthony J. Nocella II, & John Asimakopoulos, eds. *The Accumulation of Freedom: Writings on Anarchist Economics*. Oakland, Calif.: AK Press, 2012.

Shantz, Jeff. *Living Anarchy: Theory and Practice in Anarchist Movements*. Bethesda, Md.: Academica Press, 2009.

Shapiro, Ian. *The State of Democratic Theory*. Princeton, N.J.: Princeton University Press, 2003.

Smith, Marc. "About Slam Poetry." In *The Spoken Word Revolution: slam, hip hop, & the poetry of a new generation*. Edited by Mark Eleveld. Naperville, Ill.: Sourcebooks MediaFusion, 2003, 116–20.

Smith, Marc Kelly, and Joe Kraynak. *The Complete Idiot's Guide to Slam Poetry*. Indianapolis, Ind.: Alpha Books, 2004.

———. *Take the Mic: The Art of Performance Poetry Slam, and the Spoken Word*. Naperville, Ill.: Sourcebooks, Inc., 2009.

Solis, Daniel S. "Aftermath: The Wider Community." In *A Bigger Boat: The Unlikely Success of the Albuquerque Poetry Slam Scene*. Edited by Susan McAllister, Don McIver, Mikaela Renz, and Daniel S. Solis. Albuquerque, N.Mex.: University of New Mexico Press, 2008, 313–14.

———. "Letter from the Chair of NPS 2005 (from the Event Program)." In *A Bigger Boat: The Unlikely Success of the Albuquerque Poetry Slam Scene*.

Edited by Susan McAllister, Don McIver, Mikaela Renz, and Daniel S. Solis. Albuquerque, N.Mex.: University of New Mexico Press, 2008, 168–69.

Solomon, Robert. *A Passion for Justice: Emotions and the Origins of the Social Contract.* New York: Addison Wesley, 1990.

Somers-Willett, Susan. "Can Slam Poetry Matter?" *RATTLE* 13, no. 1 (2007): 85–90.

———. *The Cultural Politics of Slam Poetry: Race, Identity, and the Performance of Popular Verse in America.* Ann Arbor, Mich.: The University of Michigan Press, 2009.

Spannos, Chris, ed. *Real Utopia: Participatory Society for the 21st Century.* Oakland, Calif.: AK Press, 2008.

Stirner, Max. *The Ego and His Own.* London: A. C. Fifield, 1912 [1845].

Strachan, Robert. "Micro-independent record labels in the UK: Discourse, DIY cultural production and the music industry." *European Journal of Cultural Studies* 10:2 (2007): 245–65.

Thucydides. *History of the Peloponnesian War.* Translated by Richard Crawley. New York: E. P. Dutton, 1910.

Tucker, Eric, and Thomas Watkins. "Flash Mobs, No Longer Just Dance Parties and Pillow Fights, Pose Growing Criminal Threat: Cops." In *Cybercrime.* Edited by Louise I. Gerdes. Farmington Hills, Mich.: Greenhaven Press, 2013, 92–97.

Urbina, Ian. "Mobs are born as word grows by text message." *New York Times*, March 24, 2010.

Van Cleve, Genevieve. "Tour." In *Poetry Slam: The Competitive Art of Performance Poetry.* Edited by Gary Mex Glazner. San Francisco: Manic D Press, 2000, 135–39.

von Humboldt, Wilhelm. *On the Limits of State Action.* Translated by J. W. Burrow. Indianapolis, Ind: Liberty Fund, 1993.

von Ziegesar, Cecily, ed. *Slam.* New York: Alloy Books, 2000.

Wacławek, Anna. *Graffiti and Street Art.* London: Thames and Hudson, 2011.

Wakeman, John. *Anarchism and Democracy.* Freedom Pamphlet. London: Freedom Press, 1920.

Walker, Leita. "Synchronized, collective, and so far pointless." *Christian Science Monitor*, August 4, 2003.

Walter, Nicolas, ed. *Anarchism and Anarchist Communism.* London: Freedom Press, 1987.

Ward, Colin. *Anarchy in Action.* London: Allen and Unwin, 1973.

———. *Anarchism: A Very Short Introduction.* Oxford: Oxford University Press, 2004.

Warren, Mark. "What Should We Expect from More Democracy? Radically Democratic Responses to Politics." *Political Theory* 24:2 (1996): 241–70.

Wasik, Bill. "My Crowd: Or, Phase 5: A report from the inventor of the flash mob." *Harper's Magazine*, March 2006, 56–66.

———. "#Riot: Self-Organized, Hyper-Networked Revolts—Coming to a City Near You." *Wired*, December 16, 2011. http://www.wired.com/magazine/2011/12/ff_riots/all/1.

Wendel, Evan Landon. "New Potentials for 'Independent' Music: Social Networks, Old and New, and the Ongoing Struggles to Reshape the Music Industry." Masters Thesis (Comparative Media Studies), Massachusetts Institute of Technology, June 2008.

Williams, Leonard. "Anarchism Revived." *New Political Science* 29:3 (September 2007): 297–312.

Williamson, Ronald, and J. Howard Johnston. *The School Leader's Guide to Social Media*. Larchmont, N.Y.: Eye on Education, Inc., 2012.

Wilson, Charlotte. "Social Democracy and Anarchism." In *Quiet Rumours: An Anarcha-Feminist Reader*. Edited by The Dark Star Collective. Edinburgh: AK Press/Dark Star, 2002, 69–80.

Witz, Dan. *In Plain View: 30 Years of Artworks Illegal and Otherwise*. Berkeley, Calif.: Gingko Press, 2010.

Wolff, Robert Paul. *In Defense of Anarchism*. Berkeley, Calif.: University of California Press, 1998 [1970].

Wright, Erik Olin. *Envisioning Real Utopias*. London and New York: Verso, 2010.

Yoon-soo, Joung. "Flash Mobs: The Younger Generation Declares Its Cultural Independence." *Koreana*, Spring 2005, 74–77.

Index

www.ingramcontent.com/pod-product-compliance
Lightning Source LLC
LaVergne TN
LVHW040758070826
844660LV00025B/1189
* 9 7 8 1 4 3 8 4 5 9 2 0 2 *